POLICY ANALYSIS
In Social Science Research

Volume 72, Sage Library of Social Research

Sage Library of Social Research

1 Caplovitz The Merchants of Harlem
2 Rosenau International Studies & the Social Sciences
3 Ashford Ideology & Participation
4 McGowan/Shapiro The Comparative Study of Foreign Policy
5 Male The Struggle for Power
6 Tanter Modelling & Managing International Conflicts
7 Catanese Planners & Local Politics
8 Prescott Economic Aspects of Public Housing
9 Parkinson Latin America, the Cold War, & the World Powers, 1945-1973
10 Smith Ad Hoc Governments
11 Gallimore et al Culture, Behavior & Education
12 Hallman Neighborhood Government in a Metropolitan Setting
13 Gelles The Violent Home
14 Weaver Conflict & Control in Health Care Administration
15 Schweigler National Consciousness in Divided Germany
16 Carey Sociology & Public Affairs
17 Lehman Coordinating Health Care
18 Bell/Price The First Term
19 Alderfer/Brown Learning from Changing
20 Wells/Marwell Self-Esteem
21 Robins Political Institutionalization & the Integration of Elites
22 Schonfeld Obedience & Revolt
23 McCready/Greeley The Ultimate Values of the American Population

24 Nye Role Structure & Analysis of the Family
25 Wehr/Washburn Peace & World Order Systems
26 Stewart Children in Distress
27 Dedring Recent Advances in Peace & Conflict Research
28 Czudnowski Comparing Political Behavior
29 Douglas Investigative Social Research
30 Stohl War & Domestic Political Violence
31 Williamson Sons or Daughters
32 Levi Law & Politics in the International Society
33 Altheide Creating Reality
34 Lerner The Politics of Decision-Making
35 Converse The Dynamics of Party Support
36 Newman/Price Jails & Drug Treatment
37 Abercrombie The Military Chaplain
38 Gottdiener Planned Sprawl
39 Lineberry Equality & Urban Policy
40 Morgan Deterrence
41 Lefebvre The Structure of Awareness
42 Fontana The Last Frontier
43 Kemper Migration & Adaptation
44 Caplovitz/Sherrow The Religious Drop-Outs
45 Nagel/Neef The Legal Process: Modeling the System
46 Bucher/Stelling Becoming Professional
47 Hiniker Revolutionary Ideology & Chinese Reality
48 Herman Jewish Identity
49 Marsh Protest & Political Consciousness
50 LaRossa Conflict & Power in Marriage
51 Abrahamsson Bureaucracy or Participation

52 Parkinson The Philosophy of International Relations
53 Lerup Building the Unfinished
54 Smith Churchill's German Army
55 Corden Planned Cities
56 Hallman Small & Large Together
57 Inciardi et al Historical Approaches to Crime
58 Levitan/Alderman Warriors at Work
59 Zurcher The Mutable Self
60 Teune/Mlinar The Developmental Logic of Social Systems
61 Garson Group Theories of Politics
62 Medcalf Law & Identity
63 Danziger Making Budgets
64 Damrell Search for Identity
65 Stotland et al Empathy, Fantasy & Helping
66 Aronson Money & Power
67 Wice Criminal Lawyers
68 Hoole Evaluation Research & Development Activities
69 Singelmann From Agriculture to Services
70 Seward The American Family
71 McCleary Dangerous Men
72 Nagel/Neef Policy Analysis: In Social Science Research
73 Rejai/Phillips Leaders of Revolution
74 Inbar Routine Decision-Making
75 Galaskiewicz Exchange Networks & Community Politics
76 Alkin/Daillak/White Using Evaluations
77 Swanson/Cohen/Swanson Small Towns & Small Towners
78 Sensat Habermas & Marxism

Policy Analysis

In Social Science Research

**Stuart S. Nagel
Marian Neef**

Volume 72
SAGE LIBRARY OF
SOCIAL RESEARCH

 SAGE PUBLICATIONS   Beverly Hills   London

*Dedicated to analyzing and optimizing
the effects of alternative public policies*

For information address:

SAGE PUBLICATIONS, INC.
275 South Beverly Drive
Beverly Hills, California 90212

SAGE PUBLICATIONS LTD
28 Banner Street
London EC1Y 8QE

Printed in the United States of America

Library of Congress Cataloging in Publication Data

Nagel, Stuart S., 1934–
    Policy analysis: in social science research

    (Sage library of social research ; v. 72)
    Includes index.
    1. Social science research. 2. Policy sciences.
I. Neef, Marian, joint author. II. Title.
H62.N23   300'.7'2   78-11463
ISBN 0-8039-1156-4
ISBN 0-8039-1157-2 pbk.

FIRST PRINTING

CONTENTS

Chapter   *Page*

Introduction: A Hierarchy of Methodological Problems   9

PART ONE. BASIC SOCIAL SCIENCE RESEARCH

1. Determining an Optimum Level of Statistical Significance   17

   An Inventory Modeling Approach to Determining an Optimum Level of Statistical Significance—A Decision Theory Approach to Determining an Optimum Level of Statistical Significance

2. Alternative Prediction Methods and Criteria   35

   The Problems and the Data—Predicting Randomly—Predicting from Knowing How the Data Has Been Distributed on the Variable Being Predicted—Predicting from Knowing Something about the Relation Between the Variable Being Predicted and Another Variable—Conclusions

3. Determining and Rejecting Causation   69

   Coeffects and Intervening Variable Causation—Joint Causation and Cocausation—Reciprocal Causation—Integrating Diverse Forms of Causation

PART TWO. POLICY ANALYSIS METHODS

4. Combining and Relating Goals   105

   Combining Goals—Relating Goals—Processing the Combinations and the Relations

5. Finding an Optimum Choice, Level, or Mix in Public Policy Analysis   133

   Finding an Optimum Alternative Policy in General—Finding an Optimum Choice Among Discrete Alternatives—Finding an Optimum Level or Mix on a Continuum of Alternatives—Problems that Can Be Viewed as Simultaneously or Alternatively Involving Choices, Levels, or Mixes—Value Decisions and Policy Analysis—Some Conclusions

6. Deductive Modeling in Policy Analysis   177
        Modeling in General—Causal Modeling—Prescriptive Modeling—
        Some Conclusions

7. Applying Policy Analysis and Social Science Research to
    Delay Reduction   197
        Queueing Theory—Optimum Sequencing—Critical Path Method
        and Flow Chart Models—Optimum Level and Mix Analysis—
        Optimum Choice Analysis—Markov Chain Analysis—Some
        Conclusions

    Epilogue   221

    Name Index   231

    Subject Index   235

    About the Authors   240

LIST OF APPENDICES

Appendix   *Page*

1.1.   Basic Formulas in Determining an Optimum Level of
       Statistical Significance   29

2.1.   Summary of the Main Formulas in Prediction Analysis   59

3.1.   Summary of Some Major Principles in Causal Analysis   91

4.1.   Methods of Reducing the Number of Variables and
       Making Composite Variables   123

5.1.   Summary of the Main Formulas in Optimizing Analysis   151

5.2.   A Simplified Approach to Solving Optimum Level
       Problems   157

5.3.   A Simplified Approach to Solving Optimum Mix
       Problems   161

5.4.   A Bibliography of Policy Optimizing Methodologies and
       Applications   167

6.1.   Summary of Some Basic Principles of Deductive Modeling
       as Applied to Policy Analysis   189

6.2.   A Bibliography of Books on Deductive Modeling in
       Policy Analysis   193

Overview Appendix 1.   Summary of the Main Formulas in
                       Statistical Analysis   223

Overview Appendix 2.   Methods for Handling Missing Data   227

INTRODUCTION: A HIERARCHY OF METHODOLOGICAL PROBLEMS

The purpose of this book is to discuss some of the more interesting aspects of the leading methodological problems in social science and policy analysis. The book is intended for use in methodological courses and professional reading that seek to emphasize (1) the more controversial aspects of research methodology, (2) the newer policy analysis concern in social science research, and (3) the important problems of inference, prediction, causation, goals, optimizing, and deductive modeling.

The controversial problems include such questions as: When can a hypothesis be considered confirmed or refuted in light of the probability that the findings could be due to unrepresentative chance sampling error? What is the best way to predict how a person, place, or thing will be positioned on a variable, and what is the best criterion to use in deciding the best way to predict? How can one determine the presence of spurious, joint, reciprocal, and other forms of causation? How does one combine multiple and conflicting goals into an overall goal, and then relate that overall goal to various policy alternatives? Given one's goals and those relations, how does one find an optimum choice, level, or mix in public policy analysis? How can one deduce predictive or prescriptive conclusions from empirical premises, especially where important policy problems are involved that do not lend themselves to experimentation? How can one bring together the previous material on inference, prediction, causation, goal measurement, optimizing, and deduction to focus on a specific serious policy problem like how to reduce delay in the legal process?

The general framework for this book implicitly recognizes a hierarchy of social science research methods. Each level in the hierarchy presupposes an awareness of the more elementary levels, and each level logically leads to the more sophisticated subsequent levels. The basic level in social science research involves summarizing data to indicate univariate measures of both central tendency and spread for a number of data points on a given variable. For example, what is the average age of a set of state supreme court judges, and what is the range in their ages? At the same basic level, one is likely to make comparisons between averages or other measures for two or more groups. For example, how does the average age of elected judges compare with that of appointed judges? If one asks that kind of question, one is logically lead into asking to what extent the difference found may be readily attributable to chance. One intuitively recognizes that chance could be more easily the reason for the difference if the difference or if the size of the samples is small. Standard statistics textbooks provide formulas for calculating the chance probability of a given statistic really being zero (or some other number) with given sample sizes. An interesting controversy at that level of analysis is how low does the chance probability have to be before one will conclude that the difference or the statistic is not due to chance, but rather is based on a real difference, relation, or nonchance occurrence. That aspect of statistical inference is the subject of Chapter 1.

On the next level of analysis, one is not just concerned with summarizing data and indicating to what extent one can generalize from a sample, but instead one is interested in bivariate and multivariate relations for the purpose of predicting how a unit of analysis will be positioned on one variable given its position on one or more other variables, or given the distribution of the units of analysis on the main variable. For example, to what extent can we predict the decisional propensities of judges in criminal cases from knowing their ages, or from knowing that the average judge tends to favor the prosecution? That question raises two kinds of controversies. One is what is the "best" method of prediction, with the choices including predicting from another variable, predicting from the distribution on a given variable, and many variations on those two main prediction methods. The second question is what is the "best" criterion for deciding among those alternative prediction methods, with the choices mainly relating to either squaring or not squaring the deviations from each predicted score to each actual score. When one talks about "best," doing so usually arouses controversy. Those aspects of statistical prediction are the subject of Chapter 2.

Moving up in the hierarchy, one might logically ask, just because I know there is a nonchance predictive relation between the age of judges and their propensity to decide for the prosecution in criminal cases, how do I know that it is a causal relation, and especially how do I know what kind of causal relation? In other words, will being an older judge consistently correlate well with deciding for the prosecution, or does the correlation substantially change when some other variable is manipulated such as off-the-bench liberal attitudes. For example, if only liberal-old judges are compared with liberal-young judges, and only conservative-old judges are compared with conservative-young judges, the relation between age and deciding for the prosecution might tend to disappear, possibly indicating that liberalism is an intervening variable between age and decisional propensity. On the other hand, there may be a low propensity to decide for the prosecution among liberal-young, liberal-old, and conservative-young judges, but a high propensity to decide in favor of the prosecution by conservative-old judges, possibly indicating a joint causal relation by conservatism and age on decisional propensities. On still another hand, maybe being conservative causes one to decide for the prosecution, but deciding for the prosecution tends to reinforce one's conservatism, thereby possibly indicating some reciprocal causation in the model. Discussing how one determines various kinds of causation is the subject matter of Chapter 3.

After tentatively resolving some of the methodological controversies concerning hypothesis testing, prediction, and causation, one might then logically ask, so what? In other words, how does one make use of that kind of knowledge in order to arrive at a decision concerning what alternative public policies ought to be adopted that relate to one's subject matter? Not all social science has policy implications, but the more controversial social science studies are likely to have such implications. Before arriving at a decision as to what ought to be adopted, one has to clarify what goals one is seeking to maximize, minimize, or optimize, and also determine how those goals relate to the policy alternatives being considered. Clarifying goals may especially involve determining how one is going to combine multiple and sometimes conflicting goals. For example, in deciding between an elected or an appointed judicial system, we might have as our goals (1) securing judges who are either economic liberals or economic conservatives, when economic issues arise that cannot be resolved by clear precedents, and (2) securing judges who are civil libertarian liberals or conservatives, when legal or factual civil liberties issues arise. If elected judges were to score favorably or unfavorably on both goals, there would be no problem. However, when relating those goals to the alternative policies, we might find that elected judges tend to be somewhat more liberal on economic matters given their more working class backgrounds, but less liberal on civil liberties matters given their fear of being voted out of office by majoritarian pressures. Discussing how to combine those conflicting goals and how to relate the goals to the policy alternatives is the subject of Chapter 4.

Merely determining our goals and relating them to the policy alternatives are not necessarily sufficient to resolve the question of what is the optimum policy alternative. Answering that question may require working with a model involving formulas for (1) choosing among discrete alternatives without or with contingent probabilities, (2) finding an optimum level on a hill-shaped total benefits curve or a valley-shaped total cost curve, or (3) finding an optimum mix among a variety of places or activities. For example, the optimum solution to the policy problem of having an elected or appointed judiciary may involve a mix between the two, wherein one's goals are maximized by initially electing judges but providing for the long tenure that is associated with appointing judges. That mix might provide judges with liberal backgrounds for economic decision-making, but freedom from majoritarian pressures for civil libertarian decision-making. Determining what constitutes the optimum length of tenure may also be an optimum level problem because tenure that is either too short or too long may be undesirable since short tenure brings a lack of independence, but unduly long tenure may bring staleness and unresponsiveness. The controversies relevant to finding an optimum choice, level, or mix are the subject of Chapter 5.

On the highest methodological level, one might ask the question, how can I use all this knowledge about inference, prediction, causation, goals, and optimizing in order to deduce a prediction about the effect of X on Y, or to deduce a prescription as to what X should be adopted, without having to gather difficult empirical data to test those conclusions? For example, if one knows how twelve-person juries decide criminal cases under a unanimity rule, how can one deduce how six-person juries (or twelve-person juries under a nonunanimity rule) would decide criminal cases. Having to experiment with real criminal cases might be practically impossible, unfair to the defendants, and produce meaningless results because of our inability to statistically control for other variables besides jury size that influence case outcomes. For another example, if one knows or deduces the empirical relation between jury size and propensity to convict, and one tentatively accepts the Blackstonian norm that it is worse to convict one innocent person than to free ten guilty people, then how does one use those kinds of premises to deduce a prescriptive conclusion as to the optimum jury size? As social science does more analysis of hypotheses, predictions, causation, and optimizing, there develops a body of potential premises that can be used in deducing conclusions the way chemistry was able to deduce the existence of new elements before they were empirically discovered. That kind of deductive analysis (especially as applied to controversial policy problems) is the subject of Chapter 6.

After analyzing the component parts of this hierarchy of methodological problems, one might then seek to bring together the six methodological processes of inference, prediction, causation, goal measurement, optimizing, and deduction to focus on a specific serious problem like how to reduce delay in the legal process. That is the purpose of Chapter 7. In that chapter a series of six models are presented that collectively involve all of those processes. The models include (1) queueing theory, which involves *deducing* how much time will be consumed as a result of increasing or decreasing the rates at which cases arrive and are serviced, (2) optimum sequencing, which involves arranging the order in which cases are processed in order to *optimize* or minimize the sum of the waiting and processing time per case, (3) critical path methods, which emphasize *measuring* how much time is consumed and ought to be consumed at various stages in the processing of cases, (4) optimum level analysis, which seeks to arrive at an optimum quantity of time consumed per case through methods which involve *predicting* costs from time consumed, (5) optimum choice analysis, which is particularly concerned with understanding and manipulating the *causal* factors responsible for why decision-makers sometimes make time-lengthening decisions rather than time-saving decisions, and (6) Markov chain analysis, which involves probabilistic considerations somewhat related to those involved in statistical *inference*, but which also involves other methodological processes designed to determine future events by knowing the probability of one event leading to another.

Many of the methodological matters in this book are illustrated with examples from the legal process and legal policy analysis, but one can reason by analogy to a variety of other substantive applications. The notes and references frequently refer to other illustrative examples from other aspects of social science subject matters and other policy problems. The legal process is a particularly good source of illustrative examples for a number of reasons, including the fact that many political science and social science students are prelaw majors who welcome prelaw examples in a methodology course. The legal process is also frequently used to illustrate type 1 and type 2 errors in matters of prediction and causation since those concepts are such an important part of the legal process. There is also no substantial distinction between legal policy analysis and public policy analysis since all laws are governmental policies, and virtually all governmental policies are laws if by laws we include statutes, quasi-legislation, court precedents, quasi-adjudications, and constitutions. In addition, the legal process involves an adversary kind of conflict that tends to stir interest more so than other social phenomena, which partly explains the popularity of lawyers as a subject for TV programs, movies, and novels. The reader and instructor can easily apply the principles included in this book to other substantive fields by reasoning from analogy as well as drawing upon the references cited.

The authors are grateful to the Ford Foundation Public Policy Committee, the Illinois Law Enforcement Commission, and the University of Illinois Research Board for financial aid used in preparing this book. They also thank Rita Simon of the University of Illinois Sociology Department for allowing material to be used from our chapter in her book, *Research in Law and Sociology,* and they thank Nancy Munshaw of the University of Illinois Planning Department for co-authoring Chapter 7 on "Applying Policy Analysis and Social Science Research to Delay Reduction." The senior author is also grateful to the many students who have participated in his undergraduate course on "Methods of Political Analysis" and his graduate seminar on "Law, Policy, and Social Science." They have been quite helpful over the years in debugging the principles contained in this book. The senior author will be glad to provide users of this book with a set of the data-based exercises designed to give the students further experience in applying these principles.

As mentioned at the beginning of this introduction, the purpose of our book is to discuss various methodological controversies, but not necessarily to resolve them. It is, however, hoped that the discussion will provoke further discussion which may help make today's controversies into tomorrow's commonplace matters, and move us further up or out of the hierarchy to new methodological controversies in social science and policy analysis.

PART ONE

BASIC SOCIAL SCIENCE RESEARCH

Chapter 1

DETERMINING AN OPTIMUM LEVEL

OF STATISTICAL SIGNIFICANCE

The weather is something about which many people complain, but about which few people do anything. Likewise, statistical significance levels are also something about which there are complaints of arbitrariness, inflexibility, conservatism, deceptiveness, and other complaints.[1] Like the weather, however, few of the complainers or other social scientists do anything feasible to lessen the causes of those complaints, although some statistical analysts do offer general suggestions as to what ought to be done.[2] Typical reactions to determining a desirable level of statistical significance include Hubert Blalock's statement that "The decision as to the significance level selected depends on the relative costs of making the one or the other type of error and should be evaluated accordingly."[3] Most statistical analysts like Sidney Siegel agree that "Although the desirability of such a technique for arriving at decisions is clear, its practicality in most research in the behavioral sciences at present is dubious, because we lack the information which would be basic to the use of loss [i.e., cost] functions."[4]

The purpose of this chapter is to discuss a meaningful and feasible approach to determining the optimum level of statistical significance to use in any statistical inference situation in order to choose the level that will maximize perceived benefits minus perceived costs. More specifically, the chapter will first deal with choosing an optimum level of significance in light of an inventory modeling perspective whereby one seeks to minimize the sum of the holding costs (or type 1 error costs) and the outage costs (or type 2 error costs). The chapter then deals with choosing an optimum level in light of a decision theory perspective whereby one seeks to maximize the expected value of accepting or rejecting a hypothesis or presumption. Both perspectives are meaningful, but only the decision theory perspective seems feasible in view of the simple data it needs in order to be applied.

We will illustrate the concepts and methods involved in these two perspectives by applying them to the decisional problem of what is the optimum threshold probability of guilt to merit a conviction in criminal procedure, and to the statistical hypothesis that black defendants are treated the same as white defendants in sentencing or other aspects of criminal procedure. The first problem is referred to as the conviction criterion problem, and the second problem as the racial disparity problem. Each perspective or approach to determining an optimum significance level can be graphically applied to each of the two problems, resulting in the four graphs or figures which summarize the basic ideas of this chapter.

By level of statistical significance, we mean the probability of being right above which we would accept a hypothesis as being true and below which we would reject the hypothesis. Thus, if we operate at a .05 level of statistical significance, we are in effect saying that if the data or other facts indicate that our hypothesis has only a .15 probability of being true, then we will tentatively reject it; whereas if the data indicates our hypothesis has a .02 probability of being true, then we will tentatively accept the hypothesis as reflecting reality rather than chance occurrence.[5]

An Inventory Modeling Approach to Determining an Optimum Level of Statistical Significance

In deciding an optimum inventory level for a business firm, one must be careful not to have too much inventory because that will generate unduly high storage and spoilage costs. Likewise, one must be careful not to have too little inventory because that would generate unduly high outage costs whereby orders are lost because they cannot be met. Operations researchers have developed meaningful quantitative techniques for arriving at an inventory level for a given product of a given firm that minimizes the sum of the holding costs and the outage costs.

THE CONVICTION CRITERION PROBLEM

The conviction criterion problem is like an inventory level problem because if we set the threshold probability of guilt too high, then too many truly guilty defendants will be acquitted, analogous to having too high an inventory level. Likewise, if we set the threshold probability of guilt too low, then too many truly innocent defendants will be convicted, analogous to having too low an inventory level. The prevailing conviction criterion level in the United States is usually stated in words like "beyond a reasonable doubt." When it is expressed quantitatively, the figure of about a .90 probability of guilt is usually given by judges.[6]

Those concepts are graphically illustrated by Figure 1.1. The horizontal axis shows conviction criteria or threshold probabilities from zero to 1.00. The vertical axis shows the three kinds of costs. As the

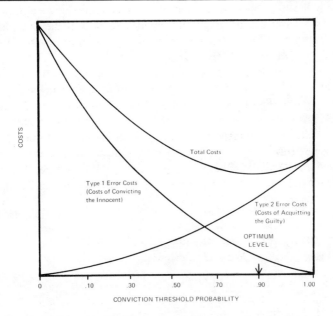

The above cost curves are consistent with the cost considerations of those who consider an optimum conviction threshold probability to be about .90.

Figure 1.1: AN INVENTORY MODELING APPROACH TO DETERMINING AN OPTIMUM THRESHOLD PROBABILITY: As Applied to Criminal Convictions

conviction threshold probability goes up, there is an increase in type 2 error costs or the costs of acquitting the guilty. Those costs probably rise at an increasing rate as the criterion approaches 1.00. As the threshold probability goes down, there is an increase in type 1 error costs or the costs of convicting the innocent, probably at an increasing rate. The type 1 error costs are likely to rise more steeply than the type 2 error costs because it is customary to consider a type 1 error of convicting an innocent defendant to generally be more costly than a type 2 error of acquitting a guilty defendant. The total cost curve is simply the sum of the two separate cost curves. It bottoms out over the .90 threshold probability in light of what we previously said about what is generally considered the optimum threshold probability. That may be higher than the usual threshold probability applied by actual jurors or judges.

This perspective is the equivalent of saying the optimum probability is the one that maximizes benefits minus costs. Any given threshold probability corresponds to a certain amount of conviction benefits, which consist of acquittal costs avoided by rightfully convicting. Likewise any given probability corresponds to a certain amount of acquittal benefits, which consist of conviction costs avoided by rightfully acquitting. Thus, the optimum threshold probability can be equally stated as the probability that (1) maximizes conviction benefits plus acquittal benefits, (2) maximizes conviction benefits minus conviction costs, (3) maximizes acquittal benefits minus acquittal costs, or (4) minimizes conviction costs plus acquittal costs. The fourth alternative is the one expressed in figures 1 and 2 because it sounds most like minimizing the sum of type 1 error costs and type 2 error costs as used in conventional statistical language.

The type 1 and type 2 error cost curves reflect the relative or absolute value of a type 1 error versus a type 2 error, which the influential legal commentator William Blackstone evaluated at a 10 to 1 ratio.[7] Those error cost curves also attempt to reflect the empirical reality of the relation between the required threshold level and the making of such errors. That empirical reality is virtually impossible to know. For that reason, it is virtually impossible to go from curve-drawing to determining an optimum threshold level rather than to go as we have done from an accepted optimum threshold level to drawing curves. Bear in mind that there is an infinite number of shapes for type 1 error cost curves and type 2 error cost curves that when summed will bottom out over the .90 level.

THE RACIAL DISPARITY PROBLEM

The racial disparity problem is also like an inventory level problem because if we set the statistical significance level too high, then we are likely to make the mistake of deciding there is no discrimination when there really is. Likewise, if we set the significance level too low, then we are likely to make the mistake of deciding there is discrimination when there really is not. Those concepts are graphically illustrated by Figure 1.2. The two error cost curves are drawn with equal although rising slopes to reflect the values of a person who considers it equally undesirable to make a type 1 error of wrongly rejecting the hypothesis or presumption of sameness and a type 2 error of wrongly accepting the hypothesis of sameness.[8]

Given the equality of the two types of error costs, it logically follows that the optimum level of statistical significance is .50 rather

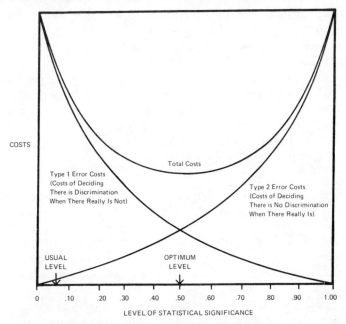

The above curves are consistent with the cost considerations of a person who considers it equally undesirable to make a type 1 or type 2 error in this context. Since the presumption is one of no difference, falsely reject-ing that presumption is a type 1 error and falsely accepting that presump-tion is a type 2 error.

Figure 1.2: AN INVENTORY MODELING APPROACH TO DETERMINING AN OPTIMUM LEVEL OF STATISTICAL SIGNIFICANCE: Applied to the Hypothesis that Black Defendants are Treated the Same as White Defendants

than the usual level of .05. Either Figure 1.2 or Figure 1.1 is capable of nicely illustrating that working with a .05 significance level results in relatively high type 1 error costs and relatively low type 2 error costs. In other words, by working with the conventional .05 level, we are in effect requiring the equivalent of proof beyond a reasonable doubt before we will reject the hypothesis that discrimination does not exist, or accept the hypothesis that it does exist. We are also in effect requiring the equivalent of what is legally referred to as a mere scintilla of proof in order to accept the hypothesis that discrimination does not exist or reject the hypothesis that it does exist.

Although figures 1.1 and 1.2 are useful in understanding the basic concepts involved in an optimum conviction criterion or significance level, they are virtually useless as a feasible method for arriving at an optimum level except for business inventories or industrial quality control, where accurate accounting or engineering data is available for generating equations to express the curves. Merely saying that the type 1 error costs are equal to or twice as important as the type 2 error costs does not tell us the shape of the curves since those curves reflect both (1) the value of a type 1 error versus a type 2 error and (2) the unknown empirical relation between various significance levels and the occurrence of such errors. In other words, total type 1 error cost for any probability level combines both a price per unit or per error, and a quantity of errors at that level. Thus, the inventory modeling perspective, while meaningful, lacks feasibility as a simple, widely applicable method for determining optimum significance levels.[9]

A Decision Theory Approach to Determining an Optimum Level of Statistical Significance

What is needed for determining an optimum conviction criterion or significance level is a method whereby one does not have to know the empirical relation between different criteria or levels and various costs or benefits, but only the relative value of a type 1 error versus a type 2 error. In other words, what we need is a meaningful way of translating Blackstone's ten to one error ratio into a threshold probability or the one to one error ratio in the racial disparity problem into a level of statistical significance without needing any intermediate curve drawing or empirical data.

Decision theory provides an approach for doing that. Decision theory can be defined as a procedure whereby one chooses among alternatives in order to maximize benefits minus costs in light of probabilistic or uncertain events. In this context, the choices are to accept or reject the hypothesis or presumption. The uncertain event is whether the hypothesis or presumption is true or false.

THE CONVICTION CRITERION PROBLEM

The method can be nicely illustrated by the conviction criterion problem, as is shown in Figure 1.3. That figure indicates we have a choice of acquitting or convicting a defendant who may be innocent or guilty. To determine an optimum threshold probability for someone like William Blackstone, we could go through the following steps:

(1) Prepare a four-cell payoff matrix with accept and reject on the vertical axis and hypothesis true or false on the horizontal axis.

(2) Of the four cells or possible outcomes, have the person whose values are relevant indicate which outcomes are undesirable and which outcomes are desirable. Blackstone would say cells 1 and 4 reading across are undesirable outcomes and cells 2 and 3 are desirable ones.

(3) Of the two undesirable outcomes, which one is the more undesirable? Blackstone would say cell 4 which involves convicting an innocent defendant rather than cell 1 which involves acquitting a guilty defendant.

(4) If we anchor the more undesirable outcome at -100, then on a scale of 0 to -100, where would you put the less undesirable outcome? Blackstone would say at -10 since he has said it is 10 times as bad to convict an innocent defendant as it is to acquit a guilty defendant.

PROBABILITY OF DEFENDANT BEING INNOCENT

		Defendant Guilty (P)	Defendant Innocent (1−P)	EXPECTED VALUE
ALTERNATIVE DECISIONS AVAILABLE	Accept Hypothesis, i.e., Acquit	−B e.g., −10 (Type 2 error)	+A e.g., +100 (Type 2 accuracy)	$EV_A = (-B)(P) + (+A)(1-P)$ $= (-10)(P) + (+100)(1-P)$
	Reject Hypothesis, i.e., Convict	+B e.g., +10 (Type 1 accuracy)	−A e.g., −100 (Type 1 error)	$EV_R = (+B)(P) + (-A)(1-P)$ $= (+10)(P) + (-100)(1-P)$

General Presumption: Defendant is innocent. Type 1 error rejects presumption when true. Type 2 accepts presumption when false.

The values in this table are those for William Blackstone, who said 10 guilty persons should go free rather than convict one innocent person.

Optimum level for Rejection: $P^* = A/(A+B) = 100/(100+10) = .91$, meaning Blackstone would require greater than .91 probability of guilt before he would convict.

Figure 1.3: A DECISION THEORY APPROACH TO DETERMINING AN OPTIMUM THRESHOLD PROBABILITY: As Applied to the Hypothesis or Presumption that a Defendant is Innocent

(5) If our respondent is a logically consistent person, then whatever value he assigns to a type 1 error (wrongly rejecting the hypothesis) should also be assigned to a type 2 accuracy (rightly accepting the hypothesis), but opposite in sign. Likewise, whatever value he assigns to a type 2 error (wrongly accepting the hypothesis) should also be assigned to a type 1 accuracy (rightly accepting the hypothesis), but opposite in sign. In other words, the benefits of accepting a true hypothesis consist of avoiding the costs of rejecting a true hypothesis, and the benefits of rejecting a false hypothesis consist of avoiding the costs of accepting a false hypothesis. Thus, the payoff matrix for William Blackstone would involve values of -10, $+100$, $+10$, and -100 reading across.

(6) Determine the expected value of accepting the hypothesis by summing the expected positive benefits ($+A$ or $+100$ for Blackstone discounted by the probability that the defendant is innocent) and the expected negative costs (-10 discounted by the probability that the defendant is guilty). This is the equivalent of the expected benefits minus the expected costs. Also determine the expected value of rejecting the hypothesis by determining the expected benefits ($+10$ discounted by or multiplied by P) and the expected costs (-100 discounted by $1-P$). To express these expected values does not require knowing the probability that the defendant is innocent, but only requires having an algebraic symbol like P to complete the expression.

(7) Given the expected value of accepting the hypothesis and the expected value of rejecting the hypothesis in light of our respondent's indication of the relative undesirability to him of a type 1 and type 2 error, now set those two expected values equal to each other and solve for P. Doing so will tell us the value of P when those two expected values are equal. That algebraically determined value of P is the optimum threshold probability in the sense that when the perceived probability of guilt is above that figure, the respondent should reject the hypothesis of innocence and convict; and when the perceived probability is below that figure, the respondent should accept the hypothesis of innocence and acquit. If the respondent follows that decision rule, he will always be choosing the alternative between the two alternative choices that gives him the highest expected benefits minus expected costs. Solving for P in the algebraic expression $(-B)(P) + (+A)$ $(1-P) = (+B)(P) + (-A)(1-P)$ yields the fact that the equilibrium P, optimum P, or P^* equals $A/(A+B)$. Thus, Mr. Blackstone's threshold probability would be $100/(100+10)$ or .91, meaning he would require greater than a .91 probability of guilt before he would convict.[10] If

Blackstone had valued a type 2 acquittal error at more than 10 (e.g., 20 to 100), then his .91 probability would have been lower, but raised if Blackstone had valued a type 2 acquittal error at less than 10 (e.g., 5 to 100, rather than 10 to 100 or 1 to 10).[11]

THE RACIAL DISPARITY PROBLEM

The same simple responses and reasoning can be applied to determining an optimum significance level as is illustrated in Figure 1.4. The only difference is that the optimum level for the conviction probability threshold is normally stated in terms of the probability level above which one *rejects* the hypothesis of innocence, whereas the optimum level for statistical significance is normally stated in terms of the probability level above which one *accepts* the hypothesis of no difference. The simplified formula for the former optimum level is $A/(A+B)$, and the simplified formula for the latter optimum level is the complement or $B/(A+B)$. Assuming a type 1 error is anchored at -100 as the more undesirable of the two errors, then all one has to do is determine one number, namely on a 0 to -100 scale what is the relative undesirability of a type 2 error or the value of B. In other words, the optimum significance level can be considered as simply equal to $B/(100+B)$. Applying that simplification to a person who considers it twice as undesirable to make a type 1 error as a type 2 error, we arrive at a P* or

PROBABILITY OF THE HYPOTHESIS BEING TRUE

		Hypothesis False (P)	Hypothesis True (−P)	EXPECTED VALUE
ALTERNATIVE DECISIONS AVAILABLE	Accept Hypothesis, i.e., Sameness is True	−B e.g., −50 (Type 2 error)	+A e.g., +100 (Type 2 accuracy)	$EV_A = (-100)(P) + (+100)(1-P)$
	Reject Hypothesis, i.e., Disparity is True	+B e.g., +50 (Type 1 accuracy)	−A e.g., −100 (Type 1 error)	$EV_R = (+100)(P) + (-100)(1-P)$

General Presumption: There is no difference between black and white defendants.

The values in this table are those of a person who considers it twice as undesirable to make a type 1 as a type 2 error in this context.

Optimum Level for Acceptance: P* = B/(A+B) = 50/(100+50) = .33, meaning that a difference between matched black and white defendants that has a chance probability greater than .33 should be accepted as a real difference rather than a chance difference, and the converse for a difference with less than a .33 chance probability. Matching should generally be done at least on the crime and having a prior record.

Figure 1.4: A DECISION THEORY APPROACH TO DETERMINING AN OPTIMUM LEVEL OF STATISTICAL SIGNIFICANCE: As Applied to the Hypothesis or Presumption that Black Defendants are Treated the Same as White Defendants

optimum significance level of 50/(100+50) or .33. Sometimes a type 2 error may be considered more undesirable than a type 1 error, and then we use the marginal formula of B/(A+B) which then becomes 100/(A+100).[12]

This decision theory approach is obviously far more simple and thus more feasible to apply than any approach that involves determining type 1 error costs and type 2 error costs for different levels of statistical significance. It is also far more simple than alternative decision theory approaches which require placing in the payoff cells absolute units like dollars, rather than purely relative units like we have used. It is also simpler than alternative decision theory approaches which require placing in the cells probabilities that the various kinds of errors or accuracies will occur.[13]

This approach also allows one to work backwards and say what a given threshold probability means in terms of the relative undesirability of a type 1 error versus a type 2 error. For example, if we start with the .05 level as a given, what does that tell us about how social science researchers have in effect or implicitly been evaluating type 1 and type 2 errors? Answering that question simply involves solving for B in the equation .05 = B/(100+B). The value of B in that equation is 5.26 (or 5/.95) meaning the traditional .05 significance level implies that a type 1 error is 100 to 5.26, or 19 to 1 times as undesirable as a type 2 error.

Another related purpose for this approach is for translating a chance probability into an undesirability ratio. For example, if we find that a difference or a relation has a .33 chance probability, we can say that such a relation ought to be accepted as a real rather than as a chance relation if we are willing to accept a type 2 error as being only half as bad as a type 1 error rather than the usual 1/19 times as bad. What we in effect did is solve for B in the equation .33 = B/(100+B), which yields a B of 50 or half the A of 100.[14]

Perhaps the best approach when discussing the statistical significance of one's findings is to do so in terms of both the conventional .05 and .01 tests and the kind of benefit-cost approach presented here, rather than use this approach to replace the conventional tests. Our approach is a benefit-cost approach in the sense that we seek to accept the hypothesis if the expected benefits [i.e., A(1-P)] minus the expected costs [i.e., B(P)] of accepting are greater than the expected benefits [i.e., B(P)] minus the expected costs [i.e., A(1-P)] of rejecting. In using the benefit-cost or decision theory approach to arriving at an optimum P* value, one should be as explicit as possible in describing how one determined the relative values of A and B, i.e., the ratio between the type 1 and type 2 error costs. One might also indicate how one's conclusions that certain findings are statistically significant would be affected or not affected by changes in the values of A and B.

With this kind of decision theory approach for determining an optimum level of statistical significance, there should no longer be any reason for complaining about the arbitrariness, inflexibility, conservatism, deceptiveness, and other defects of the .05 or .01 levels of statistical significance. Instead, one should be able to evaluate most major research hypotheses in terms of the relative undesirability of a type 1 error versus a type 2 error, and then use the expected benefit-cost maximization formula to determine the optimum level of significance probability in light of that relative undesirability. One could further indicate the significance level that would correspond to various relative undesirability ratios, and one could also express the ratio that would have to exist in order to accept a relation or difference given its chance probability. The approach does seem to make meaningful Hubert Blalock's recommendation of determining a desirable level of statistical significance by evaluating the costs of making the one or the other type of error, contrary to other statistical analysts who say it cannot be done.[15]

APPENDIX 1.1: BASIC FORMULAS IN DETERMINING AN OPTIMUM LEVEL OF STATISTICAL SIGNIFICANCE

This appendix pulls together on a more abstract symbolic level the basic formulas which are mainly presented verbally and illustrated with concrete examples in the chapter. By seeing the formulas on a more abstract level, we can further clarify their interrelations and generalizability. This appendix also briefly refers to some important general matters which did not seem so appropriate to discuss in the text given the emphasis on verbal presentation and concrete illustrations.

I. BASIC SYMBOLS

P   = The probability that a given finding could be due to chance sampling error, or the probability that a hypothesis or presumption is true (or false).

P^* = The probability level above which a hypothesis or presumption is rejected (or accepted) and below which it is accepted (or rejected), i.e., a statistical significance level.

TC = Total costs, i.e., the sum of the type 1 error costs of rejecting a true hypothesis or presumption, plus the type 2 error costs of accepting a false hypothesis or presumption.

A   = Type 1 error costs. One can try to express these costs in dollars or other absolute units, or simply in relative terms, i.e., relative to the type 2 error costs.

B   = Type 2 error costs. One can try to express these costs in

29

dollars or other absolute units, or simply in relative terms, i.e., relative to the type 1 error costs.

II. AN INVENTORY MODELING APPROACH TO DETERMINING OPTIMUM P*

1.   Optimum $P^* = P$ where $\Delta TC/ \Delta P = 0$

2.   If $TC = A + B = a_1(P)^{b_1} + a_2(P)^{b_2}$ where $b_1 < 0$ and $b_2 > 0$, then $\Delta TC/ \Delta P = b_1 a_1(P)^{b_1 - 1} + b_2 a_2(P)^{b_2 - 1}$.

This follows from the rule learned in elementary calculus that if $Y = aX^b$, then a change in Y relative to a change in X equals baX^{b-1}. Saying B_1 is less than zero merely means that as the level of statistical significance goes up, the type 1 error costs go down. Likewise, saying b_2 is greater than zero means that as the level of statistical significance goes up, the type 2 error costs go up.

3.   Given point 2 above, then when $\Delta TC/ \Delta P = 0$, optimum $P^* = [-(a_1 b_1)/(a_2 b_2)]^{1/(b_2 - b_1)}$.

We want to solve for P where the slope of the total cost relative to the probability level is zero because that is where the slope has become horizontal and where the total cost curve has bottomed out.

III. A DECISION THEORY APPROACH TO DETERMINING OPTIMUM P*

1.   Optimum $P^* = A/(A+B) = X/(X+1)$ where $X = A/B$, if the significance level or probability threshold is stated in terms of the probability level above which one *rejects* the hypothesis or presumption.

2.   Optimum $P^* = B/(A+B) = 1(X+1)$ where $X = A/B$, if the significance level or probability threshold is stated in terms of the probability level above which one *accepts* the hypothesis or presumption.

The above two formulas follow from the assumption that a decision maker wants to choose the alternative decision that will give the highest expected value. The expected value of each decision is equal to its perceived benefits minus costs with both benefits and costs discounted by the probability of their occurring.

NOTES

1. James Skipper, Anthony Guenther, and Gilbert Nass, "The Sacredness of .05: A Note Concerning the Uses of Statistical Levels of Significance in Social Science," 2 *The American Sociologist* 16-18 (1967); Hanan Selvin, "A Critique of Tests of Significance in Survey Research," 22 *American Sociological Review* 519-527 (1957); Denton Morrison and Ramon Henkel (eds.), *The Significance Test Controversy: A Reader* (Aldine, 1970); Stephen Spielman, "The Logic of Tests of Significance," *Philosophy of Science* 211-225 (1974).

2. General suggestions, such as the need to consider the relative costs of type 1 and type 2 errors, are mentioned in Sanford Labovitz, "Criteria for Selecting a Significance Level: A Note on the Sacredness of .05," 3 *The American Sociologist* 200-222 (1968); William Hays and Robert Winkler, *Statistics: Probability, Inference, and Decision* (Holt, Rinehart and Winston, 1970), 375-443.

3. Hubert Blalock, *Social Statistics* (McGraw-Hill, 1972), 160.

4. Sidney Siegel, *Nonparametric Statistics for the Behavioral Sciences* (McGraw-Hill, 1956), 8.

5. Level of statistical significance should be distinguished from some related concepts. Test of statistical significance refers to the method used to determine what the probability is that a hypothesis is true. Common tests of significance include the normal curve, t-test, chi square, and F-test. Power of a test of statistical significance refers to the probability that a test will make a type 2 error of accepting a false hypothesis. The power varies mainly with the size of the data sample and the statistical test chosen. A relation may be statistically significant in the sense that it is not readily attributable to chance (i.e., it has a low chance probability), but still not be a causal relation. See Chapter 3 for a discussion of causal tests. The probability of a hypothesis being due to chance varies mainly with the size of the data sample and the size of the deviation of the observed statistic from what one would expect by chance.

6. Rita Simon and Linda Mahan, "Quantifying Burdens of Proof," 5 *Law and Society Review* 319 (1971).

7. William Blackstone, 4 *Commentaries* 358 (1961).

8. For a discussion of the problems involved in determining whether black defendants are treated the same as white defendants (other than the problem of how much of a difference constitutes a statistically significant difference), see Nagel and Neef, "Racial Disparities that Supposedly Do Not Exist: Some Pitfalls in Analysis of Court Records," 52 *Notre Dame Lawyer* 87-94 (1976).

9. In algebraic terms, the inventory model in effect says there is a type 1 error cost curve of the form $A = a_1(P)^{b_1}$ where b_1 is negative, and there is a type 2 error cost curve of the form $B = a_2(P)^{b_2}$ where b_2 is greater than one. The parameters for those power functions or log-linear functions could theoretically be determined by creating a data matrix of numerous situations in which we somehow know the type 1 error costs (A), the type 2 error costs (B) and the

statistical significance level that was used (P). We would then use the log of A as a
dependent variable and the log of P as the independent variable in one linear
regression, and then use the log of B as a dependent variable and the log of P as
the independent variable in a second linear regression. After so determining the
values of a_1, b_1, a_2, and b_2, we could then determine that the value of P where
the total costs bottom out is a simple function of those four parameters, as is
shown in the appendix to this chapter. That function follows from setting the
slope of the total costs relative to P equal to zero and then solving for P, as is also
shown in the appendix. One could assume for the sake of simplicity that a_1 equals
a_2. One cannot, however, insert 3 in place of b_1 and 1 in place of b_2 in order to
show that the type 1 error costs are 3 times as undesirable as the type 2 error
costs. This is so because the value of A to B is not simply a function of the value
of b_1 to b_2. The A/B ratio, for example, changes if b_1/b_2 is 6 to 2 rather than 3
to 1.

  10. The proof for the formula for finding the threshold P is as follows:

$(-B) (P) + (A)(1-P) = (+B)(P) + (-A)(1-P)$

$-BP + A - AP = BP - A + AP$ (Removing parentheses)

$A + A = BP + AP + BP + AP$ (Transposing

$2A = 2BP + 2 AP$ (Combing terms)

$A = BP + AP$ (Dividing by 2)

$A = P(B + A)$ (Factoring)

$P^* = A/(B + A)$ (Dividing by B + A)

  11. One could further simplify the formula $P^* = A/(A+B)$ by algebraically
reducing it to $P^* = X/(X+1)$ where X is the A/B ratio. Thus, if Blackstone had a
10 to 1 ratio, this simplified formula would reduce to $10/(10+1) = 10/11 = .91$.
The simplified formula has the advantage that the user does not have to determine
separate quantities for A and B, but only the one quantity of how many more
times A is valued than B. For further discussion of the criminal conviction
problem, see Nagel, Lamm, and Neef, "Decision Theory and Juror Decision
Making," in Bruce Sales (ed.), *The Jury, Judicial, and Trial Processes* (Plenum,
1978).

  12. One could further simplify the formula $P^* = B/(A+B)$ by algebraically
reducing it to $P^* = 1/(X+1)$ where X is the A/B ratio. Thus, if one considers it
equally bad to make a type 1 or type 2 error in the racial disparity problem, this
simplified formula would reduce to $1/(1+1) = 1/2 = .50$. As mentioned previously,
the simplified formula has the advantage that the user does not have to determine
separate quantities for A and B, but only the one quantity of how many more
times A is valued than B. In many situations it is virtually impossible to know the
probability of a type 1 error or a type 2 error even though we can meaningfully
say something about the relative cost of a type 1 error to a type 2 error. For
example, in the criminal conviction problem we have no way of knowing out of
100 average criminal cases what the probability is of a truly innocent defendant
being convicted (a type 1 error) or a truly guilty defendant being acquitted (a
type 2 error), although we know that about 60 percent of all defendants are
convicted in jury trials and about 40 percent are acquitted. Even if jurors operate
at a .95 threshold probability such that they will only convict a defendant if he
has more than a .95 probability of guilt, that does not mean that 5 percent of the

time they will wrongly convict innocent defendants. The number of innocent defendants convicted is mainly dependent on how many innocent defendants are tried, which is an unknown and probably unknowable quantity.

13. See Hays and Winkler, note 2, especially pages 383-399.

14. After arriving at an optimum probability level of statistical significance, one should then determine the probability that the hypothesis being tested is true or false. That determination can be made by calculating a chance probability using the tests of statistical significance that are referred to in note 1 as has been done with data concerning the difference between sentences received by black defendants and white defendants. See Nagel, "Disparities in Criminal Procedure," 14 *UCLA Law Review* 1272-1305 (1967). That determination can also be made in a more subjective way where the perceived probability is not a ratio between favorable occurrences and total opportunities, but rather a measure of intensity of certainty. That is the kind of probability involved in the criminal conviction problem.

15. See notes 3 and 4.

Chapter 2

ALTERNATIVE PREDICTION METHODS AND CRITERIA

The Problems and the Data

One purpose of this chapter is to analyze alternative methods for predicting or saying in advance how persons, places, or things will be positioned on a given variable. Such prediction can occur mainly by knowing how the units of analysis have been positioned in the past, or by knowing something about the relation between the variable being predicted and another variable. A second purpose of this chapter is to analyze alternative criteria for judging the accuracy of the alternative prediction methods.

Statistics textbooks generally do not include the important concept of prediction in their tables of contents.[1] When the concept is sometimes mentioned in their indexes, it usually only refers to prediction from a regression equation, implying that regression is the most accurate kind of prediction when it quite often may not be.[2] The unusual statistics textbook that deals with alternative methods of prediction not only tends to accept regression analysis as the optimum method, but also tends to accept with little justification the least squares criterion as the optimum criterion for determining the optimum method. For example, Guilford and Fruchter justify the least squares criterion by saying statisticians "demand a predicted measurement from which the sum of the squared deviations is a minimum."[3] This in effect uses the least squares criterion to justify itself. There may often be meaningful justifications for using a regression equation to predict and for using a prediction criterion of minimizing squared deviations between predicted scores and actual scores, but the usefulness of the results may sometimes be increased by using an alternative prediction method or accuracy criterion.

Table 2.1:   Basic Data to Illustrate Alternative Prediction Methods and Criteria

A. THE PRETRIAL RELEASE DATA (Actual data to illustrate dichotomous measurement)

		Prior Record (X)		
		Two or More Prior Arrests (0)	None or One Prior Arrest (1)	
Appearance on Court Date (Y)	Defendant Appeared (1)	a 231 (87%)	c 455 (93%)	686 (91%)
	Failed to Appear (0)	b 34 (13%)	d 36 (7%)	70 (9%)
		265 (100%)	491 (100%)	756 (100%)

B. THE DAMAGES AWARDED DATA (Hypothetical data to illustrate continuous measurement)

Personal Injury Case #	Damages Awarded (Y) (in $1,000's)	Medical Expenses (X) (in $100's)
1	3	1
2	3	4
3	5	3
4	10	6
	21/4=$5.25	14/4=$3.50

The analysis of alternative prediction methods and criteria will be illustrated in this chapter by two sets of data. One set deals with attempting to predict whether an arrested suspect will appear or fail to appear for his or her court date. Being able to predict how defendants will be positioned on that variable is quite important for determining whether a defendant should be released or held in jail pending trial. This data is summarized in Table 2.1A. It consists of a random sample of 756 cases from Charlotte, North Carolina, compiled in 1973 by Professor Stevens Clarke of the University of North Carolina.[4] A relatively important predictor variable was having or not having two or more prior arrests. That actual data can be used to illustrate prediction with dichotomous measurement which is the simplest form of prediction.

The second set of data deals with the important civil law problem of predicting the damages to be awarded in personal injury cases. That kind of prediction is important to personal injury lawyers in deciding whether to take certain clients on a contingency fee basis, how to bargain with opposing counsel, and whether to bring the cases to trial. This hypothetical data is summarized in Table 2.1B. It just consists of four past cases for which the damages awarded and medical expenses are known. Lawyers often try to predict damages awarded from medical expenses using various rules of thumb such as damages awarded tend to equal three to five times the medical expenses. The hypothetical data involves a larger ratio than that, but can nicely serve to illustrate in a simple way prediction with continuous variables that can take many or an infinite quantity of values.

Predicting Randomly

One would not recommend random prediction in order to obtain accurate results. The value of discussing random prediction is to obtain a better understanding of the baseline from which one can try to improve. Over a large number of cases or instances, random prediction will result in the worst possible prediction since it relies on pure chance rather than on information concerning how the units of analysis have been distributed in the past or how they are presently positioned on some other variable.[5] In making random predictions of how cases will be positioned on a variable, one does not use any information concerning how those cases are positioned on another variable, or what has been the past distribution of the cases on the variable being predicted.

Instead one merely knows how many possible categories there are on the variable being predicted, and one gives each category an equal probability of being the predicted category.

Table 2.2A shows what is likely to happen if one randomly predicts whether a defendant will appear in court on his or her court date, or will fail to appear. Random prediction in this two-choice context means that 50 percent of the time one will predict appearance, and 50 percent of the time one will predict failure to appear. That at least will be the approximate distribution over a large number of cases if one flips an equally balanced coin to make the predictions. One interesting nonintuitive aspect of random prediction with two choices is that no matter what the actual distribution of the cases is, one will tend to be 50 percent right over a large number of cases. This is just as true if the actual occurrences are 100 percent appearance, 100 percent failure to appear, or any combination in between such as 91 percent appearance and 9 percent failure as in the Table 2.1A data. This can be more clearly seen by applying the analysis of Table 2.2A to any hypothetical distribution of the Table 2.1A data.

Table 2.2A like all the subsequent tables first shows the possible predicted scores which are either a 1 for appearing, or a 0 for failing to appear. Given the nature of random prediction, each of those two predicted scores would occur 50 percent of the time, or 378 out of the 756 cases. Some of the first set of 378 cases would have an actual score of 1 for appearing, and an actual score of 0 for not appearing. If the first set of 378 cases is a random sample of the total 756 cases, then 91 percent or 344 of them will be accurately predicted, and 9 percent or 34 of them will be wrongly predicted, and likewise with the second set of 378 cases that are predicted as failure to appear cases. The accurately predicted cases have a deviation per case of zero, and the wrongly predicted cases have a deviation per case of 1.00. The total deviation for a given category of cases is the deviation per case in that category times the frequency of its occurrence, which sums to the total number of wrongly predicted cases, and that will always be half the total cases in a two-choice situation. If 100 percent of the cases actually scored 0, or actually scored 1, then when 50 percent of the time we predict 1, we will always be right; and when the other 50 percent of the time we predict 0, we will always be wrong, still giving us a 50 percent accuracy score or average deviation. In the two-choice situation, there will also be no difference between the prediction criterion working with unsquared deviations or with squared deviations since 0 and 1 are the same unsquared or squared.

Table 2.2: The Average Deviation Between Predicted and Actual Scores: Predicting Randomly

Predicted Score (Y_p)	Frequency of Predicted Score (F_p)	Actual Score (Y_a)	Frequency of Actual Score (F_a)	Expected Deviation Per Case (Y_d)	Total Deviation $(Y_d)(F_a)$	Expected Deviation Per Case Squared (Y^2_d)	Total Deviation Squared $(Y_d^2)(F_a)$
A. THE PRETRIAL RELEASE DATA							
1 (Appear)	378 (50% of 756)	1	344 (91% of 378)	0	0	0	0
		0	34 (9% of 378)	1	34	1	34
0 (Fail)	378 (50% of 756)	1	344 (91% of 378)	1	344	1	344
		0	34 (9% of 378)	0	0	0	0
Totals and Averages					378/756=.50		378/756=.50
B. THE DAMAGES AWARDED DATA							
$0 to $10	.09 each	3	1	3.06	3.06	9.36	9.36
$0 to $10	.09 each	3	1	3.06	3.06	9.36	9.36
$0 to $10	.09 each	5	1	2.52	2.52	6.35	6.35
$0 to $10	.09 each	10	1	4.95	4.95	24.50	24.50
Totals and Averages					13.59/4=$3.40		49.57/4=$12.39

Table 2.2B shows what is likely to happen if one randomly predicts how much damages will be awarded to the plaintiff in each of our four hypothetical personal injury cases. Random prediction in this context means first determining how many categories are available on the variable being predicted and then giving each category an equal probability of being predicted. With continuously measured data, there are theoretically an infinite number of categories available. As a practical matter, however, one would normally divide a continuous variable into a set of finite categories either for tabular presentation, or simply because we do not figure damages in pennies or parts of pennies, and damages awarded never exceed about $10,000,000. With our hypothetical data, we could somewhat arbitrarily say there are eleven possible amounts that can be awarded, namely $0, $1, and so on up to $10 if we round off to the nearest $1,000 and drop the three zeros.

If we predict randomly with those eleven possible predicted scores, each one should come up about one-eleventh or 9 percent of the time by drawing two-digit numbers from a random numbers table or by drawing eleven pieces of numbered paper from a hat. In the first case, for example, 9 percent of the time we will predict $0 and be off by a $3 deviation since the first case had an actual score of $3. That $3 deviation, however, has to be discounted by the probability of its occurring which is only .09, and thus the expected or discounted deviation when we predict $0 for the first case is .27. Likewise, when we predict $1 for the first case, the deviation will be $2, but the expected or discounted deviation will be .18. If we follow that procedure for the other nine possible predictions, we will then have a set of eleven expected deviations for the first case. By summing those eleven expected deviations, we get the total expected deviation for case one, which is $3.06. By following the same procedure for the next three cases, we get an expected deviation for each of them of $3.06, $2.52, and $4.95, respectively. If we now sum those expected deviations and divide by four cases, we arrive at an average deviation for the set of cases of $3.40.[6]

That average deviation is affected by the distribution of the actual scores among the cases unlike the dichotomous pre-trial release data. This can easily be seen by changing the actual score on any one of the cases and then recalculating the average deviation. For example, if the second case had an actual score of $10 rather than $3, it would have a total deviation of $4.95, like the fourth case, which would raise the sum of the deviations and the average deviation. The random prediction method, however, by relying on pure chance still results in the worst possible average deviation over a large number of instances regardless whether one is working with dichotomous data or continuous data.

The continuous data example also differs from the dichotomous data in that the continuous data results in a difference between the average deviation of $3.40 and the average squared deviation of $12.39, whereas the dichotomous data resulted in a .50 average for both prediction accuracy criteria. To determine which is the more useful criterion for judging prediction accuracy is best done by using both criteria to compare two different prediction methods, such as random prediction versus predicting from a measure of central tendency, or better yet, prediction from the mode versus prediction from the mean to which we now turn.

Predicting from Knowing How the Data Has Been Distributed on the Variable Being Predicted

Suppose we have the row total information for the pretrial release Table 2.1A, or the Y column information for the damages awarded Table 2.1B, how might we then improve upon random prediction? One might immediately say predict the average or mean score. We will see, however, that doing so may result in substantially less accurate predictions than predicting the mode or most common score, although that partly depends on how one defines accuracy. We will also see that regardless which is the most accurate method of prediction from a prior distribution, that the actual method used may be a kind of event matching which seeks to beat the odds or at least make prediction more interesting.

PREDICTING FROM CENTRAL TENDENCY MEASURES

Table 2.3A shows what is likely to happen if one predicts whether a defendant will appear in court by always predicting the most frequent past occurrence, or by always predicting the mean score. If we always predict the mode or a score of 1, then we will be right 91 percent of the time and wrong 9 percent of the time, for an average deviation of .09. In other words, the average deviation with dichotomous data indicates the percent of mispredictions which makes it an especially useful criterion of prediction accuracy, at least with dichotomous data.[7] The mean score for the pretrial release data is .91, which can be arrived at

Table 2.3: The Average Deviation Between Predicted and Actual Scores: Predicting from Central Tendency Measure

Predicted Score (Y_p)	Frequency of Predicted Score (F_p)	Actual Score (Y_a)	Frequency of Actual Score (F_a)	Deviation Per Case (Y_d)	Total Deviation (Y_d)(F_a)	Deviation Per Case Squared (Y_d^2)	Total Deviation Squared (Y_d^2)(F_a)
A. THE PRETRIAL RELEASE DATA							
(1) Predicting from the Mode							
1.00 (Appear)	756	1	686 (91% of 756)	0	0	0	0
		0	70 (9% of 756)	1	70	1	70
					70/756=.09		70/756=.09
(2) Predicting from the Mean							
.91	756	1	686 (91% of 756)	.09	62	.01	6
		0	70 (9% of 756)	.91	0	.83	58
					62/756=.08		64/756=.03
B. THE DAMAGES AWARDED DATA							
(1) Predicting from the Mode							
$3	1	3	1	0	0	0	0
$3	1	3	1	0	0	0	0
$3	1	5	1	2	2	4	4
$3	1	10	1	7	7	49	49
					9/4=$2.25		53/4=$13.25
(2) Predicting from the Mean							
$5.25	1	3	1	2.25	2.25	5.06	5.06
$5.25	1	3	1	2.25	2.25	5.06	5.06
$5.25	1	5	1	.25	.25	.06	.06
$5.25	1	10	1	4.75	4.75	22.56	22.56
					9.50/4=$2.38		32.75/4=$8.19

by adding the 686 cases which have a score of 1 to the 70 cases which have a score of 0, and dividing the 686 sum by the 756 cases.[8] If we always predict that mean score of .91, then we will be off by a deviation of .09 in 686 cases or 91 percent of the 756; and we will be off by a deviation of .91 in 70 cases or in 9 percent of the 756. This will give a total deviation of 62 and an average deviation of .08, which with this data is an improvement on predicting by the mode.[9] The average square deviation of .08 with the mean is also an improvement on the average squared deviation of .09 with the mode.[10]

So far, the data tends to support the conventional wisdom that predicting from the mean is more accurate than predicting from the mode. The situation changes, however, when we deal with the damages award data, not because it is continuous data, but rather because it has a different distribution. Thus, applying the same methodology to Table 2.3B as we applied in 2.3A, we see that the average deviation of $2.38 in predicting damages awarded from the mean is worse than the average deviation of $2.25 in predicting from the mode.[11] The most interesting aspect of Table 2.3B, however, is the fact that the relative merits of mean versus modal prediction is reversed with prediction from the mean coming out better if we use as our accuracy criterion the least squares criterion shown in the last column. Indeed, one of the justifications given for the least squares criterion is that it minimizes the squared deviations from the mean. This means that by squaring the deviations, we automatically force predicting from the mean to be the "most accurate" of these two prediction methods, but is it really?

To answer that question, we might first look at the justifications that are given for the least squares criterion in the statistics textbooks which attempt to justify it other than by faith in statistical expertise and in noncircular ways, and then look at the practical consequences of working with the squared deviations rather than the simple deviations. One justification that is given for squaring the deviations is that it gets rid of the plus or minus sign that would otherwise be present in front of the deviation. We do want to get rid of that sign since normally a deviation of +2 is just as bad as a deviation of −2, but we can get rid of the sign more easily by ignoring it, as is done with the simple deviation method rather than by squaring the deviation. Another justification is that the algebra of least squares is quite manageable, although so is the algebra of not squaring, and the arithmetic may definitely be simpler by not squaring. A third justification is to argue that by using a least squares criterion we in some sense penalize the researcher for having outliers or more deviant cases, since a case with a deviation of 2 is considered four times as bad as a deviation of 1 if the 2 is squared, rather than merely twice as bad. That kind of reasoning might make sense in the social philosophy of John Rawls, who advocates trying to bring up the most downtrodden (although not necessarily bring down the most well-off), but does not seem to make much sense in dealing with data in which having an off-line point has no normative implications.

A fourth justification for rejecting a criterion that does not square the deviations is that for certain data some points could be changed without changing the best fitting line if that criterion were used. For example, if there are three data points with successively higher values on the X variable, then the line that minimizes the sum of the unsquared deviations may be a line that goes through the first and third points regardless where the second point is located, whereas the position of a least squares line would consider the position of the second point. That is no problem, however, so long as the unsquared criterion is capable of producing a unique line with a given set of data (rather than a number of equally fitting lines), although even a number of equally fitting lines would have the advantage of giving the decision-maker a choice among X values in order to achieve a given Y value. A final justification is that the least squares criterion results in predictors or estimators based on a sample of data that is most likely to capture the value of the same statistics if the universe of data were available. In other words, if we use the least squares method to estimate a slope from a random sample, then by increasing the size of the sample or the number of samples we should more quickly come close to the least squares slope of the universe of data from which the sample is drawn. This justification, however, presumes that we want to capture the least squares slope of the universe rather than the slope of a line that is fitted to the universe data using an unsquared criterion. It may be better to have a not-so-good estimator of the right thing than a good estimator of the wrong thing.[12]

Approaching the problem from the perspective of its practical consequences, which prediction method would a rational lawyer prefer given the data in Table 2.3B between predicting from the mode and predicting from the mean? For one thing, he would find predicting from the mode to be simpler, but which method would be more accurate? If we can agree that in a rational way, predicting from the mode is more accurate, then that means the average deviation method makes more sense at least for routine prediction than the average deviation squared method, since only the first method indicates modal prediction is more accurate. By "rational" in this context we mean doing what is likely to result in maximizing the benefits minus the costs of the decision maker. Suppose we say that our rational lawyer suffers a dollar loss in each case equal to the difference between his or her prediction and the actual damages awarded in the case. Thus by predicting from the mode, he will average a loss of $2.25 over the four cases. If, however, he predicts from the mean, he will average a loss of $2.38 over the four cases. Therefore, it makes more sense and is more rational to predict from the mode. As stated above, that conclusion also leads one to say that the average deviation criterion makes more rational sense than the average squared deviation criterion, since only the former criterion leads to that more rational result.

This does not mean we are advocating replacing the least squares criterion with an unsquared criterion. Instead it means that perhaps in statistical studies, more mention should be made of the average deviation or what is often referred to as the mean residual. Most studies merely present squared deviations, which are in effect presented whenever a correlation coefficient is given, since such a coefficient is the complement of the sum of the squared deviations between the actual and predicted scores divided by the sum of the squared deviations between the actual and mean scores. What is also being advocated is more of an awareness of how using a least squares criterion for judging between alternative prediction methods or fitting a regression line can sometimes lead to non-optimum or non-rational prediction results where (as in Table 2.3B) the results are sensitive to which accuracy criterion is used.[13]

PREDICTING FROM EVENT-MATCHING

Speaking of rational prediction, it is interesting to note that according to Herbert Simon, decision makers who have access to a prior distribution will sometimes deliberately not use the rational prediction method of either predicting from the mode or the mean. Instead, they will try to beat the odds of central tendency prediction, by doing what Simon refers to as event-matching.[14] More specifically in the pretrial release context, a decision maker who only knows that 91 percent of the defendants appear for their court dates might feel bored and unchallenged to always predict the defendant will appear. Instead, out of every ten cases, he might guess 9 will appear and 1 will fail to appear in accordance with the prior distribution, thereby seeking 100 percent accuracy rather than 91 percent. If he merely guesses which 9 will appear and which 1 will fail to appear, he is likely to predict better than purely random prediction, but substantially worse than always predicting the modal category over a large number of cases.

This can be seen from the data in Table 2.4A. Our event-matching decision maker will predict 686 of the defendants will appear or 91 percent of the 756, if he or she is going to match the row totals distribution. Of those 686 cases, 91 percent or 624 cases should result in an actual appearance if pure chance is operating. Likewise, of those 686 cases, 9 percent or 62 cases should result in a failure to appear. Applying that probabilistic logic to the remaining 70 cases in which the decision-maker predicts failure to appear, and then calculating the deviations per case, the total deviations per case type, and the sum of the total deviations, we see that such a decision maker is likely to be 17 percent wrong or only 83 percent right with this data.[15] He could have been only 9 percent wrong and 91 percent right if he would have always predicted appearance rather than nonappearance. This may partly explain why arraignment judges hold in jail pending trial much higher than only 9 percent of the persons arrested. In other words, they may be event-matching to beat the odds instead of using modal prediction which may not look as intellectually discriminating, but may produce better results, especially with such a skewed distribution.

Table 2.4B applies prediction by event-matching to the damages awarded data. In that context, event-matching means knowing that the prior distribution involved two out of four cases being awarded $3 apiece, one being awarded $5, and the fourth being awarded $10, and then trying to duplicate that distribution in future predictions. This means that out of every set of predictions, such a decision maker will predict $3 fifty percent of the time, $5 twenty-five percent of the time, and $10 twenty-five percent of the time. If he were predicting the first case in which the actual score is $3, our decision maker would be off by a deviation of $0 (i.e., $3 minus $3) fifty percent of the time, by a deviation of $2 (i.e., $3 minus $5) twenty-five percent of the time, and by a deviation of $7 (i.e., $3 minus $10) twenty-five percent of the time. The expected or discounted deviations for each of those three possibilities would thus be $0 (i.e., $0 times .50), $.50 (i.e., $2 times .25), and $1.75 (i.e., $7 times .25). By summing the expected deviations for the first case, we get $2.25 which appears in the deviation per case column of Table 2.4B. Applying the same analysis to the next

Table 2.4: The Average Deviation Between Predicted and Actual Scores: Predicting by Event Matching

Predicted Score (Y_p)	Frequency of Predicted Score (F_p)	Actual Score (Y_a)	Frequency of Actual Score (F_a)	Deviation Per Case (Y_d)	Total Deviation $(Y_d)(F_a)$	Deviation Per Case Squared (Y_d^2)	Total Deviation Squared $(Y_d^2)(F_a)$
A. THE PRETRIAL RELEASE DATA							
1 (Appear)	686 (91% of 756)	1	624 (91% of 686)	0	0	0	0
		0	62 (9% of 686)	1	62	1	62
0 (Fail)	70 (9% of 756)	1	64 (91% of 70)	1	64	1	64
		0	6 (9% of 70)	0	0	0	0
					126/756=.17		126/756=.17
B. THE DAMAGES AWARDED DATA							
3, 3, 5, or 10	.25 each	3	1	2.25	2.25	5.06	5.06
3, 3, 5, or 10	.25 each	3	1	2.25	2.25	5.06	5.06
3, 3, 5, or 10	.25 each	5	1	2.25	2.25	5.06	5.06
3, 3, 5, or 10	.25 each	10	1	4.75	4.75	22.56	22.56
					11.50/4=$2.88		37.74/4=$9.44

three cases yields an expected deviation per case of $2.25, $2.25 and $4.75 respectively. Summing those deviations yields an average expected deviation of $2.88, which is more than the $2.38 from always predicting the mean, and still more than the $2.25 average deviation from always predicting the mode, although better than the $3.40 average deviation by randomly predicting any one of eleven categories rather than more selectively working with the three categories.

Event-matching is probably more likely to be used in preference to the more boring, but more accurate, central-tendency prediction when the decision maker is a risk-preferer rather than someone who is risk-adverse or more risk-neutral. It is also more likely to be used when less is at stake such as winning pennies in a psychology experiment designed to predict whether a star or circle will appear on a cathode ray tube, rather than when one's physical well-being depends on the accuracy of the predictions. Event-matching may also be more likely to occur when fewer categories are available, thereby making the method simpler. Regardless under what circumstances event-matching is more likely to occur, it does seem to be a frequent occurrence as a prediction method, and should therefore be considered in the prediction literature more so than it has been.

Predicting from Knowing Something about the Relation Between the Variable Being Predicted and Another Variable

In contrast to predicting just on the basis of the row totals in four-cell tables or the data distribution on a dependent variable, one could also attempt to predict the positioning of persons, places or things on one variable by knowing how they are positioned on one or more other variables. This basically involves two kinds of predictions. One deals with predicting from correlation information, and the other deals with predicting from an equation relating the Y variable being predicted to the X variable from which the predictions are made.

PREDICTING FROM KNOWING INFORMATION ABOUT THE DIAGONALS OR CORRELATION OF A TABLE

Statistical studies quite often present information showing correlation coefficients between each variable and each other variable involved in the study. That kind of correlation analysis has been especially facilitated by canned computer programs that can easily intercorrelate 100 or more variables. Such research often does not involve much thinking about causal relations among the variables and tends to be especially nontheoretical in developing useful mathematical models for predicting the effects of changes in one variable by changes in another variable in light of various contingent probabilities, intervening events, and constraints. Unfortunately, however, such studies often imply that a correlation relation may be useful for prediction purposes, although they recognize that correlation does not necessarily indicate causation. One purpose of this section is to show how misleading the notion of correlation can be even in arriving at accurate predictions.

In the context of a four-cell table like Table 2.1A dealing with pretrial release data, there is a positive correlation between the X variable and the Y variable if there is a concentration of entries on the bc diagonal rather than the ad diagonal. More specifically, there is a positive correlation if b times c is greater than a times d, and there is a negative correlation if a times d is greater than b times c. Knowing that might lead one to explicitly or implicitly say that if there is a positive correlation between X and Y, then when a case scores 1 on X, predict a 1 on Y; and when a case scores 0 on X, predict a 0 on Y, and the opposite when there is a negative correlation. What's wrong with that?

The answer is partly shown in Table 2.5A with the pretrial release data. If we follow the above prediction method or decision rule, the table indicates that of the 756 cases, there are 491 in which the defendant scored a 1 on prior record, and we would thus predict a 1 on his appearing. Of those 491 cases, we will be right 455 times for a 0 deviation, and wrong 36 times for a deviation of 1. Where we predict a 0 on the Y appearance variable (when the defendant scores a 0 on the X prior record variable) in the remaining 265 cases, we will then be wrong 231 times for a deviation of 1, and right 34 times for a deviation of 0. The total number of wrong cases is thus 267, for an average deviation of .35, or 35 percent wrong. This would be the worst average deviation of all the prediction methods other than purely random prediction. How bad this prediction method comes out depends mainly on how close the correlation is to a perfect correlation.[16] The data in Table 2.1A involves a correlation of only .09.

The correlation approach to prediction will often not only be worse than predicting from merely knowing the prior distribution of the cases on the dependent variable, but will sometimes even be worse than predicting in a direction opposite to the sign of the correlation coefficient. In other words, one might be able to achieve a substantially lower average deviation by predicting a 0 on Y when there is a 1 on X, and predicting a 1 on Y when there is a 0 on X, even though the correlation

Table 2.5: The Average Deviation Between Predicted and Actual Scores: Predicting from the Correlation Direction

Predicted Score (Y_p)	Frequency of Predicted Score (F_p)	Actual Score (Y_a)	Frequency of Actual Score (F_a)	Deviation Per Case (Y_d)	Total Deviation (Y_d) (F_a)	Deviation Per Case Squared (Y_d^2)	Total Deviation Squared (Y_d^2) (F_a)
A. THE PRETRIAL RELEASE DATA							
1 (Appear)	491 (1 on X)	1	455 (1 on Y)	0	0	0	0
		0	36 (0 on Y)	1	36	1	36
0 (Fail)	265 (0 on Y)	1	231 (1 on Y)	1	231	1	231
		0	34 (0 on Y)	0	0	0	0
					267/756=.35		267/756=.35
B. THE DAMAGES AWARDED DATA							
0 (Low)	1	0	1	0	0	0	0
0	1	0	1	0	0	0	0
0	1	0	1	0	0	0	0
1 (High)	1	1	1	0	0	0	0
					0/4=0		0/4=0

is positive rather than negative. That will always be the situation whenever a + d is greater than b + c, even though b x c is greater than a x d. In other words, predicting contrary to the "main diagonal" will always result in fewer mispredictions if between the two diagonals, the diagonal which has the higher product (of its cell entries) has the lower sum. For example, suppose we have a four-cell table like Table 2.6. If we follow the correlation approach with that data, we will be wrong 8 times, and right only 6 times, for an average deviation of .57. On the other hand, if we use what might be referred to as the anti-correlation approach, we will be wrong only 6 times and right 8 times, for an average deviation of .43. Note especially that predicting on the basis of the correlation (with that hypothetical data) is so bad that the average deviation comes out higher than the .50 one could get by pure chance over a large set of cases.[17]

The notion of predicting from knowing a correlation can be applied to tables larger than a two-by-two table, especially if one expands the notion of diagonal cells to include the cells immediately adjacent to the diagonal cells. Predicting from the correlation does however require having some notion of a break in the independent variable between the low and the high categories, and likewise a break on the dependent variable. The method could, for example, be applied to the damages awarded data if we were to split the cases at the mean of $3.50 on the medical expenses variable so that medical expenses below $3.50 are considered low or scored 0, and medical expenses above $3.50 are considered high or scored 1. We could then do likewise with the damages awarded variable, splitting at the mean of $5.25. Such splitting is often done in social science research in order to simplify an analysis or a tabular presentation, although it obviously throws out possibly valuable information. That approach is used in Table 2.5B, although it

Table 2.6: A Cross-Tabulation Table in Which the Diagonal with the Bigger Product Does not Have the Bigger Sum

		X	
		0	1
Y	1	7	3
	0	3	1

is highly nonrecommended even though it generates perfect prediction
with a 0 average deviation. It illustrates how perfect prediction may
sometimes not be what we want if what we are predicting to is
meaningless for our purposes. In this example, it would probably be not
very meaningful for a lawyer to simply know that a case is predicted as
likely to result in above the $5.25 or $5,250 average damages without
being more precise than that. In other words, we are willing to have
more than a 0 average deviation or average deviation squared in order to
get more precision on what is being predicted.

The main importance of this analysis of correlation prediction may
be in the light it sheds on regression analysis and the least squares
criterion. In order to further clarify that light, we should first indicate
how prediction from regression analysis applies to the pretrial release
data and the damages award data. We will then indicate how a kind of
antiregression analysis analogous to the anticorrelation method described above can result in a lower average deviation or smaller residuals
than traditional least squares regression analysis.

PREDICTING FROM AN EQUATION

Predicting from an equation or equations does not necessarily involve curve-fitting regression analysis. Any equation in which Y is
expressed as a function of one or more X variables qualifies as prediction from an equation. The equation can be linear in nature of the form
$Y = a + bX$, log-linear of the form $Y = aX^b$, or involve any other transformation of the Y variable or X variable. The equation can have an X
variable that is Y at an earlier point in time of the form $Y_t = a + Y_{t-n}$,
or an X that is time itself of the form $Y = a + bt$ as in the projection of
a trend line. The prediction can also involve a combination of equations
such as where the relation between Y and X is linear for certain values
of X, and is another linear or non-linear equation for others values of X.
The equation can be derived from the curve fitting of regression analysis,
from deductive logic via prior equations, or from intuitive hunches.[18]

The most common type of prediction from an equation does involve
a least-squares regression equation. In the context of the dichotomous
pretrial release data, this simply means predicting the 1 or 0 value on
the Y variable from the 1 or 0 value on the X variable by noting (1) the
percentage that is in cell *a* which is the Y-intercept, and (2) the
difference between the percentages in cell *c* and cell *a* which is the
slope. Thus, the prediction equation is $Y = .87 + .06X$. The .87 tells us
that when X is scored 0, the most likely value of Y will be .87 using a
least squares criterion of "most likely." The .06 tells us that if there is a

one unit change in X from 0 to 1, there is "most likely" to be .06 of a unit change on Y from .87 to .93, again using the criterion of minimizing the total squared deviations.

Table 2.7A shows what the average deviation and average squared deviation would be if we applied that regression equation to the 756 pretrial release cases. In the 491 cases that are scored 1 on prior record, there would be a deviation per case of .07 for the 455 cases in which the defendant appeared (i.e., 1.00 - .93), and a deviation per case of .93 for the 36 cases in which the defendant failed to appear (i.e., 0 - .93). Applying that analysis to the 265 cases that are scored 0 on prior record, we arrive at an average deviation per case of .17, and an average squared deviation of .07 per case.[19] Those deviations are substantially less than merely predicting from the direction of the correlation in Table 2.5, because we are taking the degree of relation into consideration and especially the starting point or Y-intercept.[20] If we ignored the Y-intercept, we would in effect be operating as if there were a zero Y-intercept, and we would then have a much higher average deviation and quantity of mispredictions.[21]

A regression equation for continuous data like the damages awarded data in Table 2.7B cannot be derived by simply calculating some percentages. Now that electronic pocket calculators have been wired to do bivariate regression analysis, however, one can quickly determine that the regression equation which "best fits" the data of Table 2.1B is $Y = .81 + 1.27X$. We put "best fits" in quotation marks because regression analysis is not likely to provide the best fitting equation in the sense of minimizing the average deviation, but only the best fitting equation in the sense of minimizing the average squared deviation. We have already seen (in analyzing Table 2.3B with regard to mode and mean prediction) that the least squares criterion is not the more rational criterion in the sense of maximizing benefits minus costs, or minimizing costs where only costs or deviations are involved. This is just as true regardless whether we are talking about central tendency prediction or prediction from an equation. It is also just as true regardless how powerful the X variable is we choose to predict from.[22]

The inability of regression analysis to minimize deviations or residuals can best be illustrated by simply offering a regression equation of the form $Y = a + bX$ that will produce a lower total and average deviation than that given in either Table 2.7A or 2.7B. For example, in Table 2.6A the equation $Y = .87 + .13X$ produces a deviation per case for cell a of .13 (times 231 cases), for cell b of .87 (times 34 cases), for cell c of 0 (times 455 cases), and for cell d of 1.00 (times 36 cases).

Table 2.7: The Average Deviation Between Predicted and Actual Scores: Predicting from a Regression Equation

Predicted Score (Y_p)	Frequency of Predicted Score (F_p)	Actual Score (Y_a)	Frequency of Actual Score (F_a)	Deviation Per Case (Y_d)	Total Deviation (Y_d)(F_a)	Deviation Per Case Squared (Y_d^2)	Total Deviation Squared (Y_d^2)(F_a)
A. THE PRETRIAL RELEASE DATA (Y = .87 + .06X)							
.93	491 (1 on X)	1.00	455 (1 on Y)	.07	32	0	0
		0	36 (0 on Y)	.93	33	.86	29
.87	265 (0 on X)	1.00	231 (1 on Y)	.13	30	.02	1
		0	34 (0 on Y)	.87	30	.76	23
					125/756=.17		53/756=.07
B. DAMAGES AWARDED DATA (Y = .81 + 1.27X)							
$2.08	1	3	1	.92	.92	.85	.85
$5.88	1	3	1	2.88	2.88	8.29	8.29
$4.62	1	5	1	.38	.38	.14	.14
$8.42	1	10	1	1.58	1.58	2.50	2.50
					5.76/4=$1.44		11.78/4=$2.94

54

This produces a total deviation of only 96 and an average deviation of only .13 for the 756 cases, as contrasted to the total deviation of 125 and the average deviation of .17 shown in Table 2.7A. The regression equation in Table 2.7B can be improved upon by changing the slope from 1.27 to 1.50. Doing so yields a deviation in the first case of .69, the second case of 3.81, the third case of .31, and the fourth case of .19. This means a total deviation of 5.00, and an average deviation of only 1.25 for the four cases as contrasted to the higher average deviation of 1.44 using least squares regression analysis.

It is easy to improve on a regression analysis equation if improvement means lowering the average deviation, since traditional regression equations are not designed to minimize the average deviation, but rather the average squared deviation, or more precisely the total deviations squared.[23] To "improve" a regression equation, all one has to do is increase or decrease the slope or Y-intercept, and then recalculate the total deviation to see if it is lower than what it formerly was, although one must not go too far in the increasing or decreasing since there is a U-shaped relation between the size of those parameters and the total deviation.[24] By trial and error with a bivariate dichotomous relation, one could probably find the linear equation that converges at the minimum point on that U-shaped total deviation curve.[25] However, it is more difficult to find a linear equation that minimizes the total unsquared deviations for more complicated data because doing so normally involves finding the zero point on the slope or derivative of the total unsquared deviations relative to the parameters. This is impossible to do by ordinary calculus since there is no way to differentiate or find the slope of an expression that has bars in it, as does the symbolism for the absolute or unsigned deviation rather than the squared deviation.[26] This brings out the practical value of working with squared deviations in regression analysis even though unsquared deviations may in other contexts make more rational sense.

A big defect in predicting from regression analysis regardless whether the equation minimizes squared or unsquared deviations is the fact that what is predicted may be quite meaningless. Given the nature of the measurement in Table 2.1A, it is not meaningful to predict a Y-score of any value other than 0 or 1, as was mentioned in discussing prediction from the mean. Therefore, if one is working with a four-cell table where only 0s and 1s are meaningful, then the only possible regression equation is one of the form $Y = 0 + 1X$ corresponding to a positive correlation prediction, or $Y = 1 - 1X$ corresponding to a negative correlation prediction. One could derive such regression equations by using a restricted least squares regression analysis in which the Y-intercept is restricted to 0 or 1, and the slope is restricted to +1 or -1. If such a computer program were applied to the dichotomous pre-trial release data in Table 2.1A, it would generate an equation of the form $Y = 0 + 1X$ for an average deviation of .35, as shown in the correlation prediction Table 2.5, regardless whether one minimizes unsquared or squared deviations.[27]

If, however, one were to apply such a computer program to four-cell Table 2.6 in which the diagonal with the bigger product does not have the bigger sum, then such a least squares regression analysis would be a disaster on prediction accuracy, as compared to an unsquared regression analysis. The least squares approach yields the restricted regression equation $Y = 0 + 1X$, for that data, which in turn yields 8 wrong predictions and only 6 right predictions for an average deviation of .57, which is worse than pure chance. On the other hand, if one seeks to fit a regression line to the data that minimizes the total unsquared deviations, then doing so yields the restricted regression equation $Y = 1 - 1X$. That equation will produce only 6 wrong predictions and 8 right predictions for a much better average deviation or percent of mispredictions of .47.

Conclusions

In light of what has been presented, what can one conclude as to what is the best prediction method and the best prediction criterion? Actually, those are not two separate questions since the criterion chosen for judging prediction accuracy tends to determine which prediction method will be considered best. The average unsquared deviation does seem to make the most sense in terms of minimizing the costs of mispredicting. On the other hand, the average squared deviation makes the most sense in terms of its feasibility as a criterion for finding a best fitting prediction equation. Since both criteria have advantages, perhaps they should both be used. The least squares criterion can be used to arrive at prediction equations, although we may gain from experimenting with nonlinear programming algorithms that could be used to arrive at prediction equations which minimize or come satisfyingly close to minimizing the total deviations. Least squares equations, though, should probably be supplemented more often by having the researcher report the average deviation, which is usually referred to as the mean residual in computer programs.

As for the method of prediction rather than the criterion, the simplest and best method in terms of minimizing either the unsquared or squared deviations often involves predicting a central tendency measure on the dependent variable, such as the mode or the mean, especially if the data is skewed.[28] On the other hand, prediction from another variable makes the most sense in terms of developing an understanding of what causes cases sometimes to score high and sometimes to score low on the variable being predicted. Since both methods have advantages, perhaps they should both be presented, with central tendency measures emphasized for their predictive power, and predictive equations emphasized for their use in causal models and means-ends prescription.

We can also conclude some sensible hindsight caveats. First, it makes little sense to predict a dependent variable score using mean prediction or unrestricted regression analysis where the dependent variable is a discrete variable that can only be scored 0, 1, or some other integers. Second, it makes little sense to interpret correlation coefficients as having any predictive meaning as contrasted to slopes and Y-intercepts. Third, there may be substantial differences which should be studied between (1) optimum prediction as measured by squared or unsquared prediction accuracy and (2) actual prediction as reflected in the behavior of decision makers, who may prefer the variety and challenge of prediction through event-matching to the accuracy of central tendency or regression prediction.[29]

For a fourth caveat, one should be more conscious of the fact that "best fitting" regression equations and correlation coefficients as measures of "goodness of fit" do not fit the common sense rationality of minimizing deviations, but rather are best or good mainly in a mathematical convenience sense. That caveat may cause researchers and users of statistical research to seek to improve upon the regression equations that are generated by statistical research, and especially to improve upon the basic methodologies and algorithms. Such improvements should help to make statistical research more useful in arriving at individual and social decisions, as well as more useful in arriving at causal theories of individual and social behavior.

APPENDIX 2.1: SUMMARY OF THE MAIN FORMULAS IN PREDICTION ANALYSIS

This appendix pulls together on a more abstract symbolic level the basic formulas which are mainly presented verbally and illustrated with concrete examples in the chapter. By seeing the formulas on a more abstract level, we can further clarify their interrelations and generalizability. This appendix also briefly refers to some important general matters which did not seem so appropriate to discuss in the text given the emphasis on verbal presentation and concrete illustrations.

I. BASIC SYMBOLS

Y = A variable being predicted to.

Y_a = Actual scores on Y.

Y_p = Y scores predicted from X.

Y_d = The deviation or difference per case between Y_a and Y_p.

EY_d = The expected deviation between Y_a and Y_p, where Y_p is not certain but has a probability of occurring. Thus, EY_d is Y_d multiplied by the probability of its occurring.

X = A variable being predicted from.

N = Number of cases being predicted.

Σ = Sum the scores or deviations which follow.

F = Frequency of an actual score per case or case type.

59

Frequencies in a four-cell table:

a = F of cases scored 0 on X and 1 on Y.

b = F of cases scored 0 on X and 0 on Y.

c = F of cases scored 1 on X and 1 on Y.

d = F of cases scored 1 on X and 0 on Y.

II. CRITERIA FOR EVALUATING PREDICTION METHODS

A. Ungrouped Data

ΣY_d = Sum of the unsquared deviations.

ΣY_d^2 = Sum of the squared deviations.

B. Grouped Data

ΣFY_d = Sum of the unsquared deviations.

ΣFY_d^2 = Sum of the squared deviations.

III. PREDICTING RANDOMLY

Y_p = each possible Y, occurring an equal percentage of the time.

Thus, if the Y scores can be 0 and 1, then Y_p is 0 half the time and 1 the other half.

EY_d = the sum of each possible deviation multiplied by the probability of its occurring. Thus, if the Y_p scores can be 0 and 1, and the actual Y is 0, then Y_d is 0 half the time and 1 the other half. Summing those two possible deviations gives a Y_d of .50.

ΣY_d (for a four-cell table) = .50N

IV. PREDICTING FROM KNOWING HOW THE DATA HAS BEEN DISTRIBUTED ON THE VARIABLE BEING PREDICTED

A. Predicting from Central Tendency Measures

1. The mode

Y_p = the most frequent Y score.

ΣY_d (for a four-cell table) = (b+d) or (a+c), depending on whether more cases are scored 1 on Y or 0 on Y.

2. The mean

Y_p = $\Sigma Y/N$

ΣY_d (for a four-cell table) = (a+c) (b+d)/N

B. Predicting from Event-Matching

Y_p = each possible Y, occurring a percentage of the time in the predictions equal to the percentage of the time in the previous distribution of the actual scores. Thus, if the Y_p scores can be 0 and 1 and the previous distribution was one-fourth 0 and three-fourths Y, then Y_p is one-fourth 0 and three-fourths 1.

EY_d = the sum of each possible deviation multiplied by the probability of its occurring. Thus, in the above example, if Y_a is 0, then Y_d is 0 one-fourth the time and 1 the other three-fourths. Summing those two possible deviations gives a Y_d of .75.

ΣY_d (for a four-cell table) = 2(a+c) (b+d)/N.

V. PREDICTING FROM KNOWING SOMETHING ABOUT THE RELATION BETWEEN THE VARIABLE BEING PREDICTED AND ANOTHER VARIABLE

A. Predicting from Knowing Information about the Diagonals or Correlation in a Table

Y_p = 0 + 1X when there is a positive correlation, and 1 – 1X when there is a negative correlation. In other words, when X is low, predict Y to be low if there is a positive correlation; and when X is low, predict Y to be high if there is a negative correlation.

ΣY_d (for a four-cell table) = a+d or b+c, depending on whether there is a positive or negative correlation.

B.   Predicting from an Equation

Y_p $= a + bX$, if a linear relation is assumed.

Y_p $= aX^b$, if a log-linear or power function relation is assumed.

Y_p $= a + bY_{t-n}$, if one is predicting from the value of Y at a prior point in time.

Y_p $= a + bt$, if one is predicting by extending a trend line over a series of points.

Y_p $= f(X,Z)$, if Y is some function of X and other variables.

ΣY_d (for a four-cell table) $= [(2cd)/(c+d)] + [(2ab)/(a+b)]$.

NOTES

The authors thank David Hildebrand of the Department of Statistics at the University of Pennsylvania and Stephen Portnoy and Hiram Paley of the Department of Mathematics at the University of Illinois for helpful comments on some aspects of this chapter.

1. Hubert Blalock, Jr., *Social Statistics* (McGraw-Hill, 1972); John Mueller, Karl Schuessler, and Herbert Costner, *Statistical Reasoning in Sociology* (Houghton Mifflin, 1970); and Thomas Wonnacott and Ronald Wonnacott, *Introductory Statistics* (Wiley, 1972).

2. See Blalock, op. cit. note 1, at pages 362-363, and Wonnacott, op. cit. note 1, at pages 276-280.

3. J. P. Guilford and Benjamin Fruchter, *Fundamental Statistics in Psychology and Education* (McGraw-Hill, 1973).

4. Stevens Clarke, Jean Freeman, and Gary Koch, "Bail Risk: A Multivariate Analysis", 5 *Journal of Legal Studies* 341-385 (1977).

5. One can do worse than purely random prediction if one predicts so as to maximize rather than minimize the average deviation. That can happen if one predicts in accordance with the sign of the correlation coefficient as will be shown with regard to Table 2.6.

6. One might wrongly think that random prediction produces the same results as always predicting the average category. If we have eleven categories from $0 through $10, and we sum those eleven numbers and divide by eleven, the average category will be $5. Over a large number of random predictions, however, there is no reason why $5 will come up any more often than any of the other categories. They all have a 9 percent likelihood of being predicted if they all have a random or equal probability of being predicted. Thus, it would be fallacious thinking to think that random prediction means a predicted score of $5 for each

of the four cases, and thus a deviation of $2 for the first two cases, $0 for the third case, and $5 for the fourth case.

7. The average deviation indicates the percentage of mispredictions only if the deviations per case can only be 0 or 1, as with random prediction (Table 2.2A), mode prediction (Table 2.3A1) event-matching prediction (Table 2.4A), and correlation prediction (Table 2.5A), but not with mean prediction (Table 2.3A2) or regression prediction (Table 2.7A). The percentage or quantity of mispredictions is a meaningful notion only where one is predicting to a dichotomy like zero and 1. Under such circumstances, there has been a misprediction if Y_p is zero and Y_a is 1, or if Y_p is 1 and Y_a is zero. If the variable being predicted allows for more than two categories such as 1, 2, and 3, then one is faced with a question of when Y_a is 3, is a misprediction involving a Y_p of 2 to be counted as being equally bad or better than a Y_p of 1. Both mispredictions are treated as equally bad in David Hildebrand, James Laing, and Howard Rosenthal, *Analysis of Ordinal Data* (Sage, 1977). However, talking in terms of either the absolute deviation or the squared deviation between Y_a and Y_p does take the degree of misprediction into consideration.

8. Predicting from the mean can be given a Bayesian interpretation in a four-cell table. What we are in effect doing is following the formula $P(Y_1) = P(X_1)P(Y_1|X_1) + P(X_0)P(Y_1|X_0)$, as applied to the dichotomous pretrial release data in Table 2.1A. See Samuel Richmond, *Operations Research for Management Decisions* (Ronald Press, 1968) at page 543. For a four-cell table, that formula reduces to $(a+c)/N$, which is .91, meaning a defendant has a .91 probability of appearing in court.

9. Actually, it is rather meaningless to talk in terms of predicting the mean rather than the mode when one is dealing with an inherently dichotomous variable, like appearing versus not appearing. For a given defendant, one can only meaningfully predict that he or she will appear or will not appear. One cannot meaningfully say that nine-tenths of a single defendant will appear, although one can say that a single defendant has a .91 probability of appearing, or that out of a set of defendants, 91 percent are likely to appear. Thus, given the subject matter of the pretrial release data, predicting the mode is the only meaningful method of central tendency prediction.

10. We could also predict from the median category, which for dichotomous data would always be the same as the modal category. In the damages awarded data, the mode is $3.00, the mean is $5.20, and the median is $4.00. By coincidence, the sum of the absolute deviations predicting from the median comes out to be the same quantity (which is 9) as predicting from the mode. One can show that predicting from the median will always minimize the sum of the absolute deviations just as predicting from the mean will always minimize the sum of the squared deviations. Thus, if one wants to minimize the absolute deviations between the actual and the predicted as one generally would, it makes more sense to predict from the median than the mean.

11. The general formula for calculating an average deviation is $\Sigma|Y-Y_p|/N$, and the general formula for an average squared deviation is $\Sigma(Y-Y_p)^2/N$. The Y_p is the predicted Y score for each case predicting randomly, or from the mode or median, or using any other prediction method. What this article refers to as the average deviation, the average residual, or the mean residual should be distin-

guished from the mean deviation which can be expressed as $\Sigma|Y\text{-}Y_m|/N$, where Y_m is the mean of the Y scores. Those formulas for calculating the average deviation or the average deviation squared apply to all the tables in this article, although simpler nonsummation formulas can be developed for each prediction method as applied to dichotomous data in four-cell tables. For example, the average deviation using modal prediction is $(b+d)/N$, where the letters correspond to the cells in Table 2.1A and where more cases are scored 1 on Y, than 0 on Y. If more cases are scored 0 on Y, the average deviation from modal prediction would be $(a+c)/N$, or the complement of $(b+d)/N$. The average deviation for such dichotomous data using mean prediction is $(a+c)(b+d)/N^2$. Similar formulas could be developed for the average squared deviation, but they would have little value since the average squared deviation has no practical meaning. The average deviation, on the other hand, nicely indicates the likely percentage of mispredictions for most four-cell data, and its complement indicates the likely percent of accurate predictions. The average deviation also has meaningful imagery for nondichotomous data.

12. These justifications for the least squares criterion are well-presented in Wonnacott and Wonnacott, op. cit. note 1, pages 249-252. An additional justification for the least squares criterion is that one can fit a regression line to a set of data using that criterion by the minimization methods associated with ordinary calculus, whereas fitting a regression line to data using the unsquared criterion requires a searching algorithm, as is discussed in footnote 26 below and the accompanying text.

13. The problem of predicting from the mode or the mean is useful for illustrating whether the prediction criterion should be the sum of the absolute deviations between Y_a and Y_p or the sum of the squared deviations. It can also be used to illustrate that merely deciding how to calculate the deviations between actual and predicted is not the only criterion for deciding which prediction method (e.g., predicting from the mode or the mean) is the better method for predicting. Sometimes one must also look to what is going to be done with the prediction and what will be the consequences of that action if the mode rather than the mean is used. For example, if the prediction is used to determine one's bargaining limit in a bilateral bargaining arrangement, then predicting the mean may make more sense than predicting the mode.

More specifically, suppose a defense attorney in a criminal case perceives that (1) an acquittal will result in a sentence of zero years, (2) a conviction will result in a sentence of 10 years, and (3) there is a .60 probability of a conviction. Under those circumstances, predicting the mode or the most common occurrence would involve predicting a 10 year sentence. Predicting the mean or expected value would involve predicting a 6-year sentence, which in effect is saying that out of 10 cases, 6 will involve 10-year sentences, and 4 will involve zero-year sentences for an average of 6 years. Predicting the mode of 10 years would result in a smaller average deviation than predicting the mean of 6 years if 6 of the 10 cases result in 10 year sentences and 4 of the 10 cases result in zero year sentences. Predicting the mode, however, will mean the defense counsel will always accept the prosecutor's offer of a sentence less than 10 years in return for the defendant's being willing to plead guilty. Doing that will mean the defendant will plead guilty in those 4 cases where an acquittal (and thus a zero sentence) would have been received. The defendant would be better off to only be willing to plead guilty if the prosecutor offers a sentence of less than 6 years and to go to trial if the prosecutor is not willing to go below 6 years. This strategy of predicting the mean as the basis for one's bargaining limit assumes the defense counsel is accurately perceiving the conviction probability and the sentence upon conviction, and is thus accurately perceiving what an average set of 10 cases would be like. On the use of the mean or the expected value for determining bargaining limits, see Nagel and Neef, "Plea Bargaining, Decision Theory, and Equilibrium Models," 51 and 52 *Indiana Law Journal* 987-1024, 1-61 (1976).

14. Herbert A. Simon, "Theories of Decision Making in Economics and Behavioural Science," in *Surveys of Economic Theory: Resource Allocation* (Macmillan, 1966), pages 7-8; Julian Feldman, "Simulation of Behavior in the Binary Choice Experiment," in Feigenbaum and Feldman (eds.), *Computers and Thought* (McGraw-Hill, 1963); and R. R. Bush and Frederick Mosteller, *Stochastic Models for Learning* (John Wiley, 1955), Ch. 13.

15. A simplified nonsummation formula for determining the average deviation in a four-cell table using event-matching is $[2(a+c)(b+d)]/N^2$. If the corresponding cell entries are plugged in, the formula will yield an average deviation of .17, or 17 percent mispredictions through event-matching, or 87 percent accurate predictions, over a large number of cases like those in the data base of Table 2.1A.

16. A simple way to calculate a correlation coefficient for data in a form like that of four-cell Table 2.1A is to find the geometric mean of the slope going in both directions, or the square root of b_{YX} times b_{XY}. The b_{YX} slope is simply the difference between the percentages in cells c and a or, $c/(c+d)$ minus $a/(a+b)$. The b_{XY} slope is the difference between the counterpart percentages in cells b and a if the percentages added to 100 across the rows rather than down the columns, or $b/(b+d)$ minus $a/(a+c)$. One can prove that these formulas for a four-cell table algebraically equal the traditional formulas for slopes and correlation coefficients, or one can accept Blalock, op. cit. note 1, at page 380 and 385.

17. The bc diagonal is the main diagonal because its product is 9, and the ad diagonal is the off-diagonal because its product is only 7.

18. The correlation prediction method previously discussed in effect involves a linear equation of the form $Y = 0 + 1X$ when there is a positive correlation and $Y = 1 - 1X$ when there is a negative correlation. The so-called anticorrelation prediction method involves doing the opposite (i.e., predicting contrary to the main diagonal), when the sum of the entries on the off-diagonal is greater than the sum of the entries on the main diagonal.

19. One can algebraically show that the average deviation per case in a four-cell table using linear regression analysis is $(2cd)/(c+d)$ plus the quotient $(2ab)/(a+b)$, with that sum divided by N. One can also algebraically show that the average deviation per case in a four-cell table using the correlation prediction method (discussed in the text associated with Table 2.5A) and the restricted regression analysis method (discussed in note 18 and the text accompanying note 27 is $(a+d)/N$ if the main diagonal goes from southwest to northeast, and is $(b+c)/N$ if the main diagonal goes from northwest to southeast.

20. Even if the correlation method took the degree of correlation into consideration and not just the direction, it would still not make much sense as compared to regression analysis. This is so because a regression coefficient indicates the ratio of how many units the Y variable changes to a one-unit change on the X variable, i.e., $\Delta Y/\Delta X$, whereas a correlation coefficient indicates the

ratio of the explained variance to the total variance, i.e., $\Sigma\,(Y_m\text{-}Y_p)^2$ $/\Sigma\,(Y\text{-}Y_m)^2$. In other words regression coefficients measure the slope of the data dots when they are graphed on XY coordinates, and correlation coefficients measure the extent to which the data dots cluster on that slope line. Both regression coefficients and correlation coefficients, however, rely on a least squares criterion rather than a criterion of minimizing the unsquared deviations. We could have an unsquared counterpart to the correlation coefficient by simply calculating $\Sigma|\,Y_m\text{-}Y_p|\,/\Sigma|\,Y\text{-}Y_m|$.

21. Three sets of data can have the same correlation coefficient and the same slope if both X and Y have the same standard deviation, but very different Y-intercepts and meanings. For example, if Y is being imprisoned (scored 1) or put on probation (scored 0), and X is being white (0) or black (1), then a regression equation of $Y = 0 + .20X$ means that being black is a necessary condition for going to jail since only blacks go to jail. A regression equation of $Y = .80 + .20X$ means being black is a sufficient condition for going to jail since all blacks go to jail. On the other hand, a regression equation of $Y = .40 + .20X$ means being black is neither a necessary nor a sufficient condition for going to jail, even though all three equations and sets of data involve exactly the same .20 slope and .20 correlation coefficient.

22. Predicting from the least squares Y-intercept and slope can be given a Bayesian interpretation in a four-cell table. What we are in effect doing is following the formula $P(Y_1|\,X_1) = P(Y_1)P(X_1|\,Y_1)$ divided by the sum $P(Y_1)P(X_1|\,Y_1) + P(Y_2)P(X_1|\,Y_2)$, as applied to the dichotomous pre-trial release data in Table 2.1A. See Richmond, op. cit. note 8, page 544. For a four-cell table, that formula reduces to $c/(c+d)$, which is .93, meaning a defendant has a ˙93 probability of appearing if he has no prior arrests or only one prior arrest. From a related formula, one could determine that a defendant has a .87 probability of appearing if he has two or more prior arrests, although those probabilities are more easily determined by simply looking at the percentages in Table 2.1A rather than resorting to Bayesian prediction formulas.

23. To improve on the regression equation shown in Table 2.7A, all we had to do is observe that cell c in Table 2.1A has the most cases, and that if we could predict all 455 of those cases with perfect accuracy, we would probably reduce the total deviation. That is achieved by raising the slope from .06 to .13 without changing the Y-intercept so that when X is 1, Y will be predicted to be 1 as it actually is in those 455 cases. To improve on the regression equation shown in Table 2.7B involves a more unplanned trial and error approach since the variables are not limited to scores of 0 and 1.

24. When we speak of improving on traditional regression analysis, we do not mean resorting to alternatives to ordinary least squares such as multiple stage least squares, maximum likelihood methods, or least squares applied to instrumental variables, since none of those methods involve attempting to minimize the total or average unsquared deviations. It is this latter kind of minimizing that represents an important improvement in the benefit-cost sense of accurate prediction discussed above. The improved Y-intercept derived by minimizing the unsquared deviations would still be interpreted to mean the value of Y when X equals zero on that new line or linear equation, and the improved slope would still mean the change in Y when there is a one-unit change in X on that new "best fitting" line or linear equation. See M. Dutta, *Econometric Methods* (Southwestern, 1975),

pages 241-368; and Ronald Wonnacott and Thomas Wonnacott, *Econometrics* (Wiley, 1970) for a discussion of variations on ordinary least squares, especially variations that involve solving simultaneous equation and multivariate models rather than the single bivariate equation model that we are dealing with, although the problems of unsquared versus squared also apply to those more complicated models.

25. If our object is to fit a straight line to the 14 data dots of Table 2.7 that will minimize the sum of the unsquared deviations, we need not feel bound by the least squares rule which says the Y-intercept or a-coefficient has to equal $Y_m - bX_m$ (i.e., the mean Y, minus the slope times the mean X), although such a rule does make the Y-intercept a simple function of the slope. Instead we can make the Y-intercept and slope vary independently of each other until we minimize the sum of the unsquared deviations, or until we have reached a point in our trial and error approach where additional trials do not generate an improvement.

26. The minimum point on a roughly U-shaped curve representing the relation between the total unsquared deviations and the slope could probably be found by using a searching algorithm that minimizes without using derivatives. See David Himmelblau, *Applied Nonlinear Programming* (McGraw-Hill, 1972), especially pages 141-217. In order to express the total unsquared deviations as a function of the slope, one can use the same reasoning that is used to express the total squared deviations as a function of the slope, but substituting $\Sigma | Y-Y_p |$ for $\Sigma (Y-Y_p)^2$. That reasoning is described in Dutta, op. cit. note 20, pages 34-39; and Wonnacott and Wonnacott, op. cit. note 1, pages 259-261 and 289-291. See also Hoyt Wilson, "Least Squares versus Minimum Absolute Deviations Estimation in Linear Models," 9 *Decision Sciences* 322-335 (1978); R. D. Armstrong and E. L. Frome, "A Comparison of Two Algorithms for Absolute Deviation Curve Fitting," 71 *Journal of American Statistical Association* 328-330 (1976); and Harvey Wagner, "Linear Programming Techniques for Regression Analysis," 54 *Journal of American Statistical Association* 206-212 (1959).

Computer programs have now been developed whereby one can obtain the Y-intercept and the slopes for a bivariate or multivariate regression equation from a data set showing the dependent and independent variable scores for a set of cases. Such programs have names like LAD, L1, or MAD regression. They all involve a simple linear programming routine that guarantees an optimum solution if it is possible to find a least squares solution. The routine seeks to find a numerical value for the Y-intercept and the slopes that will minimize the sum of the actual Y values plus the predicted Y values across all the residuals subject to the linear constraints that every Y and Y_p value be non-negative, and that each residual $+ Y_p - Y$ be equal to 0. One need not know exactly how a LAD (least absolute deviations) program works in order to interpret and obtain the output, anymore than one needs to know how a least squares program works. R. Armstrong and E. Fromme, "A Comparison of Two Algorithms for Absolute Deviation Curve Fitting," 71 *Journal of the American Statistical Association* 328-330 (1976).

27. The disadvantage of unrestricted regression analysis, especially with more than one independent variable, is that predicted values on the dependent variable

may be meaningless by being less than 0, greater than 1, or nonprobabilities between 0 and 1. The disadvantage of using a restricted regression analysis is that by rounding the predicted values to 0 or 1, one loses information concerning how close or far the predicted values actually were to 0 or 1. A third alternative that preserves the information of unrestricted regression analysis and provides meaningful probabilities is probit regression analysis which generates true probabilities between 0 and 1 for the predicted values rather than non-probability decimals. See D. J. Finney, *Probit Analysis* (Cambridge University Press, 1971) and John C. Blydenburgh, "Probit Analysis: A Method for Coping with Dichotomous Dependent Variables," *Social Science Quarterly* 889-899 (1971). Warren Hausman and Richard Thaler of the University of Rochester School of Management have been experimenting with the application of probit analysis to pretrial release prediction. A fourth alternative might simply involve rounding off the predictions to the nearest whole number. For example, with the pretrial release data and the regression equation $Y = .87 + .06X$, if X is 0 or 1 (meaning a predicted Y of .87 or .93), then in either situation the rounded prediction would be 1.00, which is the equivalent of always predicting the median or the mode.

28. Correlation coefficients are sometimes interpreted as the relative reduction in prediction error achieved by shifting from the mean or mode as the predictor for all cases to the regression line predictions. Thus, a correlation squared of .08 should mean eight percent less errors by predicting from another variable rather than from a measure of central tendency. See Mueller, Schuessler and Costner, op. cit. note 1, where this interpretation of correlation coefficients is given for both discrete and continuous measures of correlation, especially pages 242-249 and 312-315. Unfortunately, squaring a correlation coefficient always produces a positive number, even though predicting from a regression equation may increase rather than reduce the number of errors as compared to predicting from a central tendency measure. The reduction-in-error interpretation may also lead one to think there is more relevance between correlation and prediction than there actually is.

29. Real decision-makers or predictors not only often tend to use a kind of event-matching when predicting from a prior distribution, but they also often tend to use non-optimum prediction when predicting from a prior variable. For example, if one is seeking to minimize squared or unsquared deviations in predicting from two or more dichotomous independent variables to a dichotomous dependent variable, the most effective method is a form of Bayesian prediction which adds the information for each subsequent variable to the information for each prior variable in accordance with a probability formula like that given in note 22 above. Empirical studies, however, show that experimental decision makers tend to wrongly predict contrary to the Bayesian formulas. Daniel Kahneman and Amos Tversky, "On the Psychology of Prediction," 80 *Psychological Review* 237-251 (1973); and Ward Edwards, "Conservatism in Human Information Processing," in B. Kleinmuntz (ed.), *Formal Representation of Human Judgment* (Wiley, 1968), pages 17-52. This may, however, be due to a lack of awareness of the optimum prediction methods, rather than to a desire for variety and challenge.

Chapter 3

DETERMINING AND

REJECTING CAUSATION

The purpose of this chapter is to demonstrate in a simple manner some basic concepts and methods for determining the existence of causal relations in the legal process. By legal process we mean the making and applying of law by legislatures, courts, and administrative agencies. By causal analysis in this context, we mean attempting to account for why outputs vary in the legal process by looking to variations in the inputs. A causal analysis can be considered completed when there is no other input item that will substantially change the nature of the relations between (1) the output variations being explained and (2) the input variations being used as the basis of the causal explanation.

This chapter is based on the paper "Causal Analysis and the Legal Process," which appears as Chapter 2 in Nagel and Neef, *The Legal Process: Modeling the System* (Sage Publications, 1977). The context of that chapter emphasizes the legal process subject matter, whereas the context of this chapter emphasizes the methodology of causal analysis. The present chapter also involves some important improvements, as indicated in such places as footnotes 3, 8, 10 through 20, the accompanying text, and the appendix.

The above concept of causal analysis, however, is too abstract to be very meaningful. In order to give it clearer meaning, this chapter will provide a series of examples to illustrate three different types of causal analysis. The first includes situations where the relation between an input variable and an output variable is shown to be noncausal by controlling for a third variable. The second type includes situations where one input variable cannot by itself cause the output to change, but requires a certain second input variable acting in joint causation. The third type is the reciprocal causation situation where the input causes the output, but where the output has feedback causation on the input. Like the basic concept of causal analysis, these classifications take on clearer meaning when concrete examples are presented.

Before proceeding to discuss different ways one could explain variation on an output variable, we should clarify that we are seeking generalizations concerning relations between types of inputs and types of outputs. In other words, we are not discussing the causes of a specific incident like the death of murder victim John Doe, or the skidding of Peter Roe's car at a certain intersection on a certain day. That kind of causation is very much a part of legal analysis in specific cases, rather than a part of a social science analysis designed to explain variation across cases or across other legal phenomena. Seeking the proximate cause in a specific criminal or personal injury case may also differ from our concern for causal generalizations in that proximate cause determination often involves normative judgments of blame-worthiness, rather than just empirical relations. Likewise, empirical causation in criminal and personal injury cases may emphasize medical analysis of the cause of death or an automotive engineering analysis concerning the defectiveness of a car's antiskidding qualities, rather than a social science subject matter that emphasizes interaction among people or individual psychological characteristics.[1]

Coeffects and Intervening Variable Causation

In order to understand coeffects or intervening variable causation better, the concept of noncausal relation should be clarified. A noncausal relation is a relation between an input variable and an output variable in which the relation disappears or substantially changes when one takes into consideration a third or intervening variable. The input variable (or variable being predicted from) can be symbolized X; the output variable (or variable being predicted to) can be symbolized Y;

A. COEFFECTS CAUSATION

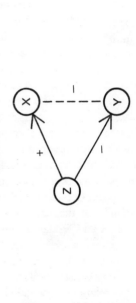

B. INTERVENING VARIABLE CAUSATION

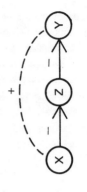

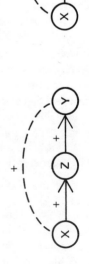

Meaning of symbols:

X = Input variable or variable being predicted from.

Y = Output variable or variable being predicted to.

Z = A third variable that is believed to explain the relation between X and Y.

Figure 3.1: Arrow Diagrams to Illustrate Coeffects and Intervening Variable Causation

and the intervening variable can be symbolized as Z, Z_1, or Z_2, depending on how many intervening variables there are. A variable is a characteristic of a person, place, or thing in which differences can occur, as with the ages of people, the per capita incomes of places, or whether the prosecutor or defendant won in various criminal cases. Some characteristics like age allow for many categories, and others like the winner in criminal cases tend to allow only for two categories, although age can be collapsed into young and old or above and below some average, and one can talk in terms of degrees of victory in criminal cases. This chapter will emphasize dichotomized variables for simplicity of presentation, although recognizing that dichotomizing sometimes causes a loss of useful information.

Relations can often be understood more clearly through the use of symbols and arrow diagrams. Thus, the arrow diagrams in Figure 3.1 provide some symbolic examples of coeffects causation and intervening variable causation. An arrow from one variable to another indicates that the first variable is hypothesized or alleged to cause the second variable to increase when the first variable increases (a plus relation), or to cause the second variable to decrease when the first variable increases (a minus relation). A broken line from one variable to another indicates that the first variable is hypothesized to have at least a partly noncausal relation with the second variable such that they increase or decrease together (a plus relation) or in opposite directions (a minus relation) due to their relations with a third variable. In the absence of the Z variable, the broken-line relation between X and Y may be zero, plus, or minus.

In a coeffects situation, the input variable X bears a noncausal relation with the output variable Y because they are both effects of a third variable Z, or are somehow otherwise related to one or more other variables. In an intervening variable situation, the input variable X bears a noncausal relation with the output variable Y, because X causes Z which in turn causes Y, rather than due to a more direct relation between X and Y. These two kinds of causation are treated together because as will be seen shortly, the methods are almost identical for analyzing whether one or the other is present.

Relations can also often be understood more clearly through the use of four-cell tables which show the percentage of persons, places, or things that are high on the input variable and also high on the output variable, and the percentage of persons, places, or things which are low on the input variable but high on the output variable. Table 3.1 provides a concrete illustration using state supreme court justices

Table 3.1: Four-Cell Tables To Illustrate Coeffects of Intervening Variable Causation

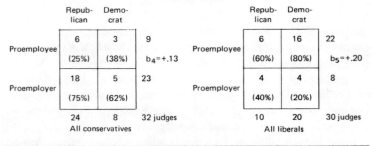

A. THE BASIC RELATION BETWEEN X AND Y

	Republican	Democrat		
Proemployee	12 (35%)	19 (68%)	31	$b_1 = +.33$
Proemployer	22 (65%)	9 (32%)	31	
	34	28	62 judges	

B. CHECKING THE RELATION BETWEEN Z AND X AND BETWEEN Z AND Y
(the positive test)

	Conservative	Liberal		
Democrat	8 (25%)	20 (67%)	28	$b_2 = +.42$
Republican	24 (75%)	10 (33%)	34	
	32	30	62 judges	

	Conservative	Liberal		
Proemployee	9 (28%)	22 (73%)	31	$b_3 = +.45$
Proemployer	23 (72%)	8 (27%)	31	
	32	30	62 judges	

C. CHECKING THE RELATION BETWEEN X AND Y HOLDING Z CONSTANT
(the negative test)

	Republican	Democrat		
Proemployee	6 (25%)	3 (38%)	9	$b_4 = +.13$
Proemployer	18 (75%)	5 (62%)	23	
	24	8	32 judges	
	All conservatives			

	Republican	Democrat		
Proemployee	6 (60%)	16 (80%)	22	$b_5 = +.20$
Proemployer	4 (40%)	4 (20%)	8	
	10	20	30 judges	
	All liberals			

NOTE: If perfect coeffects present, then $b_1 \sim \pm 1.00$, $b_2 \sim \pm 1.00$, $b_3 \sim \pm 1.00$, $b_4 \sim 0$, and $b_5 \sim 0$.

serving in 1955 as an example. The input variable is being a Democrat rather than a Republican on a bipartisan state supreme court. The output variable is being above the average of one's court with regard to the percentage of times one decided in favor of the employee rather than the employer in employee injury cases. The intervening variable or variable of which those two variables are believed to be coeffects is having a liberal attitude as measured by a mailed questionnaire.[2]

The basic relation in Table 3.1 shows that being a Democratic judge on a bipartisan state supreme court tends to correspond to having a proemployee decisional propensity. More specifically, 68 percent of the Democratic judges had such a propensity whereas only 35 percent of the Republican judges did so. The difference between those two percentages is a good measure of the degree of relationship or slope between the two variables. It means that if one goes from being a Republican (scored 0) to being a Democrat (scored 1), then the data would predict that such a judge would move up +.33 from .35 to .68 from being proemployer (scored 0) to being proemployee (scored 1).[3] This relation can be expressed by the simple equation $Y = .35 + .33(X)$ where Y refers to being proemployer or proemployee and X refers to being a Republican or a Democrat.[4]

In doing a causal analysis to determine whether the alleged Z variable is at least partly responsible for the relation between the input X variable and the output Y variable, it is logical to follow a two-step process. The positive step or test says if Z is the cause of the relation between X and Y, then Z should bear a relationship to X and a relationship to Y in conformity to one of the arrow diagrams shown in Figure 3.1 such as the first diagram under A. Both parts of this test are passed in Table 3.1B where being a liberal has a +.42 slope with being a Democrat, and where being a liberal has a +.45 slope with being proemployee. The negative step or test says if Z is the cause of the relation between X and Y, then that relation goes toward Zero when one deals separately with entities that are low on Z and separately with entities that are high on Z, thereby negating Z or holding Z constant. Both parts of this test are passed in Table 3.1C where being a Democrat has a much lower relation with being proemployee (than the original +.33) when all the judges analyzed are conservatives, and where being a Democrat has a much lower relation with being proemployee (than the +.33) when all the judges analyzed are liberals. If either part of the positive test or either part of the negative test had failed, then one would either have to look for another explanatory Z variable or at least tentatively conclude that there is a causal relation between X and Y.[5]

The reason the relation between being a Democrat and being proemployee did not go to perfect zero in either part of Table 3.1C is because liberalism apparently does not account for all of that relation, especially since the variables may have been imperfectly measured.[6] Some of that relation may involve a more direct kind of causation between party and propensity in that by being a Democrat one tends to come in contact more with people who are proemployee, thereby reinforcing one's proemployee propensities. There may also be some direct causation between being proemployee and choosing to be a Democrat since Democrats are perceived as being supportive of that value. Some of that relation may also be attributable to another Z variable like urbanism in the sense that living in an urban area where so many people are Democrats is likely to cause one to be a Democrat, and living in an urban area where unions are strong causes one more likely to be proemployee. Even if the relation in both parts of Table 3.1C did go to zero, this would only establish a noncausal relation between being a Democrat and being proemployee. It would not necessarily establish that liberalism is causally responsible since being liberal and being a Democrat might be coeffects of some additional variable like urbanism that we have not yet tabulated. If, however, no additional variable makes sense in that role, then we could tentatively conclude that a causal relation is present between being a liberal and being a Democrat.

One could have more faith that the relation between being a Democrat and being proemployee is a causal relation rather than a noncausal coeffects relation if the researcher could randomly assign some judges to be Democrats and some to be Republicans. Such randomization would eliminate the relation between being a liberal and being a Democrat. In other words, by randomly assigning judges to political parties, the proportion of liberals who are Democrats would be about the same as the proportion of conservatives who are Democrats. Stated differently, the proportion of Democrats who are liberals would be about the same as the proportion of Republicans who are liberals. Such randomization, however, is impossible to obtain since the judges themselves, not the researcher, determines which judges are Democrats and which are Republicans. Through self-selection rather than randomization, the liberal judges are more likely to call themselves Democrats, and the conservative judges are more likely to call themselves Republicans.

There are other variations on this basic type of causal analysis such as where one hypothesizes that controlling for a Z variable will cause the initial relation between X and Y to become negative if it were positive to begin with, or positive if it were negative, rather than just disappear toward zero. For example, OEO legal service agencies have a negative relation between the evaluation scores they have received (Y) and the amount of money they spent for routine case handling (X) rather than law reform activities.[7] That negative relation exists in spite of the fact that dollars for case handling and law reform tend to increase together as coeffects of an increased budget. The negative relation may be due to the fact that intense community dissatisfaction (Z_1) causes increased legal services expenditures including routine case handling (X), but community dissatisfaction may also produce low evaluation scores (Y), thereby causing X and Y to have a negative relation when they otherwise would have a positive one. Likewise, the negative relation may be due to the fact that increased legal services expenditures including routine case handling (X) may result in rising expectations and heightened goals (Z_2), but heightened goals produce low evaluation or satisfaction scores (Y) since satisfaction is a function of goals minus achievement. If data could be obtained on Z_1 and Z_2 as they have been on X and Y, then those causal models could be tested in a manner similar to that used in Table 3.1.[8]

The methodology shown in Table 3.1 applies in either the coeffects situation or the intervening variable situation as depicted in Figure 3.1. To determine which of those related models best fits a set of actual data, one has to either have data over time or have some knowledge as to whether Z precedes X in time (as in the coeffects situation) or whether X precedes Z in time (as in the intervening variable situation). Over-time data are often especially helpful in causal analysis because disruptive Z variables are more likely to be held constant when making comparisons on Y before and after a change on X in one place, than is the case if one compares two places at one point in time, one of which is high on X and one of which is low. With over-time data, one can change the arrow diagrams and tables to talk in terms of the relation between a change in X and a change in Y rather than just the relation between X and Y. The time element also is part of the basic definition of causation in that one can define a causal relation between X and Y as existing when (1) X precedes Y in time, (2) X and Y tend to vary together or in opposite directions, and (3) no third Z variable being held constant destroys or substantially changes the relation between X and Y.[9]

Joint Causation and Cocausation

Another common kind of causation in the legal process involves joint causation situations where one input variable by itself is not likely to cause the output variable to change substantially, but instead requires a second input variable interacting with it. Figure 3.2 provides some arrow diagrams illustrating two common kinds of joint causation. One situation involves two input variables that together are necessary

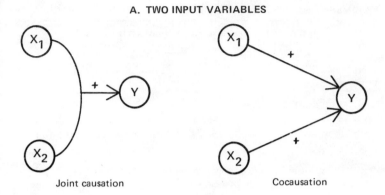

A. TWO INPUT VARIABLES

Joint causation

Cocausation

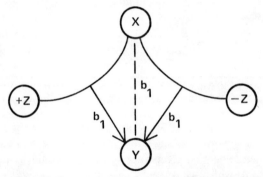

B. ONE INPUT VARIABLE AND ONE CONTROL VARIABLE

Meaning of new symbols:
+Z = Relating X to Y where all entities are in the affirmative category on Z.
−Z = Relating X to Y where all entities are in the negative category on Z.
b = The slope or degree of relation between X and Y.

Figure 3.2: Arrow Diagrams to Illustrate Joint Causation

and sufficient for the output variable to substantially increase, but which separately have little effect. Their joint causal relation is shown in the arrow diagram by the curved line which links them to the causal arrow. This situation is contrasted with a cocausation model where each input variable by itself is capable of having a substantial effect on the output variable, but the two input variables together have no greater effect than the sum of their separate effects.

The joint causation situation with two input variables is illustrated with data in Table 3.2. The data consist of questionnaire responses

Table 3.2: Four-Cell Tables To Illustrate Joint Causation with Two Input Variables

A. THE INPUT VARIABLES SEPARATELY HAVE LITTLE EFFECT

	Attitudes				Opportunities		
	Unfavorable Attitudes	Favorable Attitudes			Unfavorable Specialty	Favorable Specialty	
Represented Unpopular Clients	4 (36%)	23 (46%)	27 $b_1 = +.10$	Represented Unpopular Clients	7 (39%)	20 (47%)	27 $b_2 = +.08$
Did Not Represent	7 (64%)	27 (54%)	34	Did Not Represent	11 (61%)	23 (53%)	34
	11	50	61 lawyers		18	43	61 lawyers

B. THE INPUT VARIABLES JOINTLY HAVE A SUBSTANTIAL EFFECT

	Attitudes and Opportunities		
	Not Both Favorable	Both Favorable	
Represented Unpopular Clients	2 (10%)	25 (63%)	27 $b_3 = +.53$
Did Not Represent	19 (90%)	15 (37%)	34
	21	40	61 lawyers

NOTE: If perfect joint causation present with two input variables, then $b_1 \sim 0$, $b_2 \sim 0$, and $b_3 \sim \pm 1.00$.

from a nationwide sample of sixty-one usable attorneys in 1970. The output variable involved asking them, "Have you ever defended an unpopular client where an acceptance of the case could have damaged your career?" to which 45 percent or twenty-seven lawyers responded yes. The first input variable involved asking them whether they agreed that "Lawyers should be encouraged to represent the unpopular client" to which 82 percent or fifty lawyers responded yes. The second input variable involved asking them, "Is your legal practice primarily business and corporate?" to which 29 percent or eighteen lawyers responded yes.[10]

In Table 3.2A the relation between having a favorable attitude and representing unpopular clients is almost zero. Likewise, the relation between having favorable opportunities as reflected by having a relatively favorable legal specialty, i.e., other than a business or corporate specialty, is also almost zero. However, when one compares, as in Table 3.2B, lawyers who have both favorable attitudes and opportunities with lawyers who lack one or the other, then the relation with representing unpopular clients becomes quite substantial. If Table 3.2B had involved a degree of relation only slightly higher than the +.10, the +.08, or the sum of the two relations from Table 3.2A, then a cocausation relation might be present or at least a copredictive relation, but not a joint causation relation. To have a joint causation relation with two input variables, their interactive combined causal impact has to be in effect greater than the sum of the parts.

For further detail, Table 3.2B could have been shown with four columns instead of two. The four columns would read, (1) unfavorable attitudes and unfavorable specialty, (2) favorable attitudes and unfavorable specialty, (3) unfavorable attitudes and favorable specialty, and (4) favorable attitudes and favorable specialty. If there were a perfect joint causation relation between attitudes and opportunities on the one hand and respresenting unpopular clients on the other, then 0 percent of the lawyers in category 1 would have represented unpopular clients, 0 percent of the lawyers in category 2, and 0 percent of the lawyers in category 3, but 100 percent of those in category 4. Table 3.2B does not show a perfect joint causation, but about as close as one might expect to get given the imperfections in measuring the variables, the relevance of other variables and the somewhat small samples of lawyers involved.[11]

The same four-columns approach could be used with a cocausation relation. If the cocausation relation were perfect, then b_1 in Table 3.2A would be plus or minus 1.00, and b_2 would also be plus or minus 1.00. Zero percent of the category 1 lawyers would then be likely to represent the unpopular, and 100 percent of the category 4 lawyers would be likely to do so. One hundred percent of the category 2 and 3 lawyers would represent the unpopular if both the input variables were sufficient conditions to generate representation but not necessary conditions. However, 0 percent of the category 2 and 3 lawyers would represent the unpopular if both the input variables were necessary conditions but not sufficient conditions. It is impossible for two input variables to both be necessary and sufficient conditions even if they both have perfect covarying relations with the output variable. About 50 percent of the lawyers in category 2 and 3 would be likely to represent the unpopular if the input variables were just good correlates of the output variable, but neither one is separately a necessary or a sufficient condition for representing the unpopular, although they might jointly constitute a necessary and sufficient condition if perfect or near-perfect joint causation were present.[12]

A second common joint causation situation involves one input variable and one control variable as indicated in Figure 3.2B and in

Table 3.3 The data consist of a nationwide sample of felonious assault
and grand larceny cases for 1962 in which the defendant was convicted.
The input variable shown is race, and the output variable is whether the
convicted defendant was jailed or instead granted probation or sus-
pended sentence. The initial Table 3.2A shows a small positive relation
(+.16) between being a black rather than a white convicted defendant
and receiving a jail sentence rather than probation. If, however, we
control for the type of crime by separating the original table into an
assault table, then the relation between being black and being jailed
almost becomes negative (+.05). Likewise, if we control for the type of
crime by separating the original table into a larceny table, then the
relation becomes substantially positive (+.25). In other words, when
being black (X) is jointly combined or interacts with being an assault
defendant (−Z), the original relation drops, possibly because assault
crimes tend to be more intraracial than larceny. When, however, race
(X) is jointly combined with being a larceny defendant (+Z), the

Table 3.3: Four-Cell Tables To Illustrate Joint Causation with One Input Variable and One Control Variable

A. THE BASIC RELATION BETWEEN X AND Y

	Whites	Blacks	
Jailed	336	301	637
	(54%)	(70%)	b_1 = +.16
Probation	288	128	416
	(46%)	(30%)	
	624	429	1,053 convicted defendants

B. CHECKING THE RELATION BETWEEN X AND Y HOLDING Z CONSTANT

	Whites	Blacks			Whites	Blacks	
Jailed	141	155	296	Jailed	195	146	341
	(62%)	(67%)	b_2 = +.05		(49%)	(74%)	b_3 = +.25
Probation	86	77	163	Probation	202	51	253
	(38%)	(33%)			(51%)	(26%)	
	227	232	459		397	197	594
All assault crimes					All larceny crimes			

NOTE: If perfect joint causation present with one input variable and one control
variable, then $b_1 \sim 0$, $b_2 \sim -1.00$, and $b_3 \sim \pm 1.00$.

original relation rises, possibly because larceny crimes tend to be more interracial than assault.[13]

Joint causation with two input variables or with one input variable and one control variable can be expressed in terms of simple equations. With two input variables, we have the equation $Y = .36 + .10(X_1)$ for the data in Table 3.2A1, and the equation $Y = .39 + .08(X_2)$ for Table 3.2A2. The equation expressing the relation in Table 3.2B is $Y = .10 + .53(X_3)$ where X_3 is X_1 times X_2. In other words, if either X_1 is 0 or X_2 is 0, then that third equation would predict that Y would be a low .10. If, however, both X_1 and X_2 are scored 1, then that third equation would predict that Y would be a high .63. With one input variable and one control variable, we have the equation $Y = .54 + .16(X)$ for the relation between being jailed and being black in Table 3.3A. That initial equation, however, becomes $Y = .49 + .25(X)$ when all cases are 1 on Z. Expressing those relations in terms of equations is a useful kind of shorthand over the more detailed tabular approach although each of these equations merely involves transcribing two key numbers from the corresponding four-cell table, namely the initial percentage expressed as a decimal and the slope of the relation.[15]

An additional type of joint causation involves controlling for a third variable under circumstances which result in converting the original zero relation between two variables into a substantial positive or negative relation, which is the opposite of the basic intervening variable situation where controlling for a third variable results in converting the original substantial relation into a close-to-zero relation. For example, one may find no relation between family income and quantity of milk consumed. However, if one controls for family size, then rich large families drink more milk than poor large families, and rich small families drink more milk than poor small families. This seems strange that rich families do not drink any more milk than poor families, but yet when families are divided into large and small families, then rich families do drink more milk than poor families. The explanation is simply that rich families tend to be smaller than poor families. Thus, if the average rich family has two children and they average two quarts of milk per day, that is four quarts per rich family. The average poor family, however, may have four children (rather than two children) who average only one quart of milk per day apiece, which is also four quarts per family, meaning no difference between rich and poor families unless family size is held constant.[16]

Reciprocal Causation

A third common kind of causation in the legal process is reciprocal causation where one variable has an impact on a second variable and that second variable has a feedback effect on the first variable. This is a common legal process model by virtue of the fact that it symbolizes the law and society relationship whereby law has an impact on shaping

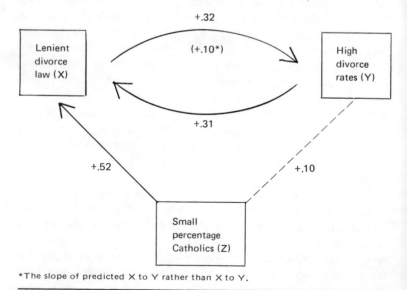

A. SYMBOLICALLY

Impact

Feedback

B. USING THE IMPACT OF DIVORCE LAWS ON DIVORCE RATES AS AN EXAMPLE
(also showing the basic slopes among the relevant variables)

+.32

(+.10*)

Lenient divorce law (X)

High divorce rates (Y)

+.31

+.52

+.10

Small percentage Catholics (Z)

*The slope of predicted X to Y rather than X to Y.

Figure 3.3: Arrow Diagrams to Illustrate Reciprocal Causation (with data at one point in time)

society, and society in turn has a reciprocal impact on shaping the law. Scholars in the field of sociology of law frequently discuss whether social behavior is more influential on social norms than social norms are on social behavior.

Although the reciprocal relation between law and behavior is often discussed, it is not so often measured, partly because the methodology for separating the impact effect from the feedback effect is not so well understood. One can illustrate that methodology by working with the relation between divorce law and divorce rates following the lead in this area of political scientist Gillian Dean.[17] Figure 3.3 provides arrow diagrams illustrating reciprocal causation both in a general symbolic way and using the divorce subject matter as an illustrative example. Table 3.4 provides the four-cell tables which clarify the slopes which are shown in Figure 3.3

All the subtables in Table 3.4 are based on forty-seven states rather than fifty states because data were unavailable for Alaska and Hawaii and because Nevada was excluded due to its atypical nature as a state specializing in divorces for short-term residents. Divorce rates refer to divorces per 1,000 married women as of 1960 according to the U.S. Public Health Service statistics. A high divorce rate means above the national average for the forty-seven states, and a low divorce rate means below the national average. Divorce law leniency refers to the results of a questionnaire by Gillian Dean directed to law professors teaching family law in all forty-seven states asking them a number of questions designed to position each state on a divorce law leniency index. Lenient states are those that are above the national average on that index, and severe states are those that are below.

Table 3.4A1 indicates that if a state moves from being severe to lenient, then it is likely to move up on the divorce rate scale from a score of .35 to a score of .67 for a slope or marginal increase of +.32. Table 3.4A2 indicates that if a state moves from being a low divorce rate state to being a high one, then it is likely to move up on the divorce law lenience scale from a score of .41 to a score of .72 for a slope of +.31. Those two tables might lead one to believe that divorce law has about the same impact on divorce rates as divorce rates have on divorce law. Such a conclusion, however, might be false by virtue of the possible fact (as indicated in the arrow diagram of Figure 3.3) that divorce rates have a causal effect on divorce law which may explain much of the +.32 relation from divorce law to divorce rates. In other words, if X is believed to cause Y, and Y is also believed to cause X, then any slope obtained by trying to predict Y from X may really be circular like trying to predict Y from Y.[18]

Table 3.4: Four-Cell Tables To Illustrate Reciprocal Causation

A. THE BASIC RELATION BETWEEN X AND Y, AND BETWEEN Y AND X

	Divorce Law					Divorce Rate		
	Severe	Lenient				Low	High	
High Divorce Rates	7 (35%)	18 (67%)	25	Lenient Divorce Law		9 (41%)	18 (72%)	27 $b_2 = +.31$
Low	13 (65%)	9 (33%)	22 $b_1 = +.32$	Severe		13 (59%)	7 (28%)	20
	20	27	47 states			22	25	47 states

B. THE RELATION BETWEEN Z AND X AND BETWEEN Z AND Y

	Percentage Catholics					Percentage Catholics		
	Large	Small				Large	Small	
Lenient Divorce Law	6 (29%)	21 (81%)	27	High Divorce Rates		10 (48%)	15 (58%)	25 $b_4 = +.10$
Severe	15 (71%)	5 (19%)	20 $b_3 = +.52$	Low		11 (52%)	11 (42%)	22
	21	26	47 states			21	26	47 states

C. THE RELATION BETWEEN PREDICTED X AND ACTUAL Y
(where X is predicted from Z)

	Predicted Divorce Law		
	Severe	Lenient	
High Divorce Rates	10 (48%)	15 (58%)	25 $b_5 = +.10$
Low	11 (52%)	11 (42%)	22
	21	26	47 states

NOTES: If perfect reciprocal causation present, then $b_1 = \pm 1.00$, $b_2 = \pm 1.00$, $b_3 = 0$, $b_4 = 0$, and $b_5 = 0$.

What we need is a way of determining the effect of X or divorce law on Y or divorce rates while somehow controlling for the feedback effect of Y on X. To be more specific, we need a method that will tell us how much of the variation on Y can be predicted by the pure variation on X. In this context, the pure variation on X refers to the variation on X that is not attributable to Y, but instead is attributable only to a third variable in the model which we have labeled Z. In this substantive context, a meaningful third variable is the smallness of the percentage of Catholics in each of the forty-seven states being used in Table 3.4. A small percentage is one that is below the national average of the forty-seven states, and a large percentage is one above the national average as of 1960.

There are a number of reasons why the percentage of Catholics in each state is a good Z variable for filtering out the feedback effect of divorce rates on divorce law in relating divorce law to divorce rates. First, as shown in Table 3.4B1, the smallness of the percentage of Catholics in a state has a high +.52 relation with the leniency of divorce law. This probably indicates that legislators in Catholic states are reluctant to make their divorce laws more lenient for fear of losing many votes. This means that percentage Catholics is capable of generating a substantial amount of variation in the leniency of divorce law separate from the feedback effect from divorce rates. Second, as shown in Table 3.4B2, the percentage of Catholics in a state has almost a zero relation with divorce rates. This probably indicates that Catholics have divorce rates close to the national average, or they tend to live in states where other groups live who have above average divorce rates which offset the lower Catholic divorce rates. It also means that divorce rates cannot influence leniency of divorce law through percentage Catholics since that relation is so low. Third, if a state adopts lenient divorce laws, that does not cause Catholics to move away from there or to move toward severe divorce law states. Thus, since X does not cause Z, the feedback effect of Y on X cannot feed into Z through X and then indirectly back on X again. In other words, percentage Catholics is a variable that is independent or exogenous from the causal influence of the two reciprocal variables which are partly dependent or endogenous on each other.

In Table 3.4C, we predict divorce rates not from divorce law but rather from predicted divorce law. By predicted divorce law in this context, we mean the score a state would be expected to receive in view of the percentage of Catholics in the state and in view of the fact that Table 3.4B1 shows a relation between divorce law and percentage Catholics that can be expressed by the equation $X = .29 + .52(Z)$. The Z variable can take the value 0 if the state has a large percentage of Catholics, and the value 1 if the state has a small percentage of Catholics. Thus, there are twenty-one states that score 0 on Z, and their predicted X score would be .29, which leads to a prediction that they would have relatively severe divorce laws. Likewise, there are twenty-six states that score 1 on Z, and their predicted X score would be .81, which leads to a prediction that they would have relatively lenient divorce laws. Table 3.4C thus shows twenty-one states in the column of states with divorce laws that are predicted to be severe from their Catholic percentages, and twenty-six states in the lenient prediction column. Of the twenty-one severe predicted states, 48 percent had high divorce rates, whereas of the twenty-six lenient predicted states, 58 percent had high divorce rates for a slope difference of +.10. Predicting a divorce law score for each state from its percentage Catholic score can be considered a first-stage prediction, and then predicting a divorce rate score for each state from its predicted divorce law score can be considered a second-stage prediction.

The +.10 slope tells us the relation between variation in divorce laws and variation in divorce rates where the only variation in divorce laws is due to variables or a variable other than divorce rates. In other words, if a state moves or varies from a severe predicted state to a lenient predicted state, then it is likely to move up on the divorce rate scale from a score of .48 to a score of .58 for a slope or marginal rate of +.10. That +.10 is substantially less than the +.32 before we controlled for the feedback effect of divorce rates changes on divorce law changes. That +.10 may, however, still indicate that there is some causal impact effect of divorce laws on divorce rates separate from the feedback effect although not much of a causal impact effect. Apparently, variation in divorce rate from state to state is much more influenced by variables other than divorce law. These variables may especially include income, education, and urbanization levels.

In the above example, we analyzed the causal impact of leniency in divorce laws (X) on the level of divorce rates (Y), filtering out the feedback effect of divorce rates on divorce laws. We could likewise analyze the impact of Y on X, filtering out the feedback effect of X on Y. Doing so would involve finding a Z variable like median educational level for each state for use in predicting divorce rates. We would then use predicted divorce rates to predict divorce law scores. The slope of that relation could then be compared with the +.10 slope going in the other direction. Doing so reveals that divorce rates have about twice the impact on divorce law in this context as divorce laws have on divorce rates. Perhaps social behavior may generally have more influence on shaping legal rules than legal rules have on shaping social behavior.[19]

An alternative approach to analyzing reciprocal causation involves obtaining data over a period of time rather than at one point in time as shown in Figure 3.4. If we find in a given state or set of states that divorce rates had been going down or had been level before the divorce law became more lenient, but that they rose afterwards, then this indicates that the law has more of a causal force on the rates than vice versa (as in Figure 3.4A1). If on the other hand we find that divorce rates had been going up before the divorce law became lenient and that they continued upward at about the same projection, then this indicates that the rates are probably having more of an influence on the law than vice versa (as in Figure 3.4A2). If, however, the rates had been going up before the legal change, but even more up after the legal change, that would tend to indicate that the rates influence the law, and the law in turn influences the rates (as in Figure 3.4A3). In that time series situation, though it is more difficult to determine the relative degrees of influence as compared to the two-stage prediction

---

A. Interrupted Time Series (multiple time points)

Rates	Rates	Rates
Before After	Before After	Before After
Law	Law	Law
Law → Rates	Rates → Law	Rates → Law → Rates

B. Cross-Lagged Panel Analysis (two points in time)

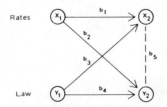

Rates → Law if $r_{X_1 Y_2 \cdot Y_1}$ is greater than $r_{Y_1 X_2 \cdot X_1}$

(where $r_{X_1 Y_2 \cdot Y_1}$ means relation between X_1 and Y_2, holding Y_1 constant)

Rates → Law if b_1 times $b_2 = b_5$, more so than b_3 times b_4

Figure 3.4: DIAGRAMS TO ILLUSTRATE RECIPROCAL CAUSATION
(with data at more than one point in time)

method with either one-point-in-time scores or change scores. Neverthe-less, the two approaches usefully supplement each other.[20]

If data can be obtained for divorce rates at two points in time (e.g., X_1 at 1950 and X_2 at 1970) and for divorce law at two points in time (Y_1 at 1950 and Y_2 at 1970), then one can determine in which direction the reciprocal causation is greater by using what is known as cross-lagged panel analysis. That approach basically involves testing whether the relation between the X_1 rates and the subsequent Y_2 law is greater or less than the relation between the Y_1 law and the subsequent X_2 rates as shown in Figure 3.4B.[21]

Integrating Diverse Forms of Causation

Legal process phenomena usually involve a combination of diverse forms of causation. For example, suppose we are trying to explain why some criminal cases involve short sentences and others long. We might partly do so by hypothesizing that the short sentence cases are more likely to be associated with Democratic judges and the long sentence cases with Republican judges. We might, however, recognize that party affiliation is not likely to directly cause sentence differences, but rather may be a coeffect along with sentence differences of a liberal attitude. We might also hypothesize that short sentences are disproportionately received by white defendants and long sentences are disproportionately received by black defendants, but especially when we only use theft crimes rather than assault crimes since theft crimes tend to be more interracial than assault crimes. We might further hypothesize that committing a misdemeanor rather than a felony causes one to be more likely to receive a short sentence rather than a long sentence, but that receiving only a short sentence may have a feedback effect causing the further committing of misdemeanors or other crimes which would not be so likely to happen if a long sentence had been given.

In the above example, we have one output variable, namely sentence length, that we are trying to explain the variation on through causal analysis. The analysis includes a coeffects relation with regard to judicial characteristics, a joint causation relation with regard to the defendant's characteristics, and reciprocal causation with regard to the nature of the crime. We could add an intervening variable causation by hypothesizing that urbanism indirectly causes short sentences by causing liberalism which in turn causes short sentences. We could also add a direct cocause that does not involve any of the other types of causation by hypothesizing that having hired counsel leads to shorter sentences than having a public defender if the severity of the crime is held constant, although we could insert an intervening variable like greater resources and lesser backlog available to hired counsel. Other examples could be given of other causal variables related to each other in a variety of ways. Those relations in a complex causal model, however, all tend to reduce to subparts of the model which deal with coeffects, joint causation, reciprocal causation, intervening variables, or direct cocausation.

Causal models can be made more complex not only by combining different types of causation into one model, but also by increasing the number of variables within each submodel. For example, a coeffects relation can involve more than two variables that relate to each other because they are all coeffects of one or more outside variables. Likewise, more than two variables can have a joint causal relation or a non-joint, cocausal relation with another variable. A reciprocal or a circular relation can also involve more than two variables where, for example, X_1 causes X_2, which causes X_3, which causes X_1. However, neither the types of causation nor the basic causal analysis methodology changes when the number of variables increases.

In looking for causes, researchers often tend to only think mechanically in terms of a list of cocauses, each of which relates directly by means of a one-way arrow to the output variable being explained. With a little more imagination, other forms of causation could be hypothesized and tested for. One could also determine how much of the total variation on the output variable is explained by each separate subpart of the model taken alone or added incrementally to the other parts of the model. The main goal, however, is not so much to compare different causal explanations, but rather to find the combination of causal explanations that will meaningfully explain the greatest percentage of the total variation on the output variable in terms of the data and the common sense of what is already known about related matters. That kind of explanatory causal analysis makes sense to strive for regardless whether one is attempting to explain the outcomes of cases, the behavior of judges or attorneys, the treatment of defendants, the effects of regulatory laws, or other legal matters. That kind of explanatory causal analysis can also be achieved if legal researchers will make more of an effort to understand the causal methods involved and to apply those methods to obtaining a better understanding of the legal process.

APPENDIX 3.1: SUMMARY OF SOME MAJOR PRINCIPLES IN CAUSAL ANALYSIS

This appendix pulls together on a more abstract level the major causal analysis principles which are illustrated in the chapter with law and society examples from judicial decision-making, attorney-client relations, comparisons across litigants, and reciprocal relations between law and society. By seeing the principles on a more abstract level, we can further clarify their interrelations and generalizability. This appendix also briefly refers to some important general matters which did not seem appropriate to discuss in the text given the emphasis on concrete legal process illustrations.

I. BASIC SYMBOLS

1. B_{YX} = The slope of the relation between dependent variable Y and independent variable X.

   a. In causal analysis, these slopes generally involve working with standardized scores on the variables, although unstandardized scores can also produce meaningful results especially where the variables are dichotomized and there is thus little difference between the two kinds of slopes.

   b. If only two variables are involved, correlation coefficients (r) can be used as a substitute for these slopes since $B_{YX} = r_{YX}$ in bivariate relations.

2. $B_{YX \cdot Z}$ = The slope of the XY relation holding a third or Z

variable constant. If the Z is preceded by a - or +, this refers to partitioning the sample into those that are in the negative category on Z and those in the positive category.

3.   High = A slope that is high relative to the other slopes that are part of the causal analysis.

4.   Low = A slope that is low relative to the other slopes that are part of the causal analysis.

5.   X → Y = The presence of variable X causes variable Y to be present or absent, or changes in variable X cause changes in variable Y.

6.   X---Y = Variable X covaries with variable Y in the same or in opposite directions, but they do not have a causal relation.

II. THE GENERAL DEFINITION OF CAUSATION

There is a causal relation between variable X and variable Y if:

1.   X precedes Y in time, or the alleged causal changes in X precede in time the alleged effect changes in Y.

2.   X substantially covaries with Y either in the same direction or in opposite directions. How much covariation or degree of correlation constitutes substantial covariation depends on the relative costs of making an error of concluding there is a causal relation when there is none versus making an error of concluding there is no causal relation when there really is one.

3.   No Z variable can be controlled for that will substantially change the covariation.

   a.   How much change constitutes substantial change depends on the same criterion as mentioned above.

   b.   When one stops looking for additional Z variables depends on the cost of doing additional research and the likely benefits in light of what is already known about the relation between the proposed Z variables and the XY relation.

III. COEFFECTS AND INTERVENING VARIABLE CAUSATION

A.   Definitions

1.   Coeffects Model: $X---Y$. $Z \to X$. $Z \to Y$.

2.   Intervening Variable Model: $X---Y$. $X \to Z$. $Z \to Y$.

B.   Conditions to Satisfy

1.   The original relations: B_{YX} = high. B_{XZ} = high. B_{YZ} = high.

2.   Partitioning the sample: $B_{YX.-Z}$ = low. $B_{YX.+Z}$ = low.

3.   Multivariate relations: $B_{YX.Z}$ = low. $B_{YZ.X}$ = high.

4.   Path analysis: B_{ZX} times B_{ZY} equals B_{YX}.

5.   Whether the coeffects model or intervening model applies depends on the known temporal order of the variables.

IV. JOINT CAUSATION

A.   Definitions

1.   Two input variables: $(X_1$ and $X_2) \to Y$, but not $X_1 \to Y$ or $X_2 \to Y$

2.   One input variable and one control variable: $X \to$ middling Y. $X \to$ low or negative Y, when all entities are -Z. $X \to$ high or positive Y, when all entities are +Z.

3.   Cocausation: $X_1 \to Y$. $X_2 \to Y$.

B.   Conditions to Satisfy

1.   Two input variables:

a.   Changing the measurement: B_{YX_1} = low. B_{YX_2} = low. $B_{YX'}$ = high, where X' is a variable such that one has to be plus on both X_1 and X_2 in order to be plus on X'.

  b.   Multivariate relations: $B_{Y X_1 . X_2 X_3} = $ low. $B_{Y X_2 . X_1 X_3} = $ low. $B_{Y X_3 . X_1 X_2} = $ high, where X_3 is the product of X_1 and X_2.

2.   One input variable and one control variable:

  a.   Partitioning the sample: $B_{Y X} = $ middling. $B_{Y X . -Z} = $ low. $B_{Y X . +Z} = $ high.

  b.   Multivariate relations: $B_{Y X . Z}$ and $B_{Y Z . X}$ tell us nothing relevant to this model.

3.   Cocausation: $B_{Y X_1} = $ high. $B_{Y X_2} = $ high. $B_{Y X_3} = $ low.

V. RECIPROCAL CAUSATION

A.   Definition: $X \to Y. \ Y \to X.$

B.   Conditions for establishing which way the causation is greater:

1.   The original relations: $B_{Y X} = $ high. $B_{X Y} = $ high.

2.   One point in time data: $B_{X Z_1} = $ high. $B_{Y Z_1} = $ low. $B_{Y Z_2} = $ high. $B_{X Z_2} = $ low. $X \to Y$ more than $Y \to X$ if $B_{Y X_p}$ is greater than $B_{X Y_p}$, where X_p is the value of X predicted from Z_1 and Y_p is the value of Y predicted from Z_2.

3.   Two points in time data:

  a.   Multivariate relations: X causes Y more than Y causes X if $B_{Y_2 X_1 . Y_1}$ is greater than $B_{X_2 Y_1 . X_1}$.

  b.   Path analysis: X causes Y more than Y causes X if $B_{X_2 X_1}$ times $B_{Y_2 X_1}$ equals $B_{Y_2 X_2}$ more so than $B_{X_2 Y_1}$ times $B_{Y_2 Y_1}$ equals $B_{Y_2 X_2}$.

4.   Multiple time points with interrupted time series (where Y is a continuous variable and X is a dichotomous variable changing once over time)

  a. X causes Y if $B_{Y X}$ substantially changes direction or degree when X changes from minus to plus, provided the other causation essentials are present.

b.   Y causes X if B_{YX} does not change direction or degree when X changes from minus to plus, provided as above.

c.   Y causes X which in turn causes Y if B_{YX} goes up before X changes and up more after X changes, or if B_{YX} goes down before X changes and goes down more after X changes, provided as above.

5.   To establish reciprocal causation rather than which way the causation is greater, both $X \rightarrow Y$ and $Y \rightarrow X$ must satisfy the general definition of causation under II.

NOTES

1. For further detail on the general methodology of causal analysis, see Hans Zeisel, *Say It With Figures* (Harper and Row, 1968), and Hubert Blalock, *Causal Inferences in Nonexperimental Research* (University of North Carolina Press, 1964), and Oliver Benson, *Political Science Laboratory* (Merrill, 1969), 302-353. For a more substantive orientation on social causation, see Robert MacIver, *Social Causation* (Harper and Row, 1964). No book or article seems to have been written dealing with the overall determination of explanatory causal generalizations in the legal process as contrasted to determining causation in specific litigation cases. A classic of the latter type is Leon Green, *The Theory of Proximate Cause* (Vernon Law Book Co., 1929).

2. The basic data shown in Table 3.1 comes from Nagel, "Political Party Affiliation and Judges' Decisions," 4 *American Political Science Review* 843-850 (1961). The questionnaire data is discussed in Nagel, "Off-the-Bench Judicial Attitudes," in Glendon Schubert, ed., *Judicial Decision-Making* (Free Press, 1963). There were, however, not enough questionnaire respondents to position all 62 judges on party affiliation, decisional propensity, and liberalism. Therefore, the data in sections B and C of Table 3.1 is partly hypothetical although consistent with the overall patterns of those judges who did respond.

3. Throughout this chapter relationships are generally expressed in three ways. One way is through an arrow diagram which emphasizes (1) whether the relation is causal or noncausal, (2) whether the causal relations are one-directional or reciprocal, and in which direction, and (3) whether the relations are positive-direct or negative-inverse. Another way of expressing relationships involves a four-cell cross-tabulation table in which the magnitude of the relation is measured by the difference between (1) the percentage of units that are positive on the independent variable and also positive on the dependent variable minus (2) the percentage of units that are negative on the independent variable and positive on

the dependent variable. A third way of expressing a relationship involves a regression equation generally of the bivariate linear form $Y = a + bX$, although more than one independent variable may be present, and non-linear relations may also sometimes be present. A fourth way that adds little to these perspectives (but is often used) involves an analysis of variance or a testing of the likelihood of attributing to chance the difference between two averages. The above two percentages from the four-cell cross-tabulation tables can be considered as being averages since the 34 Republicans in Table 1a would receive an average score of .35 on being proemployee if proemployee were scored 1 and proemployer were scored zero. Likewise, the 28 Democrats would receive an average proemployee score of .68.

4. The percentage of Democratic judges who are proemployee may be higher than the percent of Republican judges who are proemployee because Democrats have traditionally tended to empathize more with the working class and with minority ethnic groups. The percentage of Democratic judges who are proemployee is not 100 percent, however, and the percent of Republican judges who are proemployee is not zero percent because: (1) party choice is frequently determined by considerations other than the similarity between one's values and those of the party he has chosen, including such considerations as the party of one's relatives or friends; (2) a person may have average Democratic or Republican values on most issues, making him a Democrat or a Republican, but not necessarily be like an average Democrat or Republican on attitudes toward all employer-employee conflicts; and (3) two judges may have the same value systems and thus possibly be of the same party, but one of the two judges may hold his values with a greater intensity and thus may frequently dissent without being joined by his less vigorous associate of the same party.

5. Instead of comparing Democrats and Republicans on being proemployee first with all conservative judges and then with all liberals, there are two related approaches one could use to test whether the relation between being a Democrat and being pro-employee is caused by a liberalism variable. One approach involves determining whether b_6 goes close to zero where b_6 is defined as $(b_1 - b_2 \cdot b_3) / \sqrt{(1 - b_2{}^2)(1 - b_3{}^2)}$ which equals $(.33 - .42 \cdot .45) / \sqrt{(1 - .42^2)(1 - .45^2)}$, which in turn equals .17. That figure is not zero, but it is substantially less than the original b_1 of .33. This method known as partial correlation tells us the approximate relation between being a Democrat and being proemployee adjusting for liberalism, but it has the disadvantage of not truly holding liberalism constant the way we do in Table 3.1C assuming liberalism is a meaningful dichotomous or binary variable. It has the advantage though of not requiring dichotomous variables and of not requiring that each column in Table 3.1C involve a substantial number so that the percentages will be meaningful. As the formula indicates, the partial correlation coefficient or b_6 relates positively to the original b_1 relation, but inversely to the b_2 and b_3 relations.

The second alternative approach involves determining whether b_7 equals b_1 where b_7 is defined as b_2 times b_3, which equals .42 times .45, which in turn equals .19. That figure is not a .33, but it is substantially higher than zero in the direction toward .33. This method, known as path analysis, in effect says that if b_2 and b_3 were 1.00, then our arrow diagram would predict that b_1 would be 1.00. The b_7 or predicted b_1 is 1.00 discounted by the extent to which b_2 and b_3 are proportionately less than 1.00. In other words, b_1 is predicted to be 1.00

(.42)(.45). Both of these alternative approaches normally use correlation coefficients rather than slopes, but correlation coefficients are closely approximated by slopes when one is working with a four-cell table, especially if the ratio between the row totals roughly equals the ratio between the column totals. Technically speaking, a correlation coefficient shows the percentage of the variation on Y which is accounted for by X, and a slope shows the number of units that Y changes when X changes one unit.

6. In order to concentrate on the causal analysis, this article does not discuss in detail problems relating to reliability of measurement and generalizing from samples. For further detail on those matters, see J.P. Guilford and B. Fruchter, *Fundamental Statistics in Psychology and Education* (McGraw-Hill, 1973); Hubert Blalock, *Causal Models in the Social Sciences* (Aldine, 1971); and E. Caulcott, *Significance Tests* (Routledge and Kegan Paul, 1973).

7. Data dealing with the relation between evaluation scores of OEO Legal Services agencies and how they allocate their funds between routine case handling and law reform activities is analyzed in Nagel, *Minimizing Costs and Maximizing Benefits in Providing Legal Services to the Poor* (Sage Publications, 1973).

8. Another variation on the coeffects or intervening variable causation model involves controlling for a Z variable like liberalism in Table 3.1 and finding the relations between party affiliation and being proemployee goes down to almost zero when all the subjects are conservatives but not when they are liberals, or down to zero when all the subjects are liberals but not when they are conservatives. In other words, the Z variable could be only partly an intervening variable or a variable having a coeffects relation on the X and Y variables. An example of that might be that one could find female judges are more liberal than male judges. However, if one only compares older female judges with older male judges, the liberalism difference tends to disappear since older female judges tended to share similar values with their male counterparts. On the other hand, if one only compares younger female judges with younger male judges, the liberalism difference may still be strong since younger females are less likely to feel they need to act like males in order to be accepted. The same might be true with a comparison between black and white judges on liberalism, holding age constant.

9. For further detail on coeffects and intervening causation, see Herbert Simon, "Spurious Correlation: A Causal Interpretation," 49 *Journal of the American Statistical Association* 457-479 (1954); and Donald Campbell and J. Stanley, "Experimental and Quasi-Experimental Designs for Research on Teaching," in N.L. Gage, ed., *Handbook of Research on Teaching* (Rand McNally, 1963).

10. For further detail concerning this data, see Nagel, Champagne, and Neef, "Attorney Attitudes Toward the Unpopular and the Poor," in Nagel, *Improving the Legal Process: Effects of Alternatives* (Lexington-Heath, 1975). The data presented here slightly exaggerates the joint causation relation beyond the data presented in that article in order to more clearly distinguish joint causation from cocausation. The data presented here removes the inconsistencies that appeared in previous versions of this analysis in Nagel and Neef, *The Legal Process: Modeling the System* (Sage, 1977), 52; and Nagel and Neef, "Causal Analysis and the Legal Process," in Rita Simon (ed.), *Research in Law and Sociology* (Johnson Associates, 1977).

11. The relation between two independent variables and one dependent

variable can always be shown in a 4 by 2 table (i.e., four columns and two rows) if all three variables are dichotomized. Doing so often provides useful insights into what is happening regardless of the type of intervening variable causation or joint causation that is being hypothesized or that may be present.

12. The possible interaction between the certainty of being caught and the severity of punishment as determinants of crime occurrence represents another important legal process situation which some researchers have claimed is an example of joint causation. For example, Tittle in effect says that crime rates for various places will be high if either certainty or severity is low, but crime rates will be low if and only if both certainty and severity are high. See C. Tittle, "Crime Rates and Legal Sanctions," 16 *Social Problems* 409-423. Kritzer, however, presents data which tend to refute the joint causation relation and instead shows that crime rates, severity, and certainty vary together because they are co-effects of cultural variables like region, education, and urbanism. M. Kritzer, "Sanctions and Deviance," 3 *Justicia* 18-28 (1975).

Another important legal process example of joint causation with two input variables deals with combining the characteristics of judges or juries and those of defendants or plaintiffs. For instance, when black judges were compared with white judges in Atlanta on sentencing, there were almost no differences. Likewise, when black defendants were compared with white defendants on being sentenced, there were almost no differences. The situation changes, however, when four categories are created of (1) black judges with black defendants, (2) black judges with white defendants, (3) white judges with black defendants, and (4) white judges with white defendants. Categories 1 and 4 involved relatively lenient treatment, and categories 2 and 3 involved relatively severe treatment. See James L. Gibson, "Racial Discrimination in Criminal Courts: Some Theoretical and Methodological Considerations" (mimeographed paper available on request from the author at the University of Wisconsin at Milwaukee). Closely related is the fact that when female-dominated juries were compared with male-dominated juries in a nationwide sample on damages awarded, there were almost no differences. Likewise, when female plaintiffs were compared with male plaintiffs there were almost no differences. The situation changes, however, when four categories are created of (1) female-dominated juries with female plaintiffs, (2) female-dominated juries with male plaintiffs, (3) male-dominated juries with female plaintiffs, and (4) male-dominated juries with male plaintiffs. Categories 1 and 4 involved relatively high awarding of damages, and categories 2 and 3 involved relatively low awarding of damages. See Nagel and Weitzman, "Sex and the Unbiased Jury," 56 *Judicature* 108-111 (1972).

13. For further detail concerning this data, see Nagel, *The Legal Process from a Behavioral Perspective* (1969), 81-112. Cases not containing information on race, type of sentence, and type of crime were ignored in developing Table 3.3 from the data.

Another important legal process example of possible joint causation with an input and a control variable deals with explaining variation in decisional propensities across judges. There is some relation between the liberalism-conservatism of judges and their decisional propensities to favor the defendant in criminal cases. See Nagel, "Judicial Backgrounds and Criminal Cases," 53 *Journal of Criminal Law, Criminology & Police Science* 333-339 (1962). The strength of those relations has been questioned by Joel Grossman in "Social Backgrounds and

Judicial Decision-Making," 79 *Harvard Law Review* 1551-1564 (1966). There is also some relation between the activism-restraint attitudes of judges and their decisional propensities, as reported in Joel Grossman, "Role-Playing and the Analysis of Judicial Behavior: The Case of Mr. Justice Frankfurter," 11 *Journal of Public Law* 285 (1962). The strength of those relations, though, has also been questioned by Harold Spaeth, "Judicial Power as a Variable Motivating Supreme Court Behavior," VI *Midwest Journal of Political Science* 54-82 (1962). From a joint causation perspective, however, James Gibson finds that liberalism and activism have little predictive power when each variable is used alone, but a great deal of predictive power when they are used jointly. Thus, knowing a judge is liberal or conservative at least with Gibson's sample may provide little predictability, and likewise with knowing whether a judge is an activist or a restrainer. If, however, one knows a judge is an activist liberal, an activist conservative, or in between a restrained liberal or restrained conservative, this may give substantial predictability. See James Gibson, "Judges' Role Orientations, Attitudes and Decisions: An Interactive Model," *American Political Science Review* (1978). In other words, by comparing activist liberals with activist conservatives (i.e., holding constant activism), the liberal-conservative decisional differences are accentuated, although by comparing restrained liberals with restrained conservatives, the liberal-conservative decisional differences are lessened.

14. An alternative way of applying the regression equation perspective to a joint causation situation is to have a computer calculate the correlation coefficient squared (R^2) corresponding to the equation $Y = a_1 + b_1X_1 + b_2X_2$ and make a similar calculation for the equation $Y = a_1 + b_1X_1 + b_2X_2 + b_3X_1X_2$. Doing so determines how much additional variance is accounted for by adding that joint causation, interaction, or multiplicative term. A more complete way to test for the additional variance accounted for by joint causation would involve four different interaction terms and equations. In the first equation, having a favorable attitude would be coded 1 and an unfavorable attitude would be coded zero, and having a favorable specialty would be coded 1 and an unfavorable specialty would be coded zero. In the second equation the coding might be 0-1 and 0-1, instead of 1-0 and 1-0. The third equation might code the categories 1-0 and 0-1, and the fourth equation 0-1 and 1-0. That gets at all the possible ways in which the two categories on each of the independent variables could interact so as to produce a potent joint causation combination. One of those combinations could conceivably be more potent than being favorable on both variables.

15. For further detail on joint causation, see Hubert Blalock, *Social Statistics* (McGraw-Hill, 1972), 308-309 (one input variable and one control variable), 463-464 (two input variables), and 337-347, 463-464, and 483-489 (miscellaneous related matters).

16. This example comes from Zeisel, note 1, 142-143. A related example is given in Benson, note 1, 314-315, which involves no relation between party affiliation and attitudes toward urban renewal until income is held constant. Then, the high income Republicans are seen to be more conservative on urban renewal than the high income Democrats, and the low income Republicans are also seen to be more conservative than the low income Democrats. The original zero relation is due to the fact that there are more Democrats among low income people and more Republicans among high income people (just as there are more children among low income families), and to the fact that low income people who

are subject to being evicted are more unfavorable to urban renewal than high income people whose business or property interests may benefit from urban renewal. Thus the more numerous high-income relatively-favorable Republicans offset the less numerous low-income Republicans generating a collectively neutral position on urban renewal, which roughly equals the collectively neutral position of the Democrats due to the more numerous relatively-unfavorable low-income Democrats offsetting the less numerous high-income Democrats.

17. Gillian Dean, "Divorce Policy and Divorce: An Empirical Study," unpublished paper available from the author at Vanderbilt University (1973); and Gillian Dean, "Impact and Feedback Effects: Divorce Policy and Divorce in the American States," unpublished paper available from the author at Vanderbilt University (1975). The data presented in Table 3.4 is consistent with Dean's general findings as presented in those two papers, but does not reflect her data in detail since her data is not presented in four-cell tables.

18. The slope of Y predicted from X may be substantially different in magnitude from the slope of X predicted from Y depending on the relation between the spread on the Y variable and the spread on the X variable. There is no way, however, that those two slopes can be opposite in sign. This shows that merely reversing the direction of the regression analysis cannot get at reciprocal causation because sometimes reciprocal causation does involve relations that are opposite in sign. For example, an increase in capital punishment may decrease the murder rate over a set of places or time points. However, if there is an increase in the murder rate, that is likely to result in an increase in the use of capital punishment. There is thus a negative slope in one causal direction, and a positive slope in the other. For discussions of the reciprocal causation between crime rates and law enforcement, see Daniel Nagin, "Crime Rates, Sanction Levels, and Constraints on Prison Population" (Center for the Study of Justice Policy, Duke University, 1977); and David Greenberg, Ronald Kessler and Charles Logan, "Crime Rates and Arrests Rates: A Causal Analysis" (paper presented at the Law and Society Association meeting, 1978).

19. For further discussion of reciprocal causation and of the methodology of separating the impact effect from the feedback effect, see A. Miller, "Logic of Causal Analysis: From Experimental to Non-Experimental Designs," in Hubert Blalock (ed.), *Causal Models in the Social Sciences* (Aldine, 1971); E. Fowler and Robert Lineberry, "Comparative Policy Analysis and the Problem of Reciprocal Causation," in C. Liske, et al., *Comparative Public Policy: Issues, Theories and Methods* (Sage-Halsted, 1975); and Howard Erlanger and Halliman Winsborough, "The Subculture of Violence Thesis: An Example of a Simultaneous Equation Model in Sociology," 5 *Sociological Methods and Research* 231-246 (1976). The Fowler-Lineberry example deals with the extent to which an increase in the percentage of owner-occupied dwellings has a negative effect on local property taxes (due to the resistance of homeowners to such taxes), as contrasted to the extent to which high property taxes have a negative effect on the percentage of owner-occupied dwellings (due to the possibility of homeowners moving away from where property taxes are high and more commercial developments being encouraged to move in). They conclude that property taxes have more of a negative impact on the percent of homeowners in the community than the percent of homeowners has on lowering property taxes. The Erlanger-Winsborough example deals with the extent to which being violent produces prestige

among one's blue collar peers as contrasted to the extent that having such peer esteem produces violence. They conclude that being relatively high in the prestige hierarchy causes one to fight more so than fighting causes one to have high prestige.

Analyzing reciprocal causation not only indicates which way the causation is stronger and how much stronger, but it may also indicate whether there is any causation in both directions. In other words, one may find from the analysis that although Y is highly predictable from X, the predictability is due to Y causing X, not to X causing Y, and not to X and Y causing each other. That kind of analysis has important policy implications with regard to such matters as does antidiscrimination legislation cause a reduction in discrimination, or does a reduction in discrimination cause antidiscrimination legislation? Likewise, does marijuana decriminalization cause an increase in the use of marijuana or does an increase in the use of marijuana cause marijuana decriminalization, or both, or neither?

20. For further detail on analyzing time series that are subjected to the interruption of a legal change, see Donald Campbell and Laurence Ross, "The Connecticut Crackdown on Speeding: Time Series Data and Quasi-Experimental Analysis," 3 *Law and Society Review* 33-53 (1968); and Laurence Ross, Donald Campbell, and Gene Glass, "Determining the Social Effects of a Legal Reform: The British Breathalyser Crackdown of 1967," pp. 15-32 in S. Nagel (ed.), *Law and Social Change* (Sage, 1970).

A fourth graph could have been shown in Figure 3.4A where neither a change in the law causes a change in the rates, nor does a change in the rates cause a change in the law. Such a graph might involve a horizontal line indicating that although the law changed, the rates did not, and since there was no change in the rates, a change in the rates could not have been responsible for a change in the law. Such a graph could also involve a negatively sloping line. If the slope is constant, then the change in the law is not having an effect on the rates. If the slope becomes more negative after the change in the law, it would be difficult to attribute a decrease in divorce rates (as cause) to a change in the law that goes from severe before to lenient after (as effect). Likewise, a negative sloping line could not be responsible for a change in the law since it would be difficult to attribute a decrease in the divorce rates as an effect (meaning people are becoming less tolerant of divorce) to a change in the law as a cause that goes from severe before to lenient after.

21. There are two frequent forms that the cross-lagged panel approach takes. One form involves comparing (1) the partial correlation between the alleged cause X_1 and the alleged effect Y_2 holding constant the previous Y_1, and (2) the partial correlation between the alleged cause Y_1 and the alleged effect X_2 holding constant the previous X_1. If partial correlation 1 is greater than partial correlation 2, then rates have a greater effect on law than vice versa, but if partial correlation 2 is greater, then law has a greater effect on rates than vice versa. The partial correlation coefficients are calculated in a manner like that described in note 5 above.

The other form of CLPA involves comparing whether b_1 times b_2 comes closer to equaling b_5 than b_3 times b_4 does, where (1) b_1 is the slope between X_1 and X_2; (2) b_2 is the slope between X_1 and Y_2; (3) b_3 is the slope between Y_1 and X_2; (4) b_4 is the slope between Y_1 and Y_2; and (5) b_5 is the slope between X_2 and Y_2. What we are in effect saying is that X_2 and Y_2 are coeffects of either

X_1 (i.e., rates at an earlier point in time) or Y_1 (i.e., law at an earlier point in time). If the X_1 rates are the stronger cause, then the method of path analysis discussed in note 5 above says that b_1 times b_2 will more closely approximate b_5 than b_3 times b_4 will, but not if law is the stronger cause.

For further detail on cross-lagged panel analysis, see D. Heise, "Causal Inference from Panel Data," in Edgar Borgatta and G. Bornstedt (eds.), *Sociological Methodology* (Jossey-Bass, 1970); and D. Pelz and F.M. Andrews, "Detecting Causal Priorities in Panel Study Data," 29 *American Sociological Review* 836-848 (1964).

PART TWO

POLICY ANALYSIS METHODS

Chapter 4

COMBINING AND RELATING GOALS

This chapter has two purposes. The first is to discuss ways in which one can handle the evaluation of alternative public policies that involve multiple and possibly conflicting goals. Any given policy problem is likely to have many goals, including desired effects to be achieved or maximized, and undesired effects to be avoided or minimized. In order to determine which alternative policy is the most desirable, one generally needs to combine those subgoals into a strategy that involves handling each subgoal in some sequential manner, or that involves combining the subgoals into an overall goal. The first part of this chapter will deal with ways of developing such a sequential or compositing strategy.[1]

The second purpose and part of this chapter will discuss ways in which one can relate goals to alternative policies or means for achieving the goals. Making those relations often involves establishing an equation or functional relation between the goal or goals on the one hand and the policies on the other. Establishing such a relationship often involves problems in measuring the degree to which the Y goals have been achieved and the degree to which the X policies are present and solving methodological problems as to how one can determine the parameters, coefficients, or constants to relate the Y goals to the X policies.[2]

Both the combining and the relating purposes of this chapter will be illustrated mainly by the experiences which the coauthors have had in their research which has dealt with evaluating alternative policies for improving the legal process. The problems and examples, however, are general enough to be widely applicable to a great variety of policy evaluation problems.[3]

Combining Goals

As a simple illustration of the problems involved in combining goals, one cannot simultaneously maximize benefits (Y_1) and minimize costs (Y_2). This cannot be done since the way to maximize benefits is to spend huge sums of money or effort which would be contrary to cost minimization, and the way to minimize costs would be to spend nothing which would probably be contrary to benefit maximization. The simple solution that is generally recommended is to combine our concern for high benefits with low costs by creating an overall goal of maximizing benefits minus costs. Most evaluation of alternative public policies, however, does not so readily lend itself to such a simple solution, especially where the benefits and the costs are measured in terms of different units, and the costs thus cannot be meaningfully subtracted from the benefits. Likewise, there may be multiple benefits measured in different units, or multiple costs. Those are the general kinds of problems with which goal combining is concerned.[4]

HANDLING CONFLICTING GOALS SEQUENTIALLY

One way to handle the problem of benefits being measured in one type of unit and costs being measured in another is to avoid combining the two into an overall measure that involves any arithmetic operations like benefits minus costs, or benefits divided by costs. Instead, one can often handle the policy problem by talking in terms of either maximizing benefits subject to a cost constraint, or minimizing costs subject to a benefit constraint. This is especially likely to be the case where the costs are mainly dollars, and the benefits involve a nonmonetary measure like crime reduction, vote getting, or somebody's satisfaction.[5]

For example, if we are trying to allocate funds of the Law Enforcement Assistance Administration across fifty states and/or the three basic anticrime activities of police, courts, and corrections, it might be quite meaningful to say the best allocation is the one that minimizes crime (or maximizes crime reduction) while not spending more than a given national budget. It might also be meaningful to say the best allocation is the one that spends the least amount of money while not allowing crime occurrence to go higher than it was last year, plus a given percentage. Between those two alternatives, the benefit maximization alternative is usually preferred because it is unrealistic to think that if expenditures were minimized the difference between money appropriated and money spent will be returned to the treasury. It is also more difficult to talk in terms of the subjectivity satisfying a minimum benefits threshold, rather than the somewhat objective constraint of not exceeding one's budget.[6]

, Other examples might include trying to allocate (1) campaign expenditures (a) between mass media and precinct organizations or (b) among various places, or (2) funds of the Legal Services Corporation (a) between law reform and routine case handling, or (b) among specific legal services agencies. Both of those problems involve monetary costs and nonmonetary benefits. The nonmonetary benefits in the campaign expenditure problem are the votes likely to be obtained from alternative allocations. A majority or plurality of the votes may represent the minimum benefit constraint. The nonmonetary benefits in the legal services problem are represented by the satisfaction scores given to legal services agencies in the evaluations which have been periodically made. A certain score on that scale may be defined as the minimum needed to justify full refunding. In both problems, the maximum cost constraint may be the total budget available.[7]

Instead of or in addition to talking in terms of a maximum cost level or a minimum benefits level, one can also talk in terms of constraints that need to be satisfied on each of the separate subgoals. For example, in the anticrime allocation problem, there may be a maximum overall total expenditure and a minimum expenditure for each place or each type of activity. The minimum place expenditures can be determined by allocating a percentage of the total budget to each place in accordance with its population, crime rate, or other demographic characteristics. The minimum activity expenditures can be determined by seeing what is the smallest amount or proportion that has been allocated in the past in each place in various size categories to police, courts, and corrections. In the campaign expenditures example, there may be legislative constraints on how much can be spent by a candidate for mass media activity in order to hold down expenditure competition, and there may be a minimum amount that is considered necessary for precinct organization established as a rule of thumb to hold the party organization together. In the legal service example, the national office may specify for political reasons that no more than a certain percentage of an agency's budget can go for law reform, and no more than a certain percentage can go for routine case handling.

Other examples can be given where the expenditures are not monetary and where the total constraints are not just the sum of the constraints on the subgoals. For example, in the problem of how should a civil rights organization allocate its effort with regard to voting, schools, criminal justice, employment, housing, and public accommodations, the measure of effort might be a relative one measured on a five-point scale which provides for a big increase, a small increase, no change, a small decrease, and a big decrease. It might be considered meaningful to say that none of those effort expenditures should fall below a score of three, i.e., none should undergo a decrease. Another illustration might be the problem of finding an optimum mix between the freedom of newspapers to report on pending criminal trials and the freedom of defendants on trial to be free from prejudicial newspaper reporting. Both the free press subgoal and the fair trial subgoal may be subjected to legal constraints established by the U.S. Supreme Court such that free press cannot be allowed to go so far as to involve reporting on out-of-court plea bargaining, and such that fair trial cannot be allowed to go so far as to prohibit reporting on the charge and the defendant's name in an adult criminal case.[8]

In handling conflicting goals sequentially, all goals are considered. Thus, if we have two goals, Y_1 and Y_2, a sequential handling might involve specifying a minimum level that must be achieved on Y_1 and then seeking to maximize on Y_2, or specifying a minimum level on Y_2 and then seeking to maximize on Y_1. Lexicographic ordering is an alternative sequential approach that results in ignoring the goals that are not considered first unless the policies under consideration are tied on the first goal. Thus, under lexicographic ordering, if Y_1 is more important than Y_2, then policy one will be preferred over policy two if the first policy scores a 5 on Y_1 and the second policy scores a 4 on Y_1 even though the second policy scores a 10 on Y_2 and the first policy scores a 0 on Y_2. This handling of multiple goals is called lexicographic ordering because it is like choosing which of two words to place first in a dictionary where the words are analogous to policies. One simply looks to the first letter of each word and only to the second letter if there is a tie on the first letter. A related kind of sequential ordering involves maximizing on the first goal up to a maximum level and then shifting one's remaining resources to the second goal up to a maximum level and so on to each successively less important goal. Under either procedure, goals after the first goal may be ignored.[9]

HANDLING CONFLICTING GOALS SIMULTANEOUSLY

Conflicting goals can often be handled simultaneously rather than or in addition to sequentially. Doing so depends largely on whether or not the goals have a common unit of measurement.

WHEN GOALS HAVE A COMMON UNIT OF MEASUREMENT. Conflicting goals can usually be handled simultaneously without problem where the goals have a common unit of measurement. The most common unit of measurement is dollars. For example, one can develop an overall total cost goal with regard to alternative percentages of defendants to hold prior to trial by simply summing the holding costs and the releasing costs incurred at each percentage if both types of costs are measured in dollars. More specifically, the holding costs could include jail maintenance and lost gross national product, and the releasing costs could include the cost of rearresting defendants who fail to appear and a monetary cost for crimes committed while released. Minimizing total costs would then be the overall goal that would simultaneously combine those subgoals.[10]

Another example might be the anti-crime allocation problem. A meaningful overall goal might simply be to minimize the total national crime occurrence which is calculated by summing the crime occurrence in all fifty states. In that context, crimes rather than dollars would be the common unit of measurement. One might, however, not consider one crime as being equal to another crime the way one dollar is equal to another dollar. It might therefore be necessary to weight each crime on a severity scale which might provide for three notches of high, medium, and low. The overall goal would then be a weighted crime occurrence in which the quantity of each type of crime within each state would be multiplied by a 3, 2, or 1 and the overall goal would consist of the sum of those products across the fifty states rather than simply the sum of the crimes.

Still another example is the problem of finding an optimum jury size. The overall goal there might be to minimize the sum of the errors of convicting the innocent (EI) plus the errors of acquitting the guilty (EG). Errors is thus the common unit of measurement, but like crimes we might not consider one error to be equal to another the way one dollar is equal to another dollar. Blackstone said it is ten times as bad to convict an innocent person as it is to acquit a guilty person. To take that into consideration, we might define our overall goal to be (10)(EI) + (EG) in order to give the errors involving innocent defendants ten times the importance of the errors involving guilty defendants. In many of these examples, one might ask how does one measure those kind of goals. The measurement problem is separate from the problem of combining measurements sequentially or simultaneously. It is partly discussed later in the article under relating goals to alternative policies, but it is mainly a substantive problem rather than a methodological one, and thus requires consulting the specific substantive studies cited in the footnotes.[11]

Even though one has an overall goal to maximize or minimize, one might still find it meaningful to have constraints that need to be satisfied on the subgoals. That, for instance, would be the case if we were to say that our overall anticrime goal is to minimize the total national crime occurrence or the total national weighted crime occurrence, but that no state should be allowed to rise above a certain maximum crime occurrence per capita. Another example might involve alternative redistricting plans where the overall goal is to minimize the total deviation from perfect equality among the legislative districts, with total deviation being determined by summing the amount of difference between each district's population and the average district population. Along with that overall goal, might go a legal constraint that says no district shall be allowed to have a population deviating from the average population by more than five percent regardless of how small the total deviation is.[12]

Sometimes the summing of numbers representing benefits or costs to arrive at an overall goal requires discounting those numbers in light of the fact that the benefits or costs may depend on the occurrence of some contingent event. It is then appropriate to discount or multiply each of those numbers by the probability of the contingent event occurring. For example, the benefits of releasing a defendant prior to trial are contingent on the probability (P) of the defendant appearing in court, and the costs of releasing a defendant are contingent on the probability (1-P) of the defendant not appearing. Likewise, the years received as a sentence by going to trial (rather than pleading guilty) are contingent on the defendant being convicted. Thus, the expected value of going to trial equals zero years multiplied by the probability of acquittal (the expected benefits to the defendant if he is acquitted), plus the years usually given upon conviction multiplied by the probability of conviction (the expected costs to the defendant if he is convicted).[13]

WHEN GOALS DO NOT HAVE A COMMON UNIT OF MEASURE-MENT. Often the multiplicity of goals in policy problems cannot all be meaningfully measured in terms of dollars, crime, or some other common measurement unit. A frequent way of developing a composite overall goal under such circumstances is to have the overall goal consist of the product rather than the sum of the scores on the subgoals. In redistricting, for instance, the subgoals might be minimizing the total deviation from equality (E), compactness (C), and partisan proportionality (P) for the set of districts. The overall goal might then represent the product of E, C, and P. If we wanted to show that those three subgoals do not have equal importance, we could do so by attaching exponents to each of those three variables to show their relative weight. In the anticrime allocation example, it might be appropriate to have an overall goal consisting of both crime reduction and compliance with civil liberties as measured by a survey of knowledgeable persons. Those two subgoals might be combined by multiplying the two scores and having exponents to show their relative weight.

An alternative approach would involve summing the scores on the subgoals, but with each score weighted to take into consideration both the relative importance of the subgoals and the difference in the scales on which the subgoals are measured. An example of that might be the problem of determining whether adopting the rule excluding illegally received evidence in courtroom proceedings is socially desirable. The conflicting goals relate to police compliance with the law of search and seizure which tends to increase as a result of adopting the exclusionary rule, and police morale which tends to decrease as a result of adopting the rule. In one study, those two goals are measured on a five-point scale like the civil rights activities scale mentioned above which provides for a big increase, small increase, no change, small decrease, or a big decrease. In that study, if police compliance is given a weight of 2, we are in effect saying that we consider police compliance to be twice as important as police morale given the way in which those goals are measured. The exclusionary rule would thus be considered socially desirable if the increase in police compliance was more than half the decrease in police morale working with that relatively crude measurement, although such measurement may be the best available when one has to rely on subjective questionnaires for information rather than on more objective records.[14]

Giving the goal of police compliance a normative weight of 2 and police morale a normative weight of 1 may reflect the relative importance assigned to those two goals (1) by the respondents to a survey of opinions of the public, elected officials, or other persons considered to have the authority to express values; (2) by the researcher if he or she is just trying to show the effects of different weights; or (3) by doing a regression or correlation analysis between those goals and some higher goals where the weights represent relative or absolute slopes between the intermediate and the higher goals.

An additional purpose that normative weights can serve besides considering the relative importance of the goals and considering their units of measurement is to consider the possible overlapping nature of the goals.[15] For example, the goal of long life overlaps the goal of good health because if a person is high on one, he tends to be high on the other. That overlap could be eliminated by dropping one of the two goals, but then one would lose the nonoverlapping portion. To preserve both goals and simultaneously eliminate the overlap, each goal can be given less weight than it otherwise would have if only one of those two goals were included in the set of goals. Thus, if we had a set of ten goals only one of which was long life, we would give it more weight than if we had ten goals, one of which was long life and another of which was good health.[16]

A third approach to combining goals that do not have a common unit of measurement is what might be called the Gestalt or holistic approach. It involves arriving at a composite number not by multiplying or summing weighted or unweighted numbers, but rather by directly arriving at an overall number through a kind of total observation, insight, or subjective feeling. For example, in the legal services problem, the overall benefits goal was the satisfaction of the evaluators who evaluated each of the approximately 250 legal services agencies. They were instructed to score each agency on 113 dimensions including the quality of the secretarial service, the convenience of the offices to the poverty community, the aggressiveness of the lawyers, and many other dimensions. In developing an overall measure of satisfaction, the Auerbach Management Corporation did not consider it meaningful to try to sum the 113 scores for each agency with or without importance weights or measurement scale weights. Instead, the evaluators were instructed to add a 114th dimension called "overall evaluation" which provided for a twelve point scale ranging from a low of 1 corresponding to "Project has critical deficiencies—close down or cut back project," on up to a 7 corresponding to "Project operating efficiently—fund at current level," and up to a 12 corresponding to "A strong force in the war on poverty—expand if project can effectively handle additional resources."

Another example of the Gestalt approach involves the problem of the optimum decision to reach between either going to trial or settlement through plea bargaining in criminal cases. The upper bargaining limit of the defendant is equivalent to the usual sentence upon conviction given the defendant's charge, discounted by the probability of his being convicted, plus a bonus which the defendant is willing to grant the prosecutor in return for avoiding the costs of litigation. Those litigation costs include (1) the cost of sitting in jail awaiting trial if the defendant demands a trial and has not been released on bail, (2) the cost of hiring an attorney if the defendant is not eligible for a court-appointed attorney or the cost to the public defender to have to go to court, (3) the time cost involved in preparing one's case and appearing in court, (4) one's loss of reputation from the bad publicity often associated with a contested trial even if one is acquitted, and (5) the anxieties associated with prolonging the outcome of the case. Those litigation costs or nonsentence costs are difficult to measure separately and they do not involve a common unit of measurement. Preliminary analysis, however, shows that defense counsel is capable of compositing those kinds of nonsentence goals into a percentage bonus. If the usual sentence is ten years and the probability of conviction is sixty percent, then the expected or discounted value of the sentence is six years. Given the circumstances of the case, defense counsel can possibly meaningfully figure that it would be a good bargain if he could obtain an offer from the prosecutor to settle the case for eight years, meaning six years plus a 33 percent bonus to avoid those litigation costs.

Relating Goals

The problem of combining goals can be symbolized as one of determining the functional relationship between an overall goal (Y') and two or more subgoals $(Y_1$ and $Y_2)$. The problem of relating goals can be symbolized as one of determining the functional relationship

between an overall goal and one or more policies (X_1 and X_2) designed
to achieve or maximize that goal. There are basically two ways of
relating goals to policies. One involves indicating for each discrete
choice on an X policy variable what are the benefits and costs. The
other alternative involves determining linear or nonlinear parameters for
an equation-type relation between the Y' overall goal and the X policy
variable or set of X policy variables.

HANDLING DISCRETE POLICY CHOICES

A given policy problem may only involve a small set of policy
choices. For example, in the problem of how to provide legal counsel to
the poor in civil cases, the basic choices are (1) a list of volunteer
attorneys maintained by the local bar association, (2) a salaried government lawyer, as in the Office of Economic Opportunity Legal Services
Program, or (3) a judicare system whereby indigent clients go to
whatever attorney is willing to take their case and the government then
pays his fee. If the overall goal is some combination of clients served
and dollars spent, one can best relate that goal to these three policy
choices by simply determining for each choice what is the average
number of clients served in those places that have used the choice, and
what has been the total cost of the program. Those two goals can then
be combined by talking in terms of picking (1) the choice that serves as
many clients per poor population as possible, while not exceeding a
maximum total cost, (2) the choice that spends as little as possible,
while serving a minimum number of clients per capita, or (3) the choice
that spends the least per client while not exceeding a maximum total
cost or falling below a minimum number of clients served.

Discrete choices are not always few in number. In the redistricting
problem, for example, there may be millions of patterns for combining
precincts into the desired number of legislative districts in a state.
Comparing the equality, compactness, and proportionality goal criteria
for each alternative pattern choice may thus require a computerized
algorithm or set of procedures. The algorithm may be written to save
time and money by automatically excluding patterns that lack conti-
guity, and by merely seeking to satisfy certain minimum constraints (a
satisficing solution) rather than trying to maximize goals (an optimizing
solution).

The benefits and costs of discrete policy choices often need to be
discounted by the probability of certain events occurring on which
those benefits or costs are contingent. For example, in the problem of

whether to convict or acquit a defendant, the benefits of convicting should be discounted or multiplied by the probability that the defendant is actually guilty. Likewise, the costs of convicting should be discounted or multiplied by the complementary probability if the defendant is actually innocent. Measuring those initial benefits and costs before doing the discounting may be possible only on a relative scale going from −100 for the worst possibility (which would usually be convicting an innocent defendant) to +100 for the best possibility (which would usually be acquitting an innocent defendant) rather than an absolute scale of dollars or some other unit.[17]

The benefits and costs of discrete policy choices also often need to be discounted for the fact that those benefits occur at some time in the future. For example, the choices to a plaintiff's attorney in a civil case might be to accept either a $2500 offer now or a 50 percent probability of a $6000 trial victory five years from now. If we discount the trial victory by the .50 probability of its occurring, then the expected value of going to trial is $3000. That figure, however, should be further discounted for the fact that the $3000 expected value does not become a benefit until five years from now. To do that kind of discounting, one normally applies the formula $P = A/(1+r)^t$, which says the present value of money equals the future amount, divided by 1 plus the prevailing interest rate, with the exponent t equal to ,the number of years involved. Thus, if the prevailing interest rate were 6 percent, $3000 five years from now would have a value of $2,242. This means the present offer of $2500 would be more valuable than a 50 percent probability of a $6000 trial victory five years from now, especially if one deducts the inflation rate from the prevailing interest rate.

In benefit-cost analysis, it is sometimes appropriate to point out that if the net benefits from one choice is $4000 and the net benefits from a second choice is $2000, one cannot then say that the first choice is twice as valuable as the second choice. This is so because additional units of money or other benefits do not generally produce additional units of satisfaction at a constant rate, but rather at a diminishing-returns rate. Likewise, additional losses or costs do not produce additional units of dissatisfaction at a constant rate, but usually at a diminishing returns rate. Calculating what that rate might be is highly speculative and sometimes for want of a better measure, the logarithms of the net benefits for each choice will be compared rather than the untransformed net benefits. Such transformations, however, are generally irrelevant to making a decision as to which is the better choice.

This is so because if the net benefits from choice 1 are greater than the net benefits from choice 2, then choice 1 will provide more satisfaction or utility no matter what the diminishing-returns rate is, so long as increasing net benefits do not cause dissatisfaction but merely increased satisfaction at a decreasing rate.

HANDLING CONTINUUM POLICIES

Many policy problems involve X policy variables like dollars or other units that can theoretically go from negative infinity to positive infinity with all points between, or at least from zero to 100 the way percentages do. The way to relate an overall goal (Y) to that kind of policy generally involves trying to arrive at an equation of the form $Y = a+bX$ (where changes in X bring constant changes in Y); $Y = aX^b$ (where changes in X bring nonlinear or nonconstant changes in Y but the direction of the relation remains constant); or $Y = a+b_1X+b_2X^2$ (where changes in X bring nonlinear changes in Y and also a change in the direction of the relation, such that X at some levels relate positively to Y but negatively at other levels of X). There are many other equations that could be meaningfully used to relate a Y goal to an X policy, but these cover the basic ideas.

There are about three approaches to determining the "a" and "b" parameters in the above equations. The three approaches might be referred to as regression analysis, questioning of knowledgeable persons, or an assumptions approach. The regression analysis approach has a number of variations. One variation is to gather data from many places at one point in time that have adopted the X policy to various degrees, and then determine for each place how they score on the Y goal. With that data one could (1) use a linear regression analysis to determine the value of the "a" and "b" in the linear regression equation, (2) use a log-linear regression analysis for the second equation where the computer input data consists of the logarithms of the X and Y values for each city, or (3) use a linear analysis with a squaring transformation to obtain the parameters for the third equation, where the computer input data consists of scores for each place on Y, X, and X^2. As a related alternative one can gather data for many time points for a single place. The data is then processed in the same manner even though the entities, cases, or units of analysis are time points rather than places. A third variation on the regression analysis involves combining the data for many places and many time points to provide a mix of units of analysis.[18]

The second approach of questioning knowledgeable persons can be handled in a variety of ways. A way that seems most meaningful, though, is to ask those who have a familiarity with the relations between the overall goal and a policy to indicate first whether the relation is positive, negative, or both. If only positive or only negative, is it linear or nonlinear? If linear, then what is the average value of Y when X equals 0? Also, by how many units is Y likely to change if X changes 1 unit? Those last two questions give the values of "a" and "b" respectively in the equation $Y = a+bX$. If the relation is nonlinear but one-directional, then what is the average value of Y when X equals 1? Also, by what percentage is Y likely to change if X changes 1 percent? Those last two questions give the values of "a" and "b" respectively in the equation $Y = aX^b$.

If the relation is hill shaped or valley shaped, the most relevant question might be to ask at what level of X does Y reach a peak or bottom? If multiple X's are involved, as in the linear equation $Y = a+b_1X_1+b_2X_2$, all we may need to know in developing a policy strategy is which X has the largest slope or "b". If the multiple X equation is nonlinear, as in $Y = aX_1^{b_1}X_2^{b_2}$, then all we may need to know is the rank order of the elasticity coefficients or b's, not their absolute value. Other variations on these questions can be developed in light of the specific subject matter being dealt with, but the important thing is to ask questions in light of the common sense meaning of the parameters rather than their more technical statistical or mathematical meaning.[19]

The third approach of developing the parameters through assumptions may be the least valid but often necessary for lack of the kind of data needed for regression analysis and for lack of knowledgeable persons who can meaningfully respond to questions designed to determine the equation parameters. If one assumes a positive linear relation, it may often be reasonable to assume that the "a" coefficient is equal to zero. This in effect means that if one spends nothing on the X policy, then nothing will be achieved on the Y goal. Assumptions are also often made with regard to the "b" coefficients in the nonlinear relation $Y = aX^b$. For example, if one assumes that as X increases Y will increase at a diminishing rate, it may be reasonable to give "b" a value of .5, which is a square root transformation of X. Likewise, if one assumes that as X increases, Y increases at an increasing rate, where Y is a cost rather than a benefit, then it may be reasonable to give "b" a value of 2, which is a squaring transformation of X. Another reasonable assumption might be that if one assumes as X increases, Y decreases, but at a diminishing rate, then "b" can be assumed to have a value of −1, which is a reciprocal transformation. Other assumptions about the values of the parameters may also be reasonable given the subject matter involved. Where the assumed parameters are not round numbers, the assumption approach in effect becomes an approach like questioning knowledgeable persons, but the only knowledgeable person questioned is the researcher.[20]

CONTROLLING FOR ENVIRONMENTAL AND OTHER VARIABLES

A highly important aspect of relating goals to policies involves controlling for environmental and other variables which may affect the relation between policies and goals. Any variable that correlates well with both the goal measure and the policy measure may cause the goal-policy relation to appear to be stronger than it really is in a causal sense. For example, if city size correlates highly with crime occurrence and anticrime expenditures, relating those two variables may reveal a strong but meaningless relation that implies an increase in anticrime expenditures brings an increase in crime occurrence. In laboratory experiments one can randomly allocate the experimental stimulus to the subjects in order to greatly decrease the chances of confounding variables being disproportionately present between the experimental group and the control group. In policy analysis, however, it is generally impossible to randomly allocate the adoption of a policy across geographical places or other units of analysis, and one therefore generally has to resort to other types of controls. In that context one can make use of at least four different approaches to attempt to control for confounding variables other than the goals and policies being considered.[21]

One approach involves partitioning the sample of persons, places, and things into groups that are alike on whatever outside variable one is attempting to hold constant. That approach could conceivably be applied in the anticrime example by just making comparisons or correlations using big cities, and doing a separate analysis with small cities, although one might still need additional controls in order to bring out the negative relation between crime occurrence and anticrime expenditures. In the civil rights example, it might make sense to separate the data into northern cities and southern cities to bring out the possibly different relations between antidiscrimination results and antidiscrimination activities in those two regions. The partitioning of the units of analysis might also be done to control for outside variables that are not geographical in nature. For example, in the free press-fair trial study it seemed meaningful to partition the sample of questionnaire respondents into police chiefs, prosecutors, defense attorneys, and newspaper editors when relating measures of satisfaction to the occurrence of free press and fair trial. It was found, however, that the regression equations for all four groups free press received a higher slope than fair trial, and thus the optimizing solution was not sensitive to that partitioning control.

The second approach involves defining the goal variable in a relatively narrow way in order to control for variables that might otherwise disrupt the goal-policy relation. The campaign allocation problem provides an example of that approach since the goal variable there is defined as the percent of the two party vote received. That variable consists of the number of votes received divided by the total two party vote cast, and thus controls for the total vote which is the denominator of the goal variable. Likewise, working with crimes per capita for each city rather than total crime occurrence tends to partly control for city size. Different types of controls can be combined as in the campaign allocation problem where partitioning is also used by only working with nonincumbents running against nonincumbents in order to control for incumbency in relating votes received to campaign expenditures.

Another approach to controlling for variables other than the goals and policies involves developing multivariate equations in which the other variables are included as independent variables along with the policy variables. For example, in relating the percentage of defendants held in jail prior to trial (%H) to total holding costs (THC) and to total releasing costs (TRC), one can use a regression analysis that will include city population yielding log linear equations of the form $THC = a_1(\%H)^{b_1}(POP)^{c_1}$, and $TRC = a_2(\%H)^{b_2}(POP)^{c_2}$. In the pretrial release problem, it was found that the coefficients c_1 and c_2 were quite similar. This meant that city size has about an equal influence on holding costs and releasing costs. It thus has little influence on the optimum percent to hold (%H*) since %H* is a negative function of THC and a positive function of TRC, meaning as holding costs go up, the optimum percent to hold goes down, and the opposite with releasing costs.

Residual analysis is a fourth approach. It involves determining the regression equation between (1) a goal variable like crime at time t and (2) an outside variable like crime at time t-1. That equation is then used to obtain a predicted crime score for each city which is then subtracted from its actual crime score to obtain a residual crime score or a score. The residual score represents crime unexplained by either prior crime or the variables that relate to prior crime. Minimizing those residual scores can then be the controlled goal variable, thereby controlling for the variables that relate to prior crime. In the anticrime allocation problem, that kind of control was the only control that resulted in almost consistently negative relations between crime occurrence (i.e., unexplained crime occurrence) and anticrime expenditures. In other words, it was the only control in which the goal-policy slopes showed the extent to which an increase in anticrime expenditures results in a decrease in crime rather than an increase.

A special type of control may be needed where the goal and the policy have a reciprocal relation with each other. Under those circumstances, the control is needed not for an outside variable, but rather to separate the extent to which changes in the policy cause changes in the goal rather than the reverse. An example might be an analysis of the effects of divorce laws on divorce rates. If only one-point-in-time data is available, an appropriate control procedure would involve finding a variable that correlates well with divorce law but not divorce rates. One then uses that variable to obtain predicted divorce law scores (rather than use actual divorce law scores) which are then related to actual divorce rate scores. One also finds a variable that correlates well with divorce rates but not divorce laws, and uses that variable to obtain predicted divorce rate scores which are then related to actual divorce law scores. If two-points-in-time data is available, one can relate divorce law at time t back to divorce rates at time t-1, controlling for divorce law at time t-1 using a multivariate regression. Those results can then be compared with relating divorce rates at time t back to divorce law at time t-1, controlling for divorce rates at time t-1. If data is available at multiple time points, then one can observe trends in the rates before and after the law changes to see whether the rates seem to be pushing the law up, or vice versa, or both.[22]

Processing the Combinations and the Relations

After one has developed some clarity with regard to combining the goals to be achieved, avoided, maximized, or minimized and with regard to relating those combined goals to various alternative policies, the next logical question is what does one do with that information in evaluating alternative public policies. The answer is sometimes obvious, especially when one is dealing with discrete choices where one can determine how each choice scores on the overall goal or goals. The answer is, however, more complicated where continuum policies are involved, or where the discrete choices depend on continuum probabilities. Under those circumstances, the combinations and the relations often need to be processed as part of a model involving formulas associated with (1) decision theory under risk, (2) optimum level analysis, which may involve algebraically finding a peak or bottom on a hill-shaped or valley-shaped net-benefits curve, or (3) optimum mix analysis, which may involve the use of algebra or linear programming to optimally allocate scarce resources among a set of policies. Details describing those procedures are given elsewhere.[23] They are meaningful, however, only to the extent that the researcher has meaningfully clarified the goals or objectives to be achieved and related those goals to the alternative policies.

The expression "garbage in, garbage out" is sometimes used to disparage optimizing research that is based on bad data. Many policy problems, however, are capable of being insightfully analyzed by various optimizing models, even with bad data because the causal analysis or prescriptive recommendations are not affected by the extent to which the data is based on inadequate measurement, sampling, assumptions, or other details.[24] On the other hand, no matter how sophisticated an optimizing model might be, it is unlikely to produce worthwhile results if statements concerning the goals and how those goals relate to the alternative policies do not make sense. Thus, combining and relating goals does represent a highly essential part of meaningful and useful policy analysis.

APPENDIX 4.1: METHODS OF REDUCING THE NUMBER OF VARIABLES AND MAKING COMPOSITE VARIABLES

In the outline below, roman numerals always refer to methods or groups of methods, capital letters refer to specific methods, the Arabic numeral 1 defines a specific method, and Arabic numeral 2 indicates advantages and disadvantages of a specific method. All the methods described below make use of one or more programs available in the SPSS statistical programs, including transformation, correlation, partial correlation, regression, factor analysis, scalogramming, and stepwise regression.

I. SUMMATION METHODS

A. Unweighted Summation Scores (S)

1. Give each entity a score consisting of the sum of the category scores received on each variable after each variable has been recoded so that the category numbers are all in ascending order on the underlying dimension. $S = X_1 + \ldots + X_n$.

2. Advantage = simplicity. Disadvantage = ignores differential importance of the variables and their overlap.

B. Weighted Summation Score (S')

1. Multiply each category score by the correlation coefficient between each variable and the unweighted summation score. $S' = r_1 X_1 + \ldots + r_n X_n$.

       2. Advantage = weights the variables. Disadvantage = ignores overlap.

  C.   Summation Score with Partialed Weights (S'')

       1. Multiply each category score by the partial correlation coefficient between each variable and the unweighted summation score, holding the other variables constant.

       2. Advantage = weights the variables and considers overlap. Disadvantage = the dependent variable is not a least squares prediction of the summation score.

  D.   Summation Score with Regression Weights (Y)

       1. Multiply each category score by the partial slope between each variable and the unweighted summation score, holding the other variables constant. $Y = a + b_1 X_1 + \ldots + b_n X_n$.

       2. Advantage = considers weighting, overlap, and least squares prediction. Disadvantage = not oriented toward the specific subject matter being dealt with.

II. FACTOR ANALYSIS

  A.   Use a Few Factors Instead of Many Variables

       1. Input the data matrix of entities by variables into the SPSS factor analysis program to obtain a correlation matrix of variables by variables which is then used to obtain a factor matrix of variables by factors. A new data matrix of entities by the first five or so factors can then be obtained with factor scores in the cells rather than variable scores.

       2. Advantage = requires even less thought than the summation methods since those methods require picking the independent variables whereas in factor analysis all variables are treated as independent variables. Disadvantage = subjectivity of naming the factors, rotating the factors so they will have zero correlations with each other, and of deciding how many factors are enough.

B. For Each Factor, Use the Variable that Has the Highest Correlation with the Factor

1. Same steps as above except stop with the factor matrix.

2. Advantage = less subjective to interpret the results, and simpler than obtaining factor scores because one can use the variable scores for each variable chosen. Disadvantage = ignores information on unused variables that the factor-using approach above considers.

III. SCALOGRAMMING

1. Arrange a set of variables in hierarchical order on an assumed underlying dimension so as to minimize the number of inconsistencies among the respondents. If the inconsistencies are less than 10 percent of the opportunities, it is conventional to assume one has a scale. Then score the respondents or entities by giving them the number of the highest variable on which they scored positively.

2. Advantage = provides a useful visual aid and a common sense notion of unidimensional composite variable. Disadvantage = requires variables that have hierarchical order, and there is often more than one way of minimizing the number of inconsistencies.

IV. STEPWISE REGRESSION

1. Input the data matrix of entities by variables into the SPSS stepwise regression program to obtain a series of regression equations. Each subsequent equation will have one more independent variable than the previous one. The incremental independent variable will be the one next in line by looking to how the remaining variables relate to the dependent variable and to the previously-included variables. One can stop the incrementing process and just work with the most predictive variables when a point is reached where the next incre-

mental variable adds very little to the amount of variance explained on the dependent variable.

2. Advantage = a nonthinking approach like factor analysis but the results are more meaningful to interpret. Disadvantage = not oriented toward the specific subject matter being dealt with.

V. METHODS REQUIRING KNOWLEDGE OF THE SUBJECT MATTER BEING DEALT WITH

All the methods below have the advantage of making use of the researcher's knowledge about the subject matter. They all have the disadvantage of requiring some careful thinking, and of introducing subjectivities although the subjectivities tend to be clearer to the researcher and the reader than the hidden ones in more mechanical methods.

A.   Subjective Clustering

Create clusters of variables in light of some theoretical orientation that considers the subject matter. Then use one variable to represent each cluster which has the highest average correlation coefficient with all the other variables in the cluster.

B.   Recoding

Recode two or more variables to create a new variable that reflects a composite of the previous variables. For example, one might simply take the dichotomous variable of party affiliation (Democrat and Republican) and the dichotomous variable of region (North and South) to make a composite variable called party and region which has four categories (northern Democrat, northern Republican, southern Democrat, southern Republican).

C.   Subjective Variable Reduction

Think about which variables are most worth retaining in light of their known overlap and relation to what one is trying to explain in causal analysis or to what one is trying to optimize in optimizing analysis.

NOTES

1. General items dealing with combining multiple goals include Ralph Keeney and Howard Raiffa, *Decisions with Multiple Objectives: Preferences and Value Tradeoffs* (Wiley, 1976); James Cochrane and Milan Zeleny (eds.), *Multiple Criteria Decision Making* (U. of South Caroline Press, 1973); Peter C. Gardiner and Ward Edwards, "Public Values: Multiattribute Utility Measurement for Social Decision Making" in Martin Kaplan and Steven Schwartz, *Human Judgment and Decision Processes* (Academic Press, 1975), pp. 1-37; Dirk Wendt and Charles Vlek (eds.), *Utility, Probability, and Human Decision Making* (Reidel, 1975), pp. 1-133; and Allan Easton, *Complex Managerial Decisions Involving Multiple Objectives* (Wiley, 1973). These items, however, tend to emphasize business and personal goals, rather than government policy goals. They also emphasize measuring the goal achievement in terms of individual psychological utility, rather than societal social indicators.

2. General items dealing with relating goals to policies include E. J. Mishan, *Cost-Benefit Analysis* (Praeger, 1976); Werner Hirsch, *The Economics of State and Local Government* (McGraw-Hill, 1970); and William Baumol, *Economic Theory and Operations Analysis* (Prentice-Hall, 1965), pp. 169-269. The most relevant literature comes from microeconomics and deals with developing (1) production functions where output is the dependent variable or goal to be achieved, and the independent variables (analogous to policies) are variables like land, labor, capital, technology, and environmental conditions; (2) cost functions where cost is the dependent variable or goal to be avoided or minimized, and the independent variables are similar to those in production functions; and (3) consumption functions where some measure of satisfaction is the dependent variable, and the independent variables (analogous to policies) are quantities of various products along with the characteristics of the consumers being considered.

3. The general legal policy analysis literature from which the examples are drawn includes Nagel and Neef, *Legal Policy Analysis: Finding an Optimum Level or Mix* (Lexington-Heath, 1977); *The Legal Process: Modeling the System* (Sage, 1977); and *Decision Theory and the Legal Process* (Lexington-Heath, 1978). Other policy analysis examples implicitly involving problems of combining and relating goals are mentioned in Alfred Blumstein, Murray Kamrass, and Armand Weiss (eds.), *Systems Analysis for Social Problems* (Washington Operations Research Council, 1970); Saul Gass and Roger Sisson, *A Guide to Models in Governmental Planning and Operations* (Environmental Protection Agency, 1974); Martin Greenberger, Matthew Crenson, and Brian Crissey, *Models in the Policy Process* (Sage, 1976); and Walter Helly, *Urban Systems Models* (Academic Press, 1975). None of those legal or political analysis books explicitly deals with the general subject of combining multiple goals or relating goals to policies.

4. For a discussion of the concept of maximizing benefits minus costs and related criterion problems, see Roland McKean, *Efficiency in Government through Systems Analysis* (Wiley, 1958), pp. 25-49. Sometimes goals are stated in terms of maximizing a benefits/costs ratio rather than benefits minus costs. Such a ratio may be meaningful when the benefits are measured in different units than those in which the costs are measured. If a common unit of measurement is involved, however, the goal of benefits minus costs makes more sense since one

would logically prefer an investment of $100 that yields a $200 return than an investment of $10 that yields a $30 return if one's other $90 is going to remain idle. Either goal criterion will give the same results as to which of two investments is more desirable where both investments involve the same costs, i.e., both involve only $100 or only $10. E. J. Mishan, *Economics for Social Decisions: Elements of Cost-Benefit Analysis* (Praeger, 1973), pp. 134-135. Richard Zeckhauser and Elmer Schaefer, "Public Policy and Normative Economic Theory," in Raymond Bauer and Kenneth Gergen (eds.), *The Study of Policy Formation* (Free Press, 1968), pp. 72-73.

5. Constraints are generally normative or goal-oriented in nature since they specify maximums or minimums that ought not to be exceeded. Sometimes, however, constraints may merely relate to the measurement system, as is generally the case with nonnegativity constraints since they merely specify that it is meaningless to have a negative amount of dollars or some other unit.

6. On the anticrime allocation problem, see Nagel and Neef, "Allocating Resources Geographically for Optimum Results," 3 *Political Methodology* 383-404 (1976).

7. On the campaign expenditure problem see Nagel and Neef, *Operations Research Methods: As Applied to Political Science and the Legal Process* (Sage, 1976); and on the legal services problem see Nagel, *Improving the Legal Process: Effects of Alternatives* (Lexington-Heath, 1975), pp. 271-310.

8. On the civil rights allocation problem, see Nagel and Neef, *The Application of Mixed Strategies: Civil Rights and Other Multiple-Activity Policies* (Sage, 1976); and on the free press, fair trial problem see Nagel, Reinbolt, and Eimermann, "A Linear Programming Approach to Problems of Conflicting Legal Values like Free Press versus Fair Trial," 4 *Rutgers Journal of Computers and the Law* 420-61 (1975). Thanks are owed to Bernard Grofman of the University of California at Irvine and Nancy Munshaw of the University of Illinois at Urbana for their help in developing this joint causation illustration.

9. On lexicographic ordering, see Richard Zeckhauser and Elmer Schaefer, "Public Policy and Normative Economic Theory," in Raymond Bauer and Kenneth Gergen, *The Study of Policy Formation* (Free Press, 1968), pp. 27-101, especially 37-38.

10. On the pretrial release problem, see Nagel and Neef, *Too Much or Too Little Policy: The Example of Pretrial Release* (Sage, 1977), and Nagel, Neef, and Schramm, "Decision Theory and the Pretrial Release Decision in Criminal Cases," 31 *University of Miami Law Review* 1433-1491 (1977).

11. On the jury size problem, see Nagel and Neef, "Deductive Modeling to Determine an Optimum Jury Size and Fraction Required to Convict," 1975 *Washington University Law Quarterly* 933-978 (1976). On general matters relating to the measurement of goals, benefits, and costs, see Elmer Struening and Marcia Guttentag (eds.), *Handbook of Evaluation Research* (Sage, 1975); E. S. Quade, *Analysis for Public Decisions* (Elsevier, 1975); and Guy Black, *The Application of Systems Analysis to Government Operations* (Praeger, 1968).

12. On the redistricting problem, see Nagel, *The Legal Process from a Behavioral Perspective* (Dorsey, 1969), pp. 321-359; and "Computers and the Law and Politics of Redistricting" 5 *Polity* 77-93 (1972). In allocating campaign expenditure funds to 435 congressional districts by the Democratic Congressional Cam-

paign Committee, it might be meaningful to try to maximize the total number of districts that are won by democratic candidates. Doing so, however, might mean saying that no district should be given so much funds that the democratic candidate wins by more than 55 percent of the two party vote. Doing so might also mean that no district should be given more than a morale-preserving minimum where a maximum quantity of funds is not likely to result in that district reaching the 51 percent figure needed for victory. In this context, the overall goal is districts won, and each district represents a subgoal. This problem illustrates the important principle that if each subgoal is maximized, doing so may interfere with, rather than aid, the achievement of the overall goal.

13. On the plea bargaining problem, see Nagel and Neef, "Plea Bargaining, Decision Theory, and Equilibrium Models," 51 and 52 *Indiana Law Journal* 987-1024, 1-61 (1976). Combining discounted benefits and costs to create an overall goal involves the same kind of problems as combining benefits and costs that are not discounted. For example, a pretrial release judge may seek to combine the discounted benefits and costs that relate to (1) the defendant's appearing in court and (2) the defendant's not committing a crime while released. A judge could do so in a sequential manner by saying the first probability must exceed .50 and the second probability must exceed .70. An alternative would be a simultaneous approach which might involve releasing the defendant if the sum of the two probabilities is greater than 1.00. That alternative would allow a low probability on one of the two contingent events to be offset by a high probability on the other. Given the nature of the subject matter, the sequential approach with a minimum constraint on each probability makes more sense here than the simultaneous approach.

14. On the search and seizure problem, see Nagel, "Choosing Among Alternative Public Policies," in Kenneth Dolbeare (ed.), *Public Policy Evaluation* (Sage, 1975), pp. 153-174. One advantage of using the approach of summing scores with weights as multipliers (rather than multiplying scores with weights as exponents) is that the summing preserves the linear relations between the subgoals and the overall goal, whereas the multiplying introduces a non-linear or diminishing returns relation. A diminishing returns relation may make sense when one is relating policies or means to goals, but not so likely when one is relating subgoals to an overall goal.

15. Normative weights can thus be used like empirical regression coefficients which simultaneously consider the predictive power, the units of measurement, and the overlap among the independent variables in a regression equation. Normative weights, however, are generally not based on relating goals (Y_1, Y_2) to a higher goal (Y') in a regression equation of the form $Y' = a + b_1 Y_1 + b_2 Y_2$, although as mentioned above, they sometimes can be. Likewise, sometimes empirical regression coefficients are subjectively estimated just as probabilities often are, rather than stem from the processing of a data matrix showing the variable scores of a number of units of analysis.

16. On the problem of overlapping goals, see Ward Edwards, *How to Use Multi-Attribute Utility Measurement for Social Decision-Making* (USC Social Science Research Institute, 1976), especially pp. 16-18; and Nagel, "Optimizing Legal Policy," 18 *University of Florida Law Review* 577-590 (1966), especially pp. 586-588. Also see Appendix 4.1 to this chapter on "Methods of Reducing the

Number of Variables and Making Composite Variables." Another approach for dealing with the problem of overlapping goals is to estimate the correlation coefficient of every goal with every other goal if that is possible, and then insert a kind of weighted average correlation among the goals into a somewhat complicated formula in order to arrive at a relative utility score or goal attainment score. See Thomas Kiresuk and Robert Sherman, "Goal Attainment Scaling: A General Method for Evaluating Comprehensive Community Mental Health Programs," 4 *Community Mental Health Journal* 443-453 (1968).

17. On the jury decision-making problem, see Nagel, Lamm, and Neef, "Decision Theory and Juror Decision-Making," in Bruce Sales (ed.), *The Jury, Judicial, and Trial Processes* (Plenum, 1978).

18. The use of regression analysis to relate goals to policies is illustrated by the civil rights allocation problem (linear equations), the legal services problem (log-linear equations), and the pretrial release problem (equations generating a valley shaped curve).

19. Sending out questionnaires to obtain data for a regression analysis is not the same as asking knowledgeable persons for the parameters of the regression equations. Likewise, asking persons to estimate benefits, costs, utilities, or probabilities is also not the same.

20. The assumptions approach may be especially needed when one only has data on a Y goal and an X policy for a single point in time for each of a number of places, and one wants to determine the diminishing returns relation $Y = aX^b$ for each city. One can assume that $b = .5$, 2, or -1 depending on the subject matter, and then solve for the coefficient "a" by plugging into the equation the value of Y and X. That type of approach is discussed in the article dealing with the anticrime allocation.

21. In this section and elsewhere in this article, when one variable is said to be related to another, the first variable can be considered to be the dependent variable in a regression equation, and the second variable to be the independent variable.

22. For further details concerning the handling of reciprocal relations as well as spurious correlation and joint causation, see David Heise, *Causal Analysis* (Wiley, 1975); and Nagel and Neef, "Causal Analysis and the Legal Process," in Rita Simon (ed.), *Research in Law and Sociology* (Johnson Associates, 1977).

23. Samuel Richmond, *Operations Research for Management Decisions* (Ronald, 1968); Richard Zeckhauser and Elmer Schaefer, "Public Policy and Normative Economic Theory," in Raymomd Bauer and Kenneth Gergen (eds.), *The Study of Policy Formation* (Free Press, 1968); Jack Byrd, Jr., *Operations Research Models for Public Administration* (Lexington Heath, 1975); and Nagel and Neef, *Operations Research Methods: As Applied to Political Science and the Legal Process* (Sage, 1976).

24. Examples of policy analysis problems in which substantial changes in the data have little or no effect on the optimum policy levels or mixes include: (1) the pretrial release problem in which substantial changes can be made in the initial data without affecting the optimum percent to hold prior to trial since so many items and transformations are involved in determining that optimum; (2) the legal services problem in which the optimum mix between law reform work and routine case handling is the same regardless of data changes so long as the slope of

law reform remains greater than the slope of case handling; and (3) the free press, fair trial problem in which the balance among the responding occupational groups could change greatly and not affect the optimum free press, fair trial balance since all the groups gave greater weight to free press over fair trial within the constraints.

Chapter 5

FINDING AN OPTIMUM CHOICE, LEVEL, OR MIX IN PUBLIC POLICY ANALYSIS

This chapter analyzes some general matters concerning how to arrive at an optimum choice, level, or mix when confronted with alternative policy decisions, especially decisions relating to the legal process. It brings together a variety of ideas into a useful typology of problems. It also synthesizes a variety of optimizing principles with public policy and legal process illustrations.

By "optimum" in this context, we refer to the decision-making alternative or combination of alternatives that will maximize some quantitatively measured goal or goals. By "choice" we mean a situation involving alternative decisions that fit into discrete categories such as whether to provide counsel for the poor in criminal cases through volunteer counsel, assigned counsel, a public defender, or some combination of the three. By "level" and "mix," we mean a situation involving alternative decisions that fit on a continuum of possibilities such as what level of money to appropriate for a public defender's office in a given county, or what mix of available budget money to allocate between the public defender's office and the prosecutor's office.

This chapter represents a substantial extension of a paper with the same title which is scheduled to appear in the *Public Administration Review.* The chapter provides new details particularly in the four appendices.

By "public policy," we mean governmental decision-making that decides on choices, levels, and mixes with regard to controversial alternative ways of doing things. The kind of public policy problems that will be emphasized in this article are those that especially relate to the procedures whereby courts arrive at decisions but also to procedures of other governmental decision-makers and to some substantive problems as well. Given the level of methodological generality, one can easily reason by analogy from the typologies and principles given here to a variety of public policy problems. Our cited examples will often come from more detailed studies that we have made elsewhere since those are the studies with which we are most familiar and which are most illustrative of the kind of legal policy optimizing to which we are referring.

Finding an Optimum Alternative Policy in General

The methodology of finding an optimum policy in general can be reduced in its most simplified form to a one-sentence rule, namely: Choose the alternative that maximizes net benefits, where net benefits are total benefits minus total costs. That rule can be symbolized as follows: When faced with choosing between X_1, X_2, and so on, choose the X or policy alternative that gives the greatest Y, where Y symbolizes net benefits.[1]

The Y (or NB for net benefits) can be decomposed into various benefits (B_1, B_2, and so on) and various costs (C_1, C_2, and so on). A benefit is an effect of an X alternative that is considered desirable, whereas a cost is an effect of an X alternative that is considered undesirable. Sometimes benefits and costs are referred to generically simply as effects and symbolized Y_1, Y_2, and so on. The overall Y of a given X or alternative represents the sum of the separate Y scores if they are measured with a common unit and can thus be added together. Otherwise, the relation between each X and each Y must either be analyzed separately, or else each Y must be multiplied together rather than added, with exponents indicating their relative value weights.

Given those definitions of benefits and costs, it logically follows that we want to choose policy alternatives that will maximize our benefits and minimize our costs. It is, however, usually impossible to do both simultaneously since doing nothing is likely to be the alternative that will minimize our costs (i.e., bring them down to zero), but it is also the alternative that is least likely to produce any benefits. Likewise, spending great sums of money or effort may bring substantial or maximum benefits, but only at great cost. Thus, since we cannot have maximum benefits and minimum costs at the same time, a more feasible goal is to try to pick the alternative that will provide the biggest difference between total benefits $(B_1 + B_2 + \ldots + B_n)$ and total costs $(C_1 + C_2 + \ldots + C_n)$ of the alternatives available. This is analogous to a business firm seeking to maximize its profits or the difference between total income and total expenses.

That general rule about maximizing net benefits would be more useful if we were to indicate how it varies in different general situations. The main typology of situations for methodological purposes is a simple dichotomy between policy problems in which the alternatives have no logical order and policy problems in which the alternatives do have logical order. Policy problems in which the alternatives have no logical order include yes-no problems such as whether or not illegally seized evidence should be admissible in court,[2] or whether or not a given defendant should be released or held in jail prior to trial.[3] There is likewise no logical order among the alternatives where more than two nonnumerical categories are involved such as whether to provide counsel to the poor in criminal cases through a voluntary counsel system, an assigned counsel system, or a public defender system.[4] The number of categories lacking inherent order for a given policy problem can be huge as is the situation in trying to choose among all the possible ways in which 90 of the downstate Illinois counties could be made into 18 districts.[5]

Policy problems in which the policy or decisional alternatives do have inherent order include the problem of the optimum number of jurors to have among the alternatives of 6, 7, 8, 9, 10, 11, or 12,[6] or the optimum percent of defendants to hold in jail prior to trial with the alternatives being 1%, 2%, 3%, and so on including all the decimal possibilities between the integer percentages.[7] There is especially inherent order where the alternatives involve money or effort expenditures, such as how many dollars to allocate (out of every $100 available) to law reform versus case handling in the OEO Legal Services Program,[8] or how many dollars to allocate (out of every $100 available) to Illinois, Wisconsin, and other states in order to have a maximum impact on keeping down the national crime occurrence.[9]

Although our overall goal is to pick the alternative that maximizes net benefits, we often use other terminology to mean the same thing. For example, one can talk about legislatively setting bail bonds that will maximize the difference between the probability of a pretrial defendant appearing in court (PA) minus the probability of his being held in jail (PH). In that context, PA is like total benefits and PH is like total costs. One can also talk about releasing a percentage of pretrial defendants that will minimize the sum of our holding costs plus our releasing costs. In that context, holding costs can be considered a negative benefit. More specifically, holding costs are the releasing benefits (i.e, the dollars saved by not holding a defendant) which we lose by holding a defendant, and in that sense holding costs are negative releasing benefits. Thus when we say we want to minimize the sum of our holding costs plus our releasing costs, we are in effect saying we want to maximize our releasing benefits (i.e., minimize our negative releasing benefits) minus our releasing costs. In other words, costs can be considered negative benefits, and benefits can be considered negative costs. Thus, if we have considered all the relevant effects, we may be maximizing our net benefits even though we only talk about maximizing benefits or minimizing costs.[10]

Finding an Optimum Choice
Among Discrete Alternatives

Within the typology of policy problems that involve alternatives backing inherent order, we can have two kinds of policy problems, namely those that do not involve contingent probabilities and those that do involve them.

CHOOSING WITHOUT CONTINGENT PROBABILITIES

A good example of choosing without probabilities is the problem of how to provide legal counsel to the poor in criminal cases. The main alternatives are (X_1) a list of volunteer attorneys, (X_2) assigned counsel generally on a rotation basis from among practicing attorneys in the county, or (X_3) a public defender who is a salaried lawyer hired by the government to represent poor defendants. All other things being equal, the best alternative is the one that is most (Y_1) inexpensive, (Y_2) visible and accessible, (Y_3) politically feasible, and (Y_4) the most likely to result in specialized competence and aggressive representation. A benefit can be defined as being relatively high on one of these goals, and a cost can be defined as being relatively low.

Starting with the goal of inexpensiveness, volunteer counsel and assigned counsel score well. The public defender system is, however, substantially more expensive. On visibility and accessibility all three alternatives are about equal in the sense that arraigning magistrates are expected to inform poor defendants of whatever system the county uses for making counsel available to poor defendants. On political feasibility or acceptability there is not likely to be any great opposition among influential lawyers to the volunteer or public defender alternatives. They are, however, likely to object to the assigned counsel alternative since it forces lawyers against their will to devote time and resources to cases which they may find frustrating and even distateful. Volunteer counsel is unlikely to result in competent, aggressive lawyers unless substantial fees are paid to the screened volunteers, which is a system that only exists at the federal level. Likewise, assigned counsel tends to result in the appointment of lawyers who may be competent in their specialty, but that specialty is not so likely to be criminal law. The public defender system develops competent criminal defense attorneys through the specialized continuous experience although their aggressiveness may be limited by lack of funding and personnel.

The above analysis indicates three relative benefits or advantages for volunteer counsel and one relative cost or disadvantage; two benefits for assigned counsel and two costs; and three benefits for the public defender system and one cost. To resolve the tie between volunteer counsel and the public defender requires giving relative weights to the four goals. If we give more weight to the goals of visibility-accessibility and competence-aggressiveness as a more liberal policy-maker might be inclined to do, then the public defender comes out ahead. If we give more weight to the goals of inexpensiveness and political feasibility as a more conservative policy-maker might be inclined to do, then the volunteer system comes out ahead assuming that it is capable of providing sufficient counsel to satisfy the constitutional requirements.

This optimizing perspective of listing alternatives, goals, relations, weights and choices may also be applicable to obtaining insights into the best alternatives for resolving other public policy problems. The perspective can be made more sophisticated by using X's that are not mutually exclusive, thereby introducing combinations of the alternatives such as an X_4 which involves a list of volunteer attorneys for poor defendants who do not like the public defender as is done in the city of Chicago. One can also relate each X alternative to each Y goal by showing the degree of relationship and also the extent to which non-linear diminishing return are involved rather than just whether the relation is relatively positive or negative. In addition, one could indicate the extent to which a relation between an X and a Y is affected by the probabilistic occurrence of an outside event. An example might be that public defenders tend to provide aggressive representation only when they have adequate resources, but the probability of their having adequate resources is roughly .30 in the sense that only about one out of three public defenders' offices have funding above an adequate threshold of budget divided by cases, although more exact statistics are currently being developed by the National Legal Aid and Defenders' Association.

CHOOSING WITH CONTINGENT PROBABILITIES

The legal process, at least in its judicial aspects, involves a series of choices that are made by the participants on the basis of the probability of the occurrence of some contingent event. For example, the would-be criminal chooses to commit or not commit a crime partly on the basis of the probability of his getting caught and convicted. Likewise, the personal injury lawyer accepts a client partly on the basis of the probability of winning the case especially if the lawyer only gets paid if the case is won. Similar probabilistic decisions are faced by arraignment judges, sentencing judges, parole boards, prosecuting attorneys, and insurance company lawyers, although each of these decision-makers may be concerned with a different contingent event, different data, and different specific goals to be maximized.

Substantively, we could divide the above situations into criminal case decisional problems or into civil case decisional problems. From a methodological perspective, however, it would be more meaningful to divide those situations into ones that involve a single decision-maker trying to make a choice irrespective of anyone else's present choices or interaction, as contrasted to situations involving more than one decision-maker whose decisions are influenced by the interactive behavior or decisions of another decision-maker.

The one-person decision situation can be illustrated by the bond-setting decision. It involves the contingent event of the defendant appearing in court, and the contingent event of the defendant committing a crime while released. It involves the dichotomous decision of release or hold, and also the numerical decision of what dollar bond to set. The goals or Y scores (associated with each decision and contingent event) can be expressed in nonmonetary satisfaction units or in monetary dollar units. The bond-setting problem can be thought of as an individual case-by-case judicial problem, or as a more generalized problem of legislating for types of cases. In addition, the bond-setting problem illustrates distinctions between descriptive models designed to describe how the legal process operates, as contrasted to prescriptive models designed to prescribe how the legal process should operate in order to maximize given goals.[11]

The two-person interacting situation can be illustrated by the process of plea bargaining and out-of-court civil settlements. In plea bargaining, the offers of the prosecutor and the defendant or his defense counsel are partly determined by their perceptions of the probability of a conviction if the case were to go to trial. Likewise, in civil case negotiations, the offers of the plaintiff and the defendant or their attorneys are partly determined by perceptions of the probability of the defendant being found liable if the case were to go to trial. Both the criminal and the civil negotiators will choose between settlement and trial partly on the basis of what the other side offers, unlike the bond setting situation where the defendant does not bargain or make moves with the judge.[12]

The plea bargaining situation is useful not only for illustrating what is involved in making an optimum choice under probabilistic conditions, but also useful for illustrating in a generalized way the sequential steps that are likely to occur from the initial positions of the parties to the final settlement or to a determination that a settlement is impossible. That kind of sequential analysis may be especially valuable in explaining the occurrence of certain decisions. That kind of sequential analysis, plus the basic decision theory and bargaining models, may also be valuable in analyzing the effect of legal changes and other system changes on the decisional behavior of the participants. By knowing how system changes are likely to affect decisional behavior, system planners can allow for those effects when instituting various system changes such as increased pretrial release, reduced delay, or increased allocation of resources to the participants.

In discussing general optimizing, we emphasized that finding an optimum or alternative policy involves choosing the alternative that maximizes net benefits, where net benefits are total benefits minus total costs. In situations that involve making an optimum choice under probabilistic conditions, that general rule needs to be slightly modified. The modification involves saying: Choose the alternative that maximizes expected net benefits, where expected net benefits are expected total benefits minus total expected costs. In that context, expected total benefits equal the benefits to be received if a contingent event happens times the probability of its happening. Likewise, expected total costs equal the costs to be incurred if a contingent event happens times the probability of its happening. Where there is more than one benefit, each benefit to be received is multiplied by the probability on which it is contingent. Therefore, expected total benefits (or ETB) equals $P_1 B_1 + P_2 B_2 + \ldots + P_n N_n$, and likewise with expected total costs.

Finding an Optimum Level or Mix on a Continuum of Alternatives

Within the typology of policy problems that involve alternatives having inherent order (such as alternatives involving percentages or dollars), we can also have at least two kinds of policy problems. The simplest kind of policy problems with numerical alternatives is the problem where we have one policy that can be adopted to various degrees, and the problem is one of finding the optimum level or optimum degree to which the policy should be adopted. This problem is illustrated by the optimum percentage of defendants to release prior to trial and the optimum jury size problem. The other kind of policy problem with numerical alternatives is the problem where we have scarce resources, and we are trying to allocate those resources among activities, places, or other entities so as to maximize our net benefits. This problem is illustrated by the optimum allocation of civil rights effort to six civil rights activities and anticrime dollars to the 50 states.

FINDING AN OPTIMUM LEVEL

The legal process tends to be epitomized by U-shaped or valley-shaped cost curves and by hill-shaped benefit curves. This is so both with regard to judicial procedure and the more general problem of how strict or lenient should legal rules be made or applied. The due process or fair procedure aspects of the legal process involve a constant struggle between going too far in providing due process and not going far enough. If too much due process is provided, then many guilty persons will go free in criminal cases and liable persons in civil cases, which will mean high total costs to the system at that end of the due process scale. On the other hand, if too little due process is provided, then many innocent persons will be found guilty of wrongdoing in criminal cases and nonliable persons in civil cases, which will mean high total costs to the system at the low end of the due process scale. Somewhere in the middle of that valley-shaped total cost curve, the costs to the system reach a minimum. At that point we have an optimum balance or optimum level of due process.

Likewise, any legal rule can be worded or applied in an overly strict way or an overly lenient way. If environmental protection standards become too strict, we suffer unduly high cleanup costs, but if the standards become too lenient, we suffer unduly high pollution damage costs. Likewise, contract law standards can become too strict, thereby interfering with freedom of contract and possibly incurring large societal costs in terms of reduction in the free flow of business. If contract law standards become too lenient, however, then we might encourage large societal costs in terms of exploitation of the side with the lesser knowledge or weaker bargaining power. In tort law, automobile negligence standards could be so strict as to slow traffic almost to a standstill, or so lenient as to paralyze potential drivers and pedestrians from venturing into the streets. Similar problems of doing too much or too little can occur in criminal law, divorce law, housing law, or any field of law. Somewhere between those extremes, however, is an optimum point where a minimum is reached on the sum of the total costs, with or without weights to consider different valuations of each cost.

The optimum level problem can be analyzed with empirical data from the pretrial release situation. If too high a percentage of defendants is held in jail prior to trial, then high holding costs will be incurred with regard to jail maintenance, lost gross national product, and the bitterness that is generated from being held in jail in spite of the fact that one's case results in a dismissal or an acquittal. If too low a percentage of defendants is held in jail prior to trial, then high releasing costs will be incurred with regard to the cost of rearresting defendants who fail to appear for trials, and the cost of crimes that are committed by defendants prior to trial who would not have committed those crimes if they had been held in jail. The object is to find an optimum percentage of defendants to hold or release prior to trial in order to minimize the sum of the holding and the releasing costs.[13]

Another optimum level problem is the optimum jury size problem. If juries are too large, too many guilty defendants may fail to be convicted; whereas if juries are too small, too many innocent defendants may be convicted. Unlike the percentage-to-release problem, however, virtually no empirical data can be obtained which meaningfully shows for various jury sizes the quantity of defendants who are convicted, let alone the quantity of guilty or innocent defendants. This is so because when the jury size changes in a given state, the type of cases that are decided by jury trials rather than bench trials also tends to change. There is no empirical way of separating out the effect of jury size and case types on changes in the conviction percentages. Therefore, to arrive at an optimum jury size requires a substantial amount of deductive modeling from premises that are acceptable, flexible, empirical, and normative. That kind of model involves probabilistic conditions, but it is basically an optimum level model.[14]

In discussing general optimizing, we emphasized that finding an optimum alternative policy involves choosing the alternative that maximizes net benefits, where net benefits are total benefits minus total costs. In the optimum level situation, we generally convert all the relevant effects into costs and then seek to minimize the unweighted or weighted sum of the costs. One reason for making that conversion is because it is generally easier to obtain cost data than benefit data when dealing with social problems although an important type of benefit is the dollars saved (or the negation of the costs) by not having to rearrest a defendant who fails to appear, by not having to lose the gross national product lost by holding a defendant in jail, or by not incurring some other cost. Another reason for expressing effects as costs especially in the optimum level situation, is because doing so emphasizes that the optimum level problem is basically one of minimizing the sum of type 1 errors or costs (where a true hypothesis is rejected, like convicting an innocent defendant contrary to the presumption of innocence) plus type 2 errors or costs (where a false hypothesis is accepted, like acquitting a guilty defendant in accordance with the presumption of innocence).

In spite of the tendency to expose optimum level problems in terms of minimizing total costs, they can often be expressed in terms of maximizing total benefits or maximizing certain benefits minus certain costs. For example, we could express the percentage-to-release problem as the problem of finding the percentage to release at which the sum of releasing benefits (holding costs avoided) plus the holding benefits (releasing costs avoided) will be maximized. We could also express it in terms of finding the percentage to release at which the releasing benefits minus the releasing costs are maximized, or the holding benefits minus the holding costs are maximized, and still arrive at the same solution. The problem of the optimum school integration enforcement level seems to be best stated as finding the level at which we avoid both the lowered integration benefits which are associated with tokenism, as well as the lowered integration benefits which are associated with white flight and re-segregation, and we thus obtain a maximum point on a hill-shaped total benefits curve. The important thing is that we recognize both over-enforcement and under-enforcement of any law can cause us to lose benefits or suffer costs including opportunity costs, thereby necessitating a search for the optimum balance or optimum level either with empirical data, deductive models, or a combination of both.

FINDING AN OPTIMUM MIX

The legal process can be expressed as a series of probabilistic decisions or as an attempt to find an optimum balance of type 1 and type 2 errors. It can also be expressed as an attempt to allocate scarce social resources. This is especially the case with legislative and administrative programs that involve the allocation of funds for various societal purposes. Since money is a scarce resource, the object of those aspects of the legal process is to allocate those funds among activities and/or places in such a way as to maximize the total benefits that are obtained where all effects are expressed as benefits (or desirable social indicators, like increased longevity) or to minimize the total costs where all effects are expressed as costs (or undesirable social indicators, like disease or crime occurrence). The allocation or optimum mix model also applies to the legal process where nonmonetary values are being allocated, such as some measure of effort on the part of civil rights organizations or agencies.

The basic rule for handling the optimum mix problem for allocating scarce resources is to allocate to activities or places in accordance with the budget available and the slopes or marginal rates of return for each activity or place. A slope or marginal rate of return is simply the ratio between a change in output produced for an activity or place and the corresponding change in input or resources expended to that activity or place. If the relation between inputs and outputs is constant or linear, then one would allocate to the activities or places with the largest slopes after satisfying whatever minimum constraints are required. If the relation between inputs and outputs involves diminishing returns or nonlinear relations, then one would allocate to the activities or places until their changing nonlinear slopes are equalized such that nothing could be gained by shifting from one activity or place to another. Under either type of relation, all of the budget should be expended if one wants to maximize benefits without exceeding the budget, but less than all of the budget should be expended if one wants to minimize costs while providing a minimum benefit or satisfaction level.

These general principles can be illustrated with regard to allocating effort among civil rights activities relating to voting, schools, criminal justice, employment, housing, and public accommodations. The problem is one of trying to determine how to allocate the total civil rights effort to those six input activities in order to maximize the total equality improvement as the collective output activity which represents the sum of the improvements obtained in each of the six civil rights fields. The model deals with linear relations for the sake of simplicity and because the range of the data fits a linear model about as well as a nonlinear one. To further simplify the presentation, the optimum mix model can be first presented in the context of finding an optimum mix between just two civil rights activities, namely those that relate to efforts against governmental discrimination and efforts against private discrimination. The model in effect represents a combination of linear regression analysis and linear programming-optimizing. The regression analysis is especially useful for obtaining slopes between each input activity and each output criterion for use in developing an input-output matrix that enables one to see how the outputs would change given various changes in the inputs, or how the inputs would have to change in order to satisfy change in the output goals.[15]

The general principles can also be illustrated with regard to allocating dollars among geographical places in order to minimize the national crime occurrence. Here the emphasis is on places rather than activities, which changes the methodology from a single equation (relating the overall output goal to various input activities into multiple equations (in which the crime occurrence in each place is related to anticrime dollars spent in that place). The emphasis here is also on diminishing returns nonlinear relations rather than linear regression and linear programming.[16] In both examples, concern is expressed for obtaining change data or data at more than one point in time, but dollars and anticrime data lend themselves to more precise measurement than effort and antidiscrimination data. Both examples involve an attempt to deal with the crucial problem of controlling for demographic, socioeconomic, and other variables which affect crime and discrimination besides antidiscrimination effort or anticrime dollars. Likewise, both examples in differing ways involve an attempt to deal with minimum and maximum political, legal, and economic constraints on the allocation of scarce resources to either activities or places.

In discussing general optimizing, we emphasized that finding an optimum alternative policy involves choosing the alternative that maximizes net benefits, where net benefits are total benefits minus total costs. In the optimum mix situation, we in effect seek that goal by looking to the dynamic benefit-cost ratio of each activity or place to which we are considering allocating our scarce resources. By dynamic benefit-cost ratio, we mean the ratio between a change in benefits and a change in costs in moving from any one point with regard to resources allocated (for that activity or place) to any other point. By observing that benefit-cost ratio, slope, or marginal rate of return and allocating accordingly, we can at least in theory maximize the total benefits we can obtain from our total expenditures. In practice, we may run into considerable difficulty obtaining meaningful data for measuring those ratios, especially in view of our inability to hold constant or statistically control for other variables that may influence the benefits or outputs while changes are occurring in our costs or inputs.

Problems That Can Be Viewed as Simultaneously or Alternatively Involving Choices, Levels, or Mixes

In this chapter we have conceptualized the legal process as a choice model, a probabilistic model, an optimum level model, and an optimum mix model. It is useful to think of each of those models separately since they involve different concepts, methods, and to some extent, different causal and prescriptive theories. Nevertheless, there is considerable overlap among the models in that the same problem can often be viewed from more than one perspective and in that each model can often be translated into each other model. We previously mentioned that the optimum-jury-size problem can be viewed as both a probabilistic model and an optimum level model. The pretrial release problem is an example of a problem that can be viewed from three perspectives. It is a probabilistic problem in the sense that the individual judge is trying to decide whether releasing or holding the defendant produces the highest expected value in light of the probability that the defendant will appear for trial and the costs of making a type 1 error (holding a defendant who would have appeared) versus a type 2 error (releasing a defendant who would not appear). It is an optimum level problem in the sense that the system is trying to arrive at an optimum percentage of defendants to hold in order to minimize the sum of the holding costs and the releasing costs. It is an optimum mix problem in the sense that the system can also be said to be trying to arrive at an optimum mix between defendants who are held and defendants who are released.

The last point illustrates how one model can sometimes be translated into another. Any optimum level problem involving the question of what is the optimum level of due process or enforcement severity can be expressed as an optimum mix problem of finding the optimum mix between type 1 and type 2 errors or between severity and leniency although that conceptualization may be more awkward than the optimum level conceptualization. Likewise, any optimum mix problem can be reduced to an optimum level problem. This is more clearly seen when there are just two activities or two places to which to allocate. Instead of saying what is the optimum mix of $10 between place 1 and place 2, we could say, what is the optimum level to allocate our $10 to place 1 given the fact that the more we allocate to place 1, the less we will have to allocate to place 2. If there are three places, then the latter statement becomes "given the fact that the more we allocate to place 1, the less we will have to allocate collectively to places 2 and 3." That conceptualization though may also be more awkward than the optimum mix approach.

To illustrate how the optimum mix and optimum level models can sometimes be virtually interchangeable, one can use the problem of what is the optimum mix between free press and fair trial in the context of allowing newspapers to report on pending criminal trials where their reporting may tend to prejudice the defendant's case. Expressed in other terms, one is dealing with the problem of what is the optimum level of free press in that context, or what is the optimum level of fair trial in that context. The optimum mix perspective tends to appeal to political scientists because of its emphasis on policy tradeoffs in arriving at a solution. On the other hand, the optimum level perspective tends to appeal to econometricians because of its mathematical simplicity, given its emphasis on only one variable.[17]

An interesting combination methodology that combines the optimum mix perspective and the probabilistic perspective is portfolio analysis.[18] It originated in the context of trying to decide the optimum mix of stocks to purchase in order to maximize total dividends, profits from resale, or both in light of the probabilistic nature of various dividends being paid or various increases in the value of the stock occurring. One researcher has proposed the use of portfolio analysis to determine the optimum mix of prisoners in a prison between, say, armed robbers and burglars, given their differing probabilities of recommitting their crimes and the different costs to society or certain segments within society.[19]

One other set of models that crosses our typologies is that set in which the minimizing of time consumption is the primary consideration. This would include queuing models which inform us how much waiting time and processing time could be saved for court cases by adding additional judges, reducing the time needed for processing an average case, or by reducing the number of cases entering into the waiting lines. Time-oriented models would also include dynamic programming, which could inform us what is the optimum order in which to process cases so as to minimize the average waiting time plus processing time per case. A third kind of time-oriented model is PERT analysis, which can tell us what is the optimum path of alternative processing steps to follow in order to minimize time consumed by the average court case. Those three models are prescriptive time-oriented models in the sense that they tell us about means to use to minimize the anti-goal of delay. Related time-oriented models that are descriptive or causal in nature include time series analysis which relates variables to each other over time, and Markov chain analysis which indicates how a change in one variable will affect a series of other variables which are indirectly influenced by the first variable in a kind of domino effect.[20]

Value Decisions and Policy Analysis

One particularly interesting set of issues worth raising when discussing the problems of optimizing in public policy analysis are the issues that relate to the role of values in policy analysis. A number of points might be mentioned concerning those matters. On the most basic level is the issue of being value free in doing research. By definition, policy analysis at least partly involves seeking to achieve or maximize given values or social goals rather than ignoring them. Policy analysts like other researchers should, however, be value free in the sense of not allowing their values to influence how they record or present information. In fact, the concern for objectivity and replicability in policy analysis research should probably manifest itself in taking extra precautions to keep the bias of researchers from influencing their results given the stronger feelings which generally exist about policy problems, as contrasted to research problems that lack policy implications. These precautions can include drawing upon multiple sources and individuals for cross-checking information, making available raw data sets for secondary analysis, and making assumptions more explicit.

Many policy analysis problems involve taking goals as givens and determining what policies will maximize those goals. The goals, however, may be only intermediate values directed toward achieving other more general values. For example, a policy analysis problem might involve determining how to reduce pretrial jail populations (Y). The proposals might relate to methods for increasing pretrial release (X_1) and reducing delay from arrest to disposition (X_2). There might, however, be some policy-makers who think the pretrial jail population should be increased (rather than reduced) as a means for punishing arrested defendants who might otherwise escape punishment through plea bargaining or lack of admissible evidence. A second stage policy analysis could deal with the effect of the pretrial jail experience on reducing crime rates (Z) which can be taken as a higher-level goal. To make policy analysis more manageable between X and Y, one may merely refer to the possibility of doing further research on the relation between Y and Z without actually undertaking it.

Like any research tool (including a calculator or a typewriter), policy analysis can be used for good or evil purposes. A computerized analysis of the effects of alternative legislative redistricting patterns, for example, can be used to facilitate a kind of proportional representation whereby the percentage of districts dominated by Democrats roughly approximates the percentage of Democrats in the state. On the other hand, the same redistricting programs can be used to minimize Black representation in a state legislature. Quantitative policy analysis, however, is less likely to be used for purposes that are unconstitutional or on which there is a negative consensus because policy analysis does tend to make more explicit the values, assumptions, input data, and other parameters used in arriving at the decisions than more traditional decision-making does. In the computer redistricting example, one can check the programs and the input data to see what was the basis for the redistricting outputs.

Sometimes people involved in policy analysis may be asked to maximize what they consider to be socially undesirable goals. This brings out the need for policy analysts to choose carefully whom they work for, to try to improve the caliber of those people if they can, to call illegal matters to the attention of appropriate authorities, and to look elsewhere if they are dissatisfied with the goals of their government agency or employer. Normally in a democratic society, elected officials and their political appointees do try to achieve goals that will make them popular and that will be in conformity with the law. Therefore, a policy analyst's desire to do things in the public interest and be legal is not so likely to conflict with the people he or she works for.

Value decisions are particularly relevant to policy analysis in the sense that optimizing solutions are very much influenced by the values that are plugged into the analysis. In the redistricting example, the optimum plan is likely to depend on whether the goal is merely to provide equality of population across the districts or to also provide such things as proportionality of party representation and competitiveness within districts. Likewise, what constitutes an optimum jury size depends partly on how many guilty people we are willing to acquit in order to save one innocent person from conviction. A tradeoff higher than ten to one may, however, be irrelevant if the maximum reasonable jury size is 12 persons. As another example, the optimum mix of funds in the Legal Services Corporation between law reform and routine case handling may depend on who is evaluating the legal services agencies that constitute the data on which the analysis is based. Lawyer evaluators may tend to give higher ratings to agencies involved in more difficult appellate court precedent setting cases, but representatives of the poor may give higher ratings to agencies involved in easier but more immediate family, housing, and consumer negotiations. Policy analysis should be particularly concerned with presenting sensitivity analyses in their projects whereby they show how the optimum would vary when one makes changes in the values being maximized.[21]

Some Conclusions

The main thing that all the discussed models have in common is that they are capable of provoking useful insights that might otherwise be missed by viewing policy problems only from other research perspectives. Optimizing models provide insights for comparing various forms of optimum behavior with empirical behavior so that one can make policy recommendations to bring the empirical closer to the optimum, or so that one can revise the values he attributes to the policy-makers in order to bring the alleged optimum closer to the empirical. They also provide insights for understanding the effects on other variables of changing public policies and decisions, and the effects on public policies and decisions of changing other variables. They help to clarify assumptions, goals, alternative means, payoffs from alternative means, contingent probabilities and other elements essential to understanding more fully the basic simplicities and subtle complexities of the political and legal process.

APPENDIX 5.1: SUMMARY OF THE MAIN FORMULAS IN OPTIMIZING ANALYSIS

This appendix pulls together on a more abstract symbolic level the major optimizing principles which are presented verbally and illustrated with legal policy examples in the article. By seeing the principles on a more abstract level, we can further clarify their interrelations and generalizability. This appendix also briefly refers to some important general matters which did not seem appropriate to discuss in the text given the emphasis on verbal and legal-policy presentation.

I. BASIC SYMBOLS

X = A policy, means, or input. This policy can be dichotomous or continuous. It can be a single policy or a combination of policies.

Y = A goal, end, or output. This goal can be dichotomous or continuous. It can be a single goal or a combination of goals. It can be something to maximize or minimize.

B = A desirable output or a benefit.

C = An undesirable output or a cost.

b_{YX} = Slope of Y to X, meaning the change in Y with a 1 unit change in X.

Z = An occurrence or variable that affects the relation between an X policy and a Y goal.

X^* = The policy that optimizes one's goals, i.e. that maximizes a desirable Y or minimizes an undesirable Y.

151

Y^* s = The value of Y when X is X^*.

$f(X_1)$ = Function of X_1. Thus if $X_2 = 5X_1^3$, then $X_2 = f(X_1)$.

II. THE GENERAL FORMULA FOR OPTIMIZING

X^* = X → MAX (B-C) i.e., the optimum policy is the policy that causes total benefits minus total costs to be a maximum, or that simply maximizes net benefits subject to economic, legal, political, or other constraints.

III. OPTIMUM CHOICE WITHOUT PROBABILITIES

X^* = X → MAX$[\Sigma(VQ)_B - \Sigma (VQ)_C]$

V = Value per unit or normative weight. Also symbolized W_{Y_i} for the weight of output i.

Q = Quantity of units or empirical weight. Also symbolized $b_{Y_i X_j}$ for the slope of the relation between goal i and policy j.

IV. OPTIMUM CHOICE WITH PROBABILITIES

1. X^* = X → MAX(EB-EC), or MAX$[\Sigma(BP) - \Sigma (CP)]$

E = Expected Y in view of the probability of the B's and C's occurring

P = Probability of B, C, or Z occurring.

2. P^* = The threshold probability such that $X^* = +X$ if P is greater than P^*, and $X^* = -X$ if P is less than P^*. P^* = the solution for P in $(1-P)(a)+(P)(b) = (1-P)(c)+(P)(d)$.

   a. P^* = B/(A+B) or A/(A+B), depending on how the choice problem is worded.

      A = The costs of making an error of rejecting a true hypothesis.

      B = The costs of making an error of accepting a false hypothesis.

b. $P^* = (a-c)/(a-b-c+d)$, when $+Z$ has a probability of P, and $-Z$ has a probability of $1-P$.

a $= Y$ where one chooses $+X$ when Z is $-$.

b $= Y$ where one chooses $+X$ when Z is $+$.

c $= Y$ where one chooses $-X$ when Z is $-$.

d $= Y$ where one chooses $-X$ when Z is $+$.

V. OPTIMUM LEVEL PROBLEMS

A. With Relations That Go in Only One Direction (Monotonic Relations)

1. Where Y is desirable and b_{YX} is positive, $X^* =$ highest X within the constraints on X. Also applies where Y is undesirable and b_{YX} is negative.

2. Where Y is desirable and b_{YX} is negative or zero, $X^* =$ lowest X within the constraints on X. Also applies where Y is undesirable and b_{YX} is positive.

B. With Relations That Involve Valley-Shaped or Hill-Shaped Curves (Parabolic Relations)

1. $X^* = X$ where $b_{YX} = 0$.

2. If $Y = aX^b + AX^B$, then $b_{YX} = ba(X)^{b-1} + BA(X)^{B-1}$, and then if $b_{YX} = 0$, $X^* = (-ab/AB)^{1/(B-b)}$.

VI. OPTIMUM MIX PROBLEMS

A. With Linear Relations

1. Where Y is desirable and b_{YX_j} is greater in a positive direction than the slope of the other X's, then

X_j^* = highest X_j within the constraints. If there is any budget left over after maximizing X_j, give to the next highest X, and so on.

2.   Before allocating to the X with the greatest slope, provide each X with whatever minimum allocations are required. With the exception of these minimum allocations, nothing should be allocated to X's with zero slopes or negative slopes where Y is desirable.

3.   Where Y is undesirable, give to the X with the greatest negative slope, and so on.

4.   The above rules assume one wants to maximize or minimize Y within a budget. If one wants to merely reach a satisfactory level on Y and minimize budget expenditures, then allocate to the best X, and then the next best X, and so on until that satisfactory level is reached.

B.   With Nonlinear Relations

1.   If one wants to maximize or minimize Y within a budget, then spend the total budget while equalizing the slopes of the X's.

a.   For allocating to places, simultaneously solve the following types of equations:

(1) $X_1 + X_2 = G$, where G is the grand total available

(2) $ba(X_1)^{b-1} = BA(X_2)^{B-1}$, since $Y_1 = aX^b$ and $Y_2 = AX^B$

Thus X_1^* = solving for X_1 in: $X_1 + f(X_1) = G$, which requires reiterative guessing, and $X_2^* = G - X_1^*$

By reiterative guessing in this context is meant guessing successive values for X_1 to try to satisfy the equation (i.e., so the left side of the equation will equal G), although recognizing that some guesses will produce a result that is higher or lower than G until convergence is reached.

b.   For allocating to activities, simultaneously solve

the following types of equations:

(1) $X_1 + X_2 = G$

(2) $b(aX_2^B)X_1^{b-1} = B(aX_t^b)X_2^{B-1}$, since

$Y = aX_1^b X_2^B$

Thus

$X_1^* = (Gb)/(b+B)$,

and $X_2^* = (GB)/(b+B)$.

2. If one wants to merely reach a satisfactory level on Y and minimize budget expenditures, then set Y at a minimum while equalizing the slopes of the X's.

   a. For allocating to places, simulataneously solve:

   (1) Minimum $Y = aX_1^b + AX_2^B$

   (2) $ba(X_1)^{b-1} = BA(X_2)^{B-1}$

   Thus $X_1^* =$ solving for X_1 in: $aX_1^b + A(f(X_1))^B$ = Minimum Y and $X_2^* = f($Minimum Y, $X_1^*)$

   b. For allocating to activities, simultaneously solve:

   (1) Minimum $Y = aX_1^b X_2^B$

   (2) $b(aX_2^B)X_1^{b-1} = B(aX_1^b)X_2^{B-1}$

   Thus $X_1^* =$ solving for X_1 in: $aX_1^b(f(X_1))^B =$ Minimum Y and $X_2^* = f($Minimum Y, $X_1^*)$

3. If each X place or X activity is supposed to receive a minimum amount, then change the above formulas so that wherever X_1 appears, substitute $X_1 + M_1$, and wherever X_2 appears, substitute $X_2 + M_2$.

4. If there are N X's, there will be N terms in the first of the above pairs of equations, and N slopes to be equalized in the second pair. Solving each X^* may then require a computer program for solving non-linear simultaneous equations, just as a regression

analysis computer program may be needed to find the numerical values for a, b, A, B, and the other parameters.

5. If one wants to reach a different satisfactory level on each component of a composite Y and minimize budget expenditures, then simultaneously solve the following types of nonlinear equations (where the exponents are other than 1) or linear equations (where the exponents are all 1):

(1) Minimum $Y_1 = aX_1^b + AX_2^B$

(2) Minimum $Y_2 = aX_1^b + AX_2^B$

Thus $X^* =$ solving for X_1 in: $Y_1 = aX_1^b + A(f(X_1))^3$ and $X_2^* = f(\text{Minimum } Y_1, X^*)$

APPENDIX 5.2: A SIMPLIFIED APPROACH TO SOLVING OPTIMUM LEVEL PROBLEMS

O. BASIC SYMBOLS

X = A policy or input variable that has a continuous number of possible positions. In optimum level problems, there is only one policy variable, rather than a set of policies, activities, or places to which scarce resources are allocated as in optimum mix problems. In optimum level problems, the policy variable is continuous, rather than a set of discrete unordered categories as in optimum choice problems.

Y = The goal variable which may be a composite of a number of sub-goals. It is assumed to be a desirable goal or output like health, rather than an undesirable one like crime. The rules stated below generally need to be phrased in the opposite way if Y is a bad rather than a good.

I. WITH MONOTONIC RELATIONS

A. Definitions

There is a monotonic relation between a Y goal variable and an X policy variable if (1) increases in X always result in increases in Y, (2) increases in X always result in decreases in Y, or (3) increases in X always result in no change in Y. The relation may be linear, convex, concave, or partly convex and partly concave.

B. Steps

1. Determine the functional relation between Y and X, or at least determine that the relation is monotonic.

2. Determine the slope of Y relative to X, or at least the direction of that slope.

3. If the slope is positive, then the optimum X value is the maximum value that X can take given the constraints. If the slope is negative or zero, then the optimum X value is the minimum value that X can take given the constraints and given that Y is a desirable output.

II. WITH NONMONOTONIC RELATIONS

A.   Definitions

There is a nonmonotonic relation between a Y goal variable and an X policy variable if (1) increases in X result in ,increases in Y up to a peak and then result in decreases in Y, or (2) increases in X result in decreases in Y down to a trough and then result in increases in Y. There are many equations that will result in such hill-shaped or valley-shaped curves. Fortunately for ease in handling optimum level problems, there are almost never relations between policy variables and goal variables that result in curves that have more than one peak or trough, or both a peak and a trough, unless time is the independent variable.

B.   Steps

1. Determine the functional relation between Y and X. For example, $Y = a + b_1 X + b_2 X^2$. Determining that relation usually involves fitting various curves to empirical data in order to determine which curve accounts for the greatest percentage of the variance and which curve makes the greatest amount of sense in light of the subject matter.

2. Determine the slope of Y relative to X in light of the above functional relation. For example, $\Delta Y / \Delta X = 0 + b_1 + 2B_2 X^{2-1}$. Determining that slope usually involves applying combinations of the rules that (1) if $Y = a$, then $\Delta Y / \Delta X = 0$; (2) if $Y = X$, then $\Delta Y / \Delta X = 1$; (3) if $Y = bX$, then $\Delta Y / \Delta X = b$; and (4) if $Y = X^b$, then $\Delta Y / \Delta X = bX^{b-1}$.

3. Set the slope equal to zero to indicate that we are seeking the value of X when the slope of Y to X flattens out as it does at a peak or a trough. For example, $0 = b_1 + 2b_2X$.

4. Solve for X in the equation created in step 3. For example, $2b_2X = -b_1$, and $X^* = -b_1/2b_2$.

APPENDIX 5.3: A SIMPLIFIED APPROACH TO SOLVING OPTIMUM MIX PROBLEMS

O. BASIC SYMBOLS

X_1 and X_2 = The amount of scarce resources allocated to two activities or two places.

Y = The goal variable which may be a composite of a number of subgoals. It is assumed to be a desirable goal or output like health rather than an undesirable one like crime. The rules stated below generally need to be phrased in the opposite way that they are phrased if Y is a bad rather than a good. Y bears some empirical relation to X_1 and X_2.

TC = The total cost variable which is the sum of X_1 and X_2 by definition.

I. WITH LINEAR RELATIONS

These problems always involve solving for one goal equation with one unknown. The one equation is $Y = a + b_1 X_1 + b_2 X_2$ (where the X's correspond to activities), or $Y' = a_1 + b_1 X_1 + a_2 + b_2 X_2$ (where the X's correspond to places and Y' corresponds to the sum of the goal achievements $Y_1 + Y_2$ from each place). The regression parameters come from doing a linear regression analysis over a set of places at one point in time, or over a set of time points for a single place. In the above equations with one goal variable and two policy variables, one has to insert meaningful values for two of the three variables and then solve for the third.

A.   To Maximize Goal Achievement Subject to a Maximum Total Cost

0. The general rule is to spend all of Max TC in such a way as to get the highest amount of Y or Y'.

1. Insert a minimum X value for each X that has less than the highest b.

2. Insert a maximum X value for the X that has the highest b.

3. Sum the above X values to see if they equal the maximum TC.

4. If the sum of the X values exceeds Max TC, then come down on the X with the highest b until Max TC is reached, or until the minimum X value is reached, whichever comes first.

5. If the sum of the X values from step 3 falls below Max TC, then come up on the X with the next to the highest b until Max TC is reached or until a maximum X value is reached, whichever comes first. Do not, however, give more than the minimum X to an X that has a negative or zero b.

6. After making the sum of the X's equal Max TC in accordance with the above rules, then solve for Y.

7. The same rules can be applied with more than two X's by rank ordering the treatment of the X's in order of their b's.

8. If no set of X's will satisfy all the maximum and minimum X, Y, and TC constraints, then analyze the constraints to see which one or more can be most meaningfully relaxed in order to be able to simultaneously satisfy all the others while seeking as much goal achievement as possible.

B.   To Minimize Total Cost Subject to a Minimum Goal Achievement

0. The general rule is to spend as little TC as possible in such a way to get the minimum required amount of Y or Y'.

1 and 2. These rules are the same as rules 1 and 2 above on maximizing goal achievement.

3. Sum the bX products and the little a figures to see if they equal the minimum required Y.

4. If the sum from step 3 exceeds Min Y, then come down on the X with the highest b until Min Y is reached or until the minimum X value is reached, whichever comes first.

5. If the sum of the X values from step 3 falls below Min Y, then come up on the X with the next to the highest b until Min Y is reached or until a maximum X value is reached, whichever comes first. Do not, however, give more than a minimum X to an X that has a negative or zero b.

6. After making the step 3 sum equal Min Y in accordance with the above rules, then solve for TC by summing the X's.

7 and 8. These rules are the same as rules 7 and 8 above on maximizing goal achievement.

II. WITH NONLINEAR RELATIONS

These problems always involve solving for two equations in two unknowns. The first equation is a slope equalization equation of the form $b_1 a X_2^{b_2}(X_1)^{b_1-1} = b_2 a X_1^{b_1}(X_2)^{b_2-1}$ (where the X's correspond to activities), or of the form $b_1 a_1 (X_1)^{b_1-1} = b_2 a_2 (X_2)^{b_2-1}$ where the X's correspond to places). The regression parameters come from doing a log-linear regression analysis over a set of places at one point in time, or over a set of time points for a single place. The second equation depends on whether we are seeking to maximize goal achievement or minimize total cost. The same linear rules apply to nonlinear relations if all the b's are negative except one. The rules below only apply where one is allocating to two or more X's with positive b's. Any X that has a negative or zero b should always receive only the minimum X, assuming Y is a good rather than a bad.

A. To Maximize Goal Achievement Subject to a Maximum Total Cost

1. The general rule is to simultaneously solve the above

slope equalization equation along with the total cost equation $TC = X_1 + X_2$ where TC is set equal to Max TC.

2. Solving that pair of simultaneous equations involves expressing X_2 in terms of X_1 using the slope equalization equation, and then inserting that value in place of X_2 in the above total cost equation.

3. We then have one equation and one unknown of the form Max $TC = X_1 + f(X_1)$. Solving that equation is best done through the reiterative guessing of values for X_1 between zero and Max TC until the right side of the equation equals the left side. At that point, we have solved for X^*.

4. To determine X^*, subtract X^* from Max TC.

5. After thereby solving the pair of simultaneous equations, then solve for Y or Y' in the goal equation given under rule 1 below on minimizing total cost.

6. The same rules can be applied with more than two X's by equalizing all their slopes in a series of slope equalization equations, and by adding additional X's to the total cost equation in rules 1 above.

7. Same as rule 8 with linear relations.

8. If one is allocating to activities, the above rules further simplify to $X^* - (\text{Max } TC \cdot b_1)/(b_1 + b_2)$, and $X^* = (\text{Max } TC \cdot b_2)/(b_1 + b_2$.

B.   To Minimize Total Cost Subject to a Minimum Goal Achievement

1. The general rule is to simultaneously solve the above slope equalization equation along with the goal equation $Y = aX^{b_1}X^{b_2}$ (where the X's correspond to activities), or $Y' = a_1 X^{b_1} + a_2 X^{b_2}$ (where the X's correspond to places), and where Y or Y' is set to the minimum allowable goal achievement.

2. Solving that pair of simultaneous equations involves expressing X_2 in terms of X_1 using the slope equalization equation, and then inserting that value in place of X_2 in the above goal achievement equation.

3. We then have one equation and one unknown which can be solved by either doing the same thing with both sides to get X_1 to stand alone on the left side, or which can be solved by the reiterative guessing method mentioned in rule 3 above on maximizing goal achievement. At that point, we have solved for X_1^*.

4. To determine X_2^*, solve for X_2 in the above goal equation after inserting Min Y or Min Y′ and X_1^*.

5. After thereby solving the pair of simultaneous equations, then solve for TC in the total cost equation $TC = X_1 + X_2$.

6. The same rules can be applied with more than two X's by equalizing all their slopes in a series of slope equalization equations, and by adding additional X terms to the goal achievement equation in rule 1 above.

7. Same as rule 8 with linear relations.

8. If one is allocating to activities, the above rules further simplify to $X_1^* = (Min\ Y \cdot b_1^{b_2})/(a \cdot b_2^{b_2})$ raised to the power $1/(b_1 + b_2)$, and $X_2^* = (X_1^* b_2)/b_1$.

III. MISCELLANEOUS POINTS

1. If there are minimum constraints on Y_1 and Y_2, then when minimizing total costs subject to a minimum goal achievement, the problem may require satisfying three linear or non-linear minimum Y, Y_1, and Y_2 equations, or two minimum Y_1 and Y_2 equations, as well as a slope equalization equation if non-linear relations are involved.

2. If there are minimum constraints on X_1 and X_2 in the non-linear relations, then the equations should substitute $X_1 + M_1$ and $X_2 + M_2$ for X_1 and X_2 where M_1 is the minimum X_1 and M_2 is the minimum X_2.

3. The linear relations problems can also be solved with the linear programming routine available in the SOUPAC, MPDS, and other software systems. The non-linear relations problems can also be solved with such routines as PCON, ZSYSTM, and other stand-alone routines.

APPENDIX 5.4: A BIBLIOGRAPHY OF POLICY OPTIMIZING METHODOLOGIES AND APPLICATIONS

The purpose of this bibliography is to provide references describing the general methodological techniques and some specific applications of optimizing methodologies. By optimization in this context is meant methods relevant to making an alternative governmental decision that maximizes benefits minus costs of both a monetary and nonmonetary nature. The alternatives may involve discrete choices with or without contingent probabilities, or a continuum of choices relevant to deciding an optimum policy level or policy mix. In this bibliography, policy optimizing books are listed under each approach in terms of whether they emphasize methods or applications although most of the books contain some of both.

I. General Literature

These items discuss or use a wide variety of optimizing methods. The methods are collectively referred to by such phrases as operations research, management science, systems analysis, and policy analysis.

A. BASIC METHODS

1. William Baumol, *Economic Theory and Operations Analysis* (Prentice-Hall, 1965), 606 pp.

2. Ron Clayton et al., *Managing Public Systems: Concepts and Methods* (Duxbury, 1978).

3. Sheen Kassouf, *Normative Decision Making* (Prentice-Hall, 1970), 88 pp.

4. Duncan MacRae, Jr. and James Wilde, *Policy Analysis for the Citizen* (Duxbury, 1978).

5. S. Nagel and M. Neef, *Operations Research Methods: As Applied to Political Science and the Legal Process* (Sage Publications, 1976), 76 pp.

6. Edward Quade et al., *Systems Analysis: An Outline for the State-of-the-Art Survey Publications* (International Institute for Applied Systems Analysis, 1976), 41 pp.

7. Samuel Richmond, *Operations Research for Management Decisions* (Ronald Press, 1968), 615 pp.

8. Henri Theil, John Book, and Teun Kloek, *Operations Research and Quantitative Economics: An Elementary Introduction* (McGraw-Hill, 1965), 258 pp.

9. Robert Thierauf and Richard Grosse, *Decision Making Through Operations Research* (Wiley, 1970).

10. Edith Stokey and Richard Zeckhauser, *A Primer for Policy Analysis* (W.W. Norton, 1978).

B. POLICY APPLICATIONS

1. Alfred Blumstein, Murray Kamrass, and Armand Weiss (eds.), *Systems Analysis for Social Problems* (Washington Operations Research Council, 1970), 331 pp.

2. James Buchanan and Gordon Tullock (eds.), *Theory of Public Choice* (U. of Michigan, 1972).

3. Richard de Neufville and David Marks (eds.), *Systems Planning and Design: Case Studies in Modeling, Optimization, and Evaluation* (Prentice-Hall, 1974).

4. Alvin Drake, Ralph Keeney, and Philip Morse, *Analysis of Public Systems* (MIT Press, 1972).

5. Gary Fromm, William Hamilton, and Diane Hamilton, *Federally Supported Mathematical Models: Survey and Analysis* (Data Resources and Abt Associates, 1974), 79 pp.

6. Saul Gass and Roger Sisson, *A Guide to Models in Governmental Planning and Operations* (Environmental Protection Agency, 1974), 415 pp.

7.   Martin Greenberger, Matthew Crenson, and Brian Crissey, *Models in the Policy Process* (Sage, 1976), 355 pp.

8.   Walter Helly, *Urban Systems Models* (Academic Press, 1975), 185 pp.

9.   Julius Margolis (ed.), *Analysis of Public Output* (National Bureau of Economic Research, 1970).

10.   Nagel and Neef, *Legal Policy Analysis: Finding an Optimum Level or Mix* (Lexington-Heath, 1977), 327 pp.

11.   Richard Zeckhauser et al. (eds.), *Benefit Cost and Policy Analysis: An Aldine Annual on Forecasting, Decision-Making, and Evaluation* (Aldine, 1974). (Also see the 1973 volume edited by Robert Haveman, the 1972 volume edited by William Niskanen, and the 1971 volume edited by Arnold Harberger.)

II. Optimum Choice Without Probabilities

These items discuss or use methods that emphasize determining whether a given policy provides greater benefits than costs and how much greater, rather than what policy would maximize a given set of goals. Evaluation research and the measurement of benefits and costs are the predominant methods here.

A. METHODS

1.   Carl Bennett and Arthur Lumsdaine (eds.), *Evaluation and Experiment: Some Critical Issues in Assessing Social Programs* (Academic Press, 1975), 553 pp.

2.   Guy Black, *The Applications of Systems Analysis to Government Operations* (Praeger, 1968), 186 pp.

3.   Francis Caro (ed.), *Readings in Evaluation Research* (Russell Sage Foundation, 1971), 418 pp.

4.   Richard Layard (ed.), *Cost-Benefit Analysis* (Penguin, 1972), 496 pp.

5.   Ezra J. Mishan, *Cost-Benefit Analysis* (Praeger, 1976), 454 pp.

6.   Edward S. Quade, *Analysis for Public Decisions* (Elsevier, 1975), 322 pp.

7. Elmer Struening and Marcia Guttentag (eds.), *Handbook of Evaluation Research* (Sage Publications, 1975), 696 pp. and 736 pp.

8. Edward Suchman, *Evaluative Research: Principles and Practice in Public Service and Social Action Programs* (Russell Sage Foundation, 1967), 186 pp.

9. Carol Weiss, *Evaluation Research: Methods for Assessing Program Effectiveness* (Prentice-Hall, 1972), 160 pp.

B. APPLICATIONS

1. Clark Abt (ed.), *The Evaluation of Social Problems* (Sage Publications, 1976), 503 pp.

2. Marcia Guttentag and Shalom Saar (eds.), *Evaluation Studies Review Annual, Volume 2* (Sage Publications, 1977), 736 pp. (Also see Volume 1 edited by Gene Glass.)

3. Harley Hinrichs and Graeme Taylor, *Systematic Analysis: A Primer on Benefit-Cost Analysis and Program Evaluation* (Goodyear, 1972), 152 pp.

4. Roland McKean, *Efficiency in Government Through Systems Analysis: With Emphasis on Water Resources Development* (Wiley, 1958), 336 pp.

5. Peter Rossi and Walter Williams (eds.), *Evaluating Social Programs: Theory, Practice, and Politics* (Seminar Press, 1972), 326 pp.

6. Joseph Wholey, et al., *Federal Evaluation Policy: Analyzing the Effects of Public Programs* (Urban Institute, 1976), 134 pp.

III. Optimum Choice With Probabilities

These items discuss or use methods that emphasize the role of risk, uncertainty, or contingent probabilities in determining which policy provides the greatest benefits minus costs. Decision theory is the predominant method here.

A. METHODS

1. Robert Behn and James Vaupel, *Analytical Thinking for*

Busy Decision Makers (Basic Books, 1978).

2. Rex Brown, Andrew Kahr, and Cameron Peterson, *Decision Analysis for the Manager* (Holt, Rinehart and Winston, 1974).

3. R. Howard, C. Spetzler, J. Matheson, D. North, et al., *Readings in Decision Analysis* (Stanford Research Institute, 1977), 613 pp.

4. R.C. Jeffrey, *The Logic of Decision* (McGraw-Hill, 1965), 201 pp.

5. Wayne Lee, *Decision Theory and Human Behavior* (Wiley, 1971).

6. Ruth Mack, *Planning on Uncertainty: Decision Making in Business and Government Administration* (Wiley-Interscience, 1971), 233 pp.

7. Howard Raiffa, *Decision Analysis: Introductory Lectures on Choices Under Uncertainty* (Addison-Wesley, 1968), 309 pp.

8. Paul Slovic, Baruch Fischolff, and Sara Lichtenstein, "Behavioral Decision Theory," 28 *Annual Review of Psychology* 1-39 (1977).

B. APPLICATIONS

1. Elizabeth Clark and Andrew van Horn, *Risk-Benefit Analysis and Public Policy: A Bibliography* (Harvard Energy and Environmental Policy Center, 1976), 79 pp.

2. Allan Easton, *Complex Managerial Decisions Involving Multiple Objectives* (Wiley, 1973), 421 pp.

3. Albert Halter and Gerald Dean, *Decisions under Uncertainty with Research Applications* (South-Western, 1971), 266 pp.

4. Ralph Keeney and Howard Raiffa, "Illustrative Applications," pp. 354-435 in *Decisions with Multiple Objectives: Preferences and Value Tradeoffs* (Wiley, 1976), 569 pp.

5. S. Nagel and M. Neef, *Decision Theory and the Legal Process* (Lexington-Heath, 1978).

IV. Optimum Level Analysis

These items discuss or use methods that emphasize finding the point on a continuum policy which minimizes a valley shaped total cost survey, maximizes a hill shaped total benefit curve, or maximizes net benefits minus costs where doing too much or too little is socially undesirable. Calculus maximization is the predominant method here.

A. METHODS

1. Michael Brennan, *Preface to Econometrics: An Introduction to Quantitative Methods in Economics* (South-Western, 1973), 488 pp.

2. Gene Fisher, *Cost Considerations in Systems Analysis* (American Elsevier, 1971).

3. S. Henry, *Elementary Mathematical Economics* (Sage Publications, 1969), 112 pp.

4. James Shockley, *The Brief Calculus: With Applications in the Social Sciences* (Holt, Rinehart and Winston, 1971), 439 pp.

5. M.K. Starr and D.W. Miller, *Inventory Control: Theory and Practice* (Prentice-Hall, 1962).

B. APPLICATIONS

1. James Buchanan and Gordon Tullock, *The Calculus of Consent: Logical Foundations of Constitutional Democracy* (U. of Michigan Press, 1962).

2. James Hite, et al., *The Economics of Environmental Quality* (American Enterprise Institute for Public Policy Research, 1972), 113 pp.

3. S. Nagel, M. Neef, and Paul Wice, *Too Much or Too Little Policy: The Example of Pretrial Release* (Sage Administrative and Policy Studies Series, 1977), 68 pp.

4. Llad Phillips and Harold Votey, "An Economic Basis for the Definition and Control of Crime," pp. 89-109 in Stuart Nagel (ed.), *Modeling the Criminal Justice System* (Sage Publications, 1977).

5. George Stigler, *The Theory of Price* (Macmillan, 1966).

V. *Optimum Mix Analysis*

These items discuss or use methods that emphasize allocating scarce resources to maximize satisfaction within a budget constraint or to minimize expenditures while providing a minimum satisfaction level. Mathematical programming (linear, non-linear, etc.) is the predominant method here, or program budgeting on a less sophisticated level.

A. METHODS

1. Philip Kotler, *Marketing Decision Making: A Model Building Approach* (Holt, 1971), 715 pp.

2. Sang Lee, *Goal Programming for Decision Analysis* (Auerbach, 1972), 383 pp.

3. Robert Llewellyn, *Linear Programming* (Holt, 1963), 365 pp.

4. Lyden and Miller (eds.), *Planning-Programming-Budgeting: A Systems Approach to Management* (Rand McNally, 1972).

5. Claude McMillen, Jr., *Mathematical Programming: An Introduction to the Design and Applications of Optimal Decision Machines* (Wiley, 1970), 439 pp.

B. APPLICATIONS

1. Edward Beltrami, *Models for Public Systems Analysis* (Academic, 1977), 218 pp.

2. Thomas Goldman (ed.), *Cost-Effectiveness Analysis: New Approaches in Decision-Making* (Praeger, 1967).

3. Robert Haveman and Julius Margolis (eds.), *Public Expenditures and Policy Analysis* (Markham, 1970), 596 pp.

4. C. Laidlaw, *Linear Programming for Urban Development Plan Evaluation* (Praeger, 1972).

5. S. Nagel, *Minimizing Costs and Maximizing Benefits in Providing Legal Services to the Poor* (Sage Administrative and Policy Studies Series, 1973), 45 pp.

6. Donald Shoup and Stephen MeHay, *Program Budgeting for Urban Police Services* (Praeger, 1971).

VI. Time Oriented Optimizing Models

These items discuss or use methods that emphasize saving time as the key benefit-cost consideration, or that emphasize the need to think in terms of chain reactions or future values in making present choices. Queueing, dynamic programming, PERT, Markov chains, and difference-differential equations are the predominant methods here.

A. METHODS

1. Russell Archibald and Richard Villoria, *Network-Based Management Systems: PERT/CPM* (Wiley, 1967), 508 pp.

2. Kenneth Baker, *Introduction to Sequencing and Scheduling* (Wiley, 1974), 305 pp.

3. Fernando Cortes, Adam Przeworski, and John Sprague, *Systems Analysis for Social Scientists* (Wiley, 1974), 336 pp.

4. Donald Gross and Carl Harris, *Fundamentals of Queueing Theory* (Wiley, 1974), 556 pp.

5. Steven Wheelwright and Spyros Makridakis, *Forecasting Methods for Management* (Wiley, 1973), 241 pp.

B. APPLICATIONS

1. Haig Bohigian, *The Foundations and Mathematical Models of Operations Research with Extensions to the Criminal Justice System* (Gazette, 1971).

2. Jack Byrd, Jr., *Operations Research Models for Public Administration* (Lexington-Heath, 1975), 276 pp.

3. J. Chaiken et al., *Criminal Justice Methods: An Overview* (Rand, 1975), 186 pp.

4. S. Nagel and M. Neef, "Time-Oriented Models and the Legal Process: Reducing Delay and Forecasting the Future" (Paper presented at the annual meeting of the American Society for Public Administration, 1978), 70 pp.

5. John Reed, *The Applications of Operations Research to Court Delay* (Praeger, 1973), 206 pp.

NOTES

1. Roland McKean, *Efficiency in Government through Systems Analysis* (Wiley, 1958), 25-102. For general works on optimizing methods in public policy analysis, although presenting different perspectives from this article, see Edward Quade, *Analysis for Public Decisions* (Elsevier, 1975); Guy Black, *The Application of Systems Analysis to Government Operations* (Praeger, 1969); Alvin Drake, Ralph Keeney, and Philip Morris (eds.), *Analysis of Public Systems* (MIT Press, 1972); and Nagel and Neef, *Operations Research Methods: As Applied to Political Science and the Legal Process* (Sage, 1976).

2. Nagel, "Choosing Among Alternative Public Policies" in Kenneth Dolbeare (ed.), *Public Policy Evaluation* (Sage, 1975), 153-174.

3. Nagel and Neef, "Bail, Not Jail, for More Defendants," 60 *Judicature* 172-178 (1976).

4. Nagel, "How to Provide Legal Counsel for the Poor: Decision Theory," in Dorothy James (ed.), *Analyzing Poverty Policy* (Lexington-Heath, 1975), 215-222.

5. "Computers and the Law and Politics of Redistricting," in Nagel, *Improving the Legal Process: Effects of Alternatives* (Lexington-Heath, 1975), 173-190.

6. Nagel and Neef, "Deductive Modeling to Determine an Optimum Jury Size and Fraction Required to Convict," 1975 *Washington University Law Quarterly,* 933-978 (1976).

7. Nagel and Neef, "The Policy Problem of Doing Too Much or Too Little: Pretrial Release as a Case in Point" (Sage Professional Papers in Administrative and Policy Studies, March, 1977).

8. Nagel, "Minimizing Costs and Maximizing Benefits in Providing Legal Services to the Poor" (Sage Professional Papers in Administrative and Policy Studies. 1973).

9. Nagel and Neef, "Allocating Resources Geographically for Optimum Results." *Political Methodology* (December, 1976).

10. An alternative conceptualization would involve saying that in some situations, we have semantically reduced all effects to positive or negative costs. In those situations, the total benefits are zero, and the net benefits equal the total costs. Likewise, in some situations, we semantically reduce all effects to positive or negative benefits, and the net benefits then equal the total benefits.

11. Nagel, Neef, and Schramm, "Decision Theory and the Pretrial Release Decision in Criminal Cases" 31 *University of Miami Law Review* 1433-1491 (1977).

12. Nagel and Neef, "Plea Bargaining, Decision Theory, and Equilibrium Models," 51 and 52 *Indiana Law Journal* 987-1024, 1-61 (Summer and autumn, 1976); and "The Impact of Plea Bargaining on the Judicial Process," 62 *American Bar Association Journal* 1020-1022 (1976).

13. See note 7. That study involves benefit-cost data obtained from police chiefs, prosecutors, judges, defense attorneys, and bail officials in 23 cities.

14. See note 6.

15. Nagel and Neef, "The Application of Mixed Strategies: Civil Rights and Other Multiple-Activity Policies" (Sage Professional Papers in American Politics, 1976). That study involves civil rights input-output data obtained from NAACP chapter presidents in 31 cities.

16. See note 9.

17. Nagel, Reinbolt, and Eimermann, "A Linear Programming Approach to Problems of Conflicting Legal Values like Free Versus Fair Trial," 4 *Rutgers Journal of Computers and the Law* 420-461 (1975). That study involves attitudinal questionnaire data obtained from about 250 police chiefs, prosecutors, defense attorneys, and newspaper editors.

18. William Baumol, *Portfolio Theory: The Selection of Asset Combinations* (McCaleb-Seiler, 1970).

19. Peter Aranson, et al., "Post Conviction Decisions in Criminal Justice" (Research proposal to the Law Enforcement Assistance Administration, 1975).

20. Jack Byrd, Jr., *Operations Research Models for Public Administration* (Lexington-Heath, 1975), 115-220; and Haig Bohigian, *The Foundations and Mathematical Models of Operations Research with Extensions to the Criminal Justice System* (Gazette, 1971), 171-247.

21. For other discussions of value decisions in policy analysis, see Phillip Gregg, ed., *Problems of Theory in Policy Analysis* (Lexington-Heath, 1976); Duncan MacRae, Jr., *The Social Function of Social Science* (Yale University Press, 1976); Gideon Sjoberg, "Politics, Ethics and Evaluation Research," in Guttentag (ed.), *Handbook of Evaluation Research* 29-51 (Sage, 1975); Laurence Tribe, "Policy Sciences: Analysis or Ideology?" 2 *Philosophy and Public Affairs* 66-110 (1973); Peter Brown, "Ethics and Policy Research," 2 *Policy Analysis* 325-340 (1976); and S. Nagel (ed.), *Policy Studies and the Social Sciences* (Lexington-Heath, 1975) (Part VI deals with social philosophy and includes relevant chapters by John Ladd, Eugene Meehan, and Martin Golding).

Chapter 6

DEDUCTIVE MODELING IN

POLICY ANALYSIS

In recent years, interest has greatly increased in the use of deduction to determine causal relations or means-ends prescriptions. This is in sharp contrast to the low repute in which deductive analysis had previously been held as contrasted to empirical behavioral analysis. That previous low repute was partly attributable to the fact that logical deduction usually only dealt with problems that had no causal or prescriptive value, such as deductions concluding that Aristotle is mortal from the premises that he was a man and all men are mortal. In the past, deduction often involved no attempt to validate premises empirically as for example in medieval scholasticism where the premises were taken as given because their source was the Bible or some other religious auth-

This chapter is based on the introduction to *The Legal Process:Modeling the System* (Sage Publications, 1977). The context of that introduction emphasizes the legal process subject matter, whereas the context of this chapter emphasizes the methodology of deductive modeling. Te present chapter also involves some important improvements, as indicated in such places as footnote 2, the accompanying text, and the appendices.

ority. Previous deductive analysis also often oversimplified matters by ignoring measurement problems, many variables, nonlinear relations, constraints, and probabilities.

The current improved image of deductive modeling partly stems from the fact that deduction is now being applied in useful ways to both causal and policy problems. It now has a much richer supply of premises to work with, which have been or are being empirically validated by behavioral research. The current concepts and methods of deductive modeling can also consider a variety of complexities which makes such modeling more realistic.[1]

The purpose of this chapter is to clarify the nature, purposes, forms, and criteria of deductive modeling, especially as such modeling relates to empirical analysis. The emphasis will be on deduction as applied to determining causation and means-ends prescriptions, with particular emphasis on the many uses of causal and prescriptive modeling. The main examples will come from the criminal justice research of the authors, although examples could be offered from any field of social behavior or any type of social problem.[2]

Modeling in General

A deductive model is a system of premises and conclusions where the premises are derived from empirical observation, prior deductions, or are accepted without proof, and where the conclusions are derived solely from the premises. Deductive models can be reduced to the simple syllogistic form: (1) X bears a relation to Z, (2) Z bears a relation to Y, and (3) therefore, X bears a relation to Y, which follows from the first two relations. In place of saying "bears a relation to," one might use such relational terms as equals, includes, excludes, is less than, is greater than, varies directly with, varies inversely with, causes, is better than, is worse than, or some other relational term or combination of them.

A simple example from the criminal justice field might involve starting with the legal or empirical premise that all members of a jury must generally be convinced of the guilt of a defendant in order for the jury to convict. One might then note as a second premise that it is more difficult to convince twelve persons of the guilt of a defendant than to convince six persons. One could therefore conclude that twelve-person juries are less likely to convict than six-person juries. In this example the input X variable is jury size, which can be six or twelve; the output Y variable is the jury decision which can be conviction or nonconviction; and the intervening Z variable is whether or not the jurors are convinced of the guilt of the defendant. Symbolically, we are saying that Z bears a relation to Y, X bears a relation to Z, and therefore X bears a relation to Y. All these relations are causal or definitional.[3]

Deductive models can be classified in various ways. Perhaps the most important is in terms of their uses or purposes. Causal models have conclusions of the form: X causes Y. Prescriptive models have conclusions of the form: X should be adopted. In this context, miscellaneous models are those that have neither causal nor prescriptive conclusions, such as, Aristotle is mortal. Such models are not so likely to be useful in understanding why things happen the way they do, or what should be done to achieve given goals, although they may serve as the premises for causal or prescriptive models. More will be said presently about the form and uses of causal and prescriptive modeling.

Deductive models can also be meaningfully classified in terms of being simple or complex on various dimensions. One dimension relates to the number of categories provided for by the X, Y, and Z variables in the syllogistic reasoning. In the simple example given, all the variables were stated in terms of simple dichotomies, rather than multiple categories or degrees. Another dimension relates to whether there is a single input X variable, a single output Y variable, and a single intervening Z variable, as in the simple example, or instead many Xs, Ys, and Zs. A third dimension is whether the inputs bear a constant or linear relation with the outputs, or instead a nonlinear relation that changes with the values of the variables. Models can also be made more complex (and possibly more realistic and useful) by explicitly recognizing constraints on the X, Y, and Z variables so that they cannot empirically or normatively vary infinitely upward or downward. Another dimension relates to whether it is recognized that X may bear a relation to Y only a percentage of the time or as a probability depending on the occurrence of another variable. More will be said about these variations in the specific examples that are given to illustrate the policy uses of causal and prescriptive modeling.

There are at least seven important criteria of a good deductive model. These are given in random order. First, the premises about reality should be empirically validated or at least consistent with related empirical knowledge. Second, premises about normative goals should be reasonably related to the goals that relevant policy-makers are likely to have or the goals and probably their source should at least be explicitly stated. Third, the conclusions that are derived should follow from the premises by logical deduction without requiring outside information.

Fourth, the deductive model should serve a causal, prescriptive, or some other useful purpose. Fifth, the model should indicate how its conclusions would change as a result of changes in its empirical and normative premises. Sixth, the model should have broadness in time, geography, and abstractness, but still be applicable to concrete situations. Seventh, the model should be simple and understandable, but still capture the essence of an important and complex phenomenon.

The most important aspect of the relation between deductive modeling and empirical analysis is the fact that conclusions or premises about reality can often be empirically tested, or at least benefit from relevant empirical data. On the other hand, purely normative *conclusions* (like input X is desirable) cannot be empirically tested, although they can be deductively validated in terms of how they relate to their premises. Normative *premises* (like goal Y is desirable) can sometimes be empirically validated if Y is an instrumental value for achieving some higher value, but not if Y is an ultimate value. The empirical validation can take the form of determining whether Y does objectively relate to a higher value like increased health, or whether relevant respondents consider it to subjectively relate to a higher value like happiness.

Sometimes the validity of a hypothesis can be determined better by deductive rather than empirical means because of the difficulty of empirically holding constant intervening Z variables. An example is determining the exact effects on conviction rates of reducing the size of juries from twelve to six, not merely the direction of the effects. One cannot make that determination by comparing the conviction rates in states that use twelve-person juries with states that use six-person juries, because any differences we find in the conviction rates may be due to differences in the characteristics of the law, the people, or the cases in the two sets of states rather than to differences in their jury sizes. We likewise cannot compare the conviction rates in a given state before and after switching from twelve-person to six-person juries because defense counsel seem to be reluctant to bring the same relatively weak twelve-person cases before six-person juries for fear of a greater likelihood of conviction, and this change in the cases results in six-person juries convicting less not more than twelve-person juries. Using simulated six- and twelve-person juries to hear the same case may lack realism and would only involve a sample of one case, unless a lot of research money were available for having many six- and twelve-person juries hear many representative cases under realistic conditions.

On the other hand, the impact on conviction rates of changing the size of juries can be meaningfully determined by starting with the empirically validated premise that twelve-person juries unanimously convict in 64 out of 100 cases, and that individual jurors vote to convict 68 percent out of the 1,200 opportunities in those 100 representative cases. If jury decision-making were like flipping 12 independent coins, then individual jurors would have to vote to convict 96 percent of the time in order to get 64 convictions out of 100 cases, since only .96 multiplied by itself 12 times equals .64. On the other hand, if jury decision-making were more like bowling with 12 pins, where all 12 pins tend to fall or not fall together depending on how well placed the evidence ball is, then individual jurors would vote to convict 64 percent of the time in order to get 64 convictions and 36 non-convictions out of 100 cases. This tells us that jury decision-making (.68 actual vote) is more analogous to bowling (.64 deduced vote) than to coin flipping (.96 deduced vote), but somewhere in between. By using some simple arithmetic to determine how to weight and combine the two analogies one can conclude that switching from a twelve-person jury to a six-person jury while preserving the unanimity rule and the nature of the cases will only increase the probability of conviction from .64 to .66. Later we shall give other examples where deductive modeling can provide meaningful causal or prescriptive answers that can substitute for or at least supplement empirical analysis.

Causal Modeling

The general form for a deductive model that is causal in nature involves the syllogism: (1) X precedes Y, (2) X covaries with Y either in the same direction or in opposite directions, (3) no Z can be controlled for that will substantially change the covariation, and (4) therefore we conclude that X causes Y. It is normally relatively easy to determine whether X generally precedes Y, and the degree to which X covaries with Y, but controlling for possible intervening Z variables may often be quite difficult if not impossible. It generally is impossible in the social sciences to physically keep out Z variables (like urbanism when the attitudes of old and young people are compared) the way the natural sciences can create a vacuum to keep out air pressure when the falling speed of heavy and light objects are compared. The closest the social sciences usually come is for example to randomly assign some children to one teaching method and other children to another, but one cannot randomly assign some cities to adopt one law and others another law. Likewise, one cannot generally match cities with a given law against other like cities lacking the law, because it is too difficult to determine what characteristics to match, and because there are often not enough cities or especially states and countries for meaningful matching. The same is true with regard to what Z variable to control for using the statistical techniques associated with partial correlation, partial regression, or quasi-experimental analysis. Often the most meaningful way to control for possible intervening Z variables (like the strength of the defendant's case in the above jury example) is to work with a deductive model in which the conclusion about the causal relation between X and Y follows from a set of premises that are not statistical in nature, and thus do not involve virtually impossible controls on potentially intervening Z variables.[4]

Another example besides the jury size example is the causal question of the effect of imprisonment on crime rates. There are so many variables that determine crime rates besides the severity of imprisonment that it is virtually impossible empirically to demonstrate whether there is a direct, inverse, or no relation between the two variables. A simple deductive decision model, however, might provide a number of insights into the causes of crime rates and the means for reducing them. Such a model starts with the premise that would-be criminals choose to commit a crime if the benefits minus the costs of the crime exceed the benefits minus the costs of compliance with the law, where those benefits and costs are discounted by the probability of being arrested, convicted, and jailed. From that premise one can deduce that crime can be lessened, (1) by increasing the probability of being arrested, convicted, and jailed, possibly through more professional criminal justice personnel or lessened due process; (2) by decreasing the benefits of crime and thus decreasing the opportunity costs of compliance, possibly through hardening the targets of crime or redirecting peer group recognition along more constructive lines; and (3) by increasing the costs of crime and thus increasing the benefits of compliance, possibly through more severe punishment or loss of legitimate opportunities that would otherwise be realistically available to would-be criminals. This kind of deductive analysis can substantially increase our ability to generate hypotheses, deduce conclusions and integrate findings at least as a supplement to empirical analysis.[5]

Causal modeling whereby we can conclude that X causes Y has at least two important uses in making policy decisions. First, if X is increasing or decreasing, one can then try to make adjustments for the effects of changes that would otherwise occur in Y. For example, if X is increased pretrial release, such a release is likely to cause fewer guilty pleas because the prosecutor can no longer offer to reduce the charge and sentence to the time already served awaiting trial. Therefore, if we want to preserve the percentage of guilty pleas at its previous level, the prosecutor had better be prepared to find other ways to sweeten his offers, such as the increased use of probation. If he does not change the offers he makes in plea bargaining, he can still hold constant the quantity of cases going to trial by dismissing more cases. The important thing, however, is that by knowing increased pretrial release will other- wise decrease guilty pleas and increase trials, the prosecutor can plan how he will more effectively offset those undesirable effects by work- ing on other causes of guilty plea and trial rates.[6]

A second use of causal modeling in making policy decisions involves situations where, if it is desired to have Y change in a certain direction or remain constant, then X must be changed appropriately. For exam- ple, if Y is improvement in interracial equality of opportunity, and it has been established that black voter registration X precedes and covaries directly with Y regardless of region, urbanism, or other Z variables, then it makes sense to exert effort to increase X. A more meaningful analysis would take into consideration that there are other civil rights activities besides voter registration that can help produce increased equality of opportunity, such as employment training pro- grams and school desegregation activities. Ideally, such an analysis might try to determine the marginal rate of return for each such activity and either allocate one's scarce resources to the most produc- tive activity subject to minimum constraints on the other activities, or else allocate one's resources to all the activities so as to equalize their marginal rates of return where each activity may involve diminishing marginal returns.[7]

Among laymen and even among social scientists, correlation is some- times interpreted as indicating causation, although as indicated above, correlation or covariation is just one element in establishing causation. In other words, if causation is present, correlation has to be present, at least when other muddying variables are controlled, but if correlation is present, that does not indicate causation is also present. This distinction is important for deductive modeling because one can often deduce important conclusions from causal statements, but not from correlation statements. For example, if we know X causes Z, and Z causes Y, then it logically follows that X causes Y. If, however, we know that X correlates positively with Z, and Z correlates positively with Y, then we do not know from those empirically verified premises that X correlates positively with Y, unless the first two premises involve perfect correla- tions. One can show with dichotomous variables and four-cell tables a high positive correlation between X and Z, and between Z and Y, and yet a perfect negative correlation between X and Y. The causation relation is like the "less than" relation in that if X is less than Z, and Z is less than Y, then X has to be less than Y. The correlation relation is like the "inclusion" relation in that if some X is included in Z, and some Z is included in Y, then we cannot therefore deductively conclude that some X has to be included in Y, as can be shown with interlocking circles.

Even if we know the exact percentage of X that is in Z, and Z that is in Y, we still cannot deduce whether any X is in Y. Thus, if 90 percent of X is also Z, and 90 percent of Z is also Y, there could still be no units of analysis that have X characteristic that also have Y characteristic. For example, suppose we have a society with 1,000 people. Of those 1,000 people, there are 10 armed robbers (+X), and 990 people who are not armed robbers (−X). Of the 1,000 people, there are 500 males (+Z) and 500 females (−Z). Of the 10 armed robbers, 9 are male. Thus, 90 percent of X is included in Z. Of the 500 males there are also 450 heterosexuals (+Y) and 50 homosexuals (−Y). Thus, 90 percent of Z is included in Y. At first glance, one might deduce from those facts that some armed robbers are heterosexuals, especially if one only had the percentages and not the quantities. However, it is quite consistent with the above information for all 10 armed robbers in this society to be homosexuals. In other words, it is possible for 90 percent of X to be included in Z, and 90 percent of Z to be included in Y, and none of X to be included in Y. It is likewise possible to have both a .90 correlation between X and Z, and .90 correlation between Z and Y, and yet no correlation, a strong negative correlation, or even a perfect negative correlation between X and Y. One could also have a low relation between both X and Z, and also Z and Y, and yet have a perfect relation between X and Y. Traditional syllogistic logic does not deal with correlation, regression, or percentage statements, but social scientists who often do deal with such statements should probably be more aware of what one can logically deduce or not deduce when such statements are combined.

A related kind of deductive reasoning involves working with probability statements. One problem there involves the need to be more aware of the often unexpressed assumptions that go with the factual premises in deducing conclusions. For example, one might deduce from the above facts that the probability of a male armed robber being a homosexual is only .10, but doing so assumes armed robbers are typical males, which they might not be. One might also deduce that the probability of somebody being both a male armed robber and a male homosexual is only .02 times .10 (since 2 percent of the males are armed robbers, and 10 percent of the males are homosexuals), but doing so assumes that being an armed robber (or not) and being a homosexual (or not) are independent of each other, which they may not be. Likewise, with a little more information, one might deduce the probability of somebody being homosexual given that one is an armed robber and a male using the formulas associated with Bayesian conditional probability. The conclusion from such an analysis might be that a male armed robber has a .20 probability of being a homosexual, and that it is therefore unlikely that all 10 armed robbers will be homosexuals, rather than just 2 out of 10. The 2 out of 10 figure, however, like any probability figure assumes a large base, such that out of 1,000,000 trials, one would expect about 200,000 affirmative cases. With a base as small as 10, though, one would not be too surprised with an observed figure substantially higher or lower percentagewise than 2, even 10 cannot be deductively ruled out.[8]

Reasoning from analogy is a common form of reasoning in deductive modeling. In one form, it involves saying that X_1 policy or situation has been found to cause Y effect; X_2 policy or situation is like X_1 policy with regard to all that we know to be relevant to the occurrence of Y effect; and therefore we predict X_2 policy will also cause Y effect. That kind of causal modeling from analogy is illustrated by attempting to determine the effects of various judicial process changes that relate to plea bargaining (X_2), with regard to the effects on the likelihood and level of plea bargaining settlements (Y) by analogizing plea bargaining to a no-fixed-price push-cart peddler transaction (X_1). In another form, deductive causal modeling with policy implications involves saying X_1 policy has been found to cause Y effect; X_2 policy has been found to cause Y_2 effect; X_3 policy is in the middle between X_1 and X_2, with regard to its relevant characteristics; and therefore we predict that X_3 policy will cause Y_3 effect, which is in the middle between Y_1 and Y_2. That kind of causal modeling from analogy is illustrated by attempting to determine the effects on conviction rates (Y) of shifting from a twelve-person to a six-person jury (the X_3 policy) by analogizing jury decision-making to flipping twelve coins (X_1) and to bowling with 12 pins (X_2).

Prescriptive Modeling

The general form for a deductive model which is prescriptive in nature involves the syllogism, (1) X causes Y, which is a perception premise; (2) Y is desirable, which is a value premise; and (3) therefore adopt X, which is a decisional conclusion.[9] The most obvious use for prescriptive modeling is to deduce from a set of perception and value premises a conclusion as to what decision should be adopted. This can be illustrated by using our original jury example. The initial or perception premise might be that twelve-person juries are less likely to convict than six-person juries. The second or value premise might be that jury systems should err in the direction of wrongly acquitting rather than in the direction of wrongly convicting. Therefore, our decision would be to adopt a twelve-person jury system, or to conclude that twelve-person juries are better than six-person juries, assuming no other values.

A second use for prescriptive modeling is to try to change the decisional conclusions of decision-makers by influencing their perceptions and values. Suppose, for example, we know that police officers implicitly decide to arrest and book suspects rather than issue a summons to them to appear in court depending on (1) the officer's perception of the probability that the defendant will appear in court for his court date without being rearrested for another crime, and on (2) how they value the relative undesirability of making an error of releasing an unworthy person versus holding a worthy person. Thus, if we want to encourage police to issue more summons to appear rather than make arrests, we should try to influence those perceptions and values.

A third use of prescriptive modeling involves attempting to determine the implicit values of decision-makers by knowing what their decisions and perceptions are. For example, if (1) we know that judges generally decide against instructing juries in quantitative rather than verbal terms as to the meaning of "beyond a reasonable doubt," and (2) we assume that judges perceive that convictions will be more difficult to obtain if juries are told that "beyond a reasonable doubt" means greater than a .90 or .95 probability of guilt, then (3) we can deduce that judges must generally place a positive value on keeping the conviction rate up, assuming no other deduced value position is capable of reconciling the decisions reached with the factual perceptions.

A fourth use is a corollary of the third use. It involves attempting to determine the implicit perceptions of decision-makers by knowing what their decisions and values are. For example, students at the University of Illinois were asked to play the role of jurors and were given a variety of instructions concerning the threshold probability needed to convict a defendant (the value in this context). It was found, however, that regardless of the required threshold probability of guilt, the student jurors still tended to convict at the same rate (the decision). From that information one can deduce that they must be adjusting their perceptions of the actual probability of guilt in order to be able to hold constant their decisions, since their decisions were determined by their perceptions and values. In other words, when the required value threshold goes up from say .51 to .90, and the decisions remain the same for a variety of factual cases for nearly all the students, then it seems they must in effect be deciding first and then adjusting their perception of the defendant's guilt in light of the new required values. The only exception might be with cases in which the perception of guilt was always .91 or above, so that a conviction decision would result regardless of whether the student-jurors were told the conviction threshold was .51 or .90.

A fifth purpose involves (1) determining what decision ought to be reached in light of certain perceptions and values, (2) observing the deviations between what ought to be and what is, and (3) then attempting to decrease those deviations by reconsidering the perceptions and values one has attributed to the decision-makers. For example, in an analysis of pretrial release in twenty-three cities, it was found that the actual percentage of defendants held in jail prior to trial was 27 percent, but the optimum percentage was calculated to be 4 percent. Perhaps the 4 percent optimum was too low because it did not take into consideration the opportunity cost of punishing arrested persons by jailing them prior to trial, which would be partly lost by arraignment judges if they substantially lowered their percentage of defendants held.[10]

A sixth purpose is a corollary of the fifth. It involves attempting to reconcile the deviations between the deduced optimum decision and the observed actual decisions by trying to influence the decision-makers to change their decisions rather than have the researcher change his or her deductions as to what the optimum decision is. For example, perhaps a 4 percent pretrial release really does reflect the benefit-cost values of arraignment judges, but is substantially lower than the 27 percent actual pretrial release because arraignment judges may often think that defendants will fail to appear in court or that they will commit crimes while released, and perhaps the judges may be responsive to statistical data that would lessen such misperceptions. More important, however, may be the fact that arraignment judges are operating under the value principle that when one's perceptions are in doubt, one should hold rather than release, since releasing errors are more embarrassing, even though the law says release rather than hold. If that is so, then the model that emphasizes decisions as a function of perceptions and values might lead one to seek to publicize the extent to which individual judges are or are not complying with the presumption in favor of the defendant by making public for each judge his holding rates and his appearance rates for those defendants he releases, thereby increasing the cost of making holding errors.

Some Conclusions

Political and social scientists are increasingly in a better position (1) to apply deductive modeling in useful ways from both a theoretical and policy perspective, (2) to work with a rich supply of premises which have been or are being empirically validated by behavioral research, and (3) to consider a variety of complexities that make such modeling more realistic. The benefits of such applications are mainly the increased ability to generate hypotheses, integrate findings, and deduce conclusions, especially concerning matters that do not lend themselves so well to empirical testing. What is needed now are more people who are willing to do more of the hard but enjoyable thinking involved in building deductive models relevant to policy analysis, political science, and social relations.

APPENDIX 6.1 : SUMMARY OF SOME BASIC PRINCIPLES OF DEDUCTIVE MODELING AS APPLIED TO POLICY ANALYSIS

This appendix pulls together on a more abstract symbolic level the major deductive modeling principles which are mainly presented verbally and illustrated with concrete policy analysis examples in the chapter. Be seeing the principles on a more abstract level, we can further clarify their interrelations and generalizability.

I. MODELING IN GENERAL

    A.   Definition or General Form

        1.   Premises

            a.   X bears a relation to Z

            b.   Z bears a relation to Y

        2.   Conclusion

        Therefore, X bears some relation to Y, which follows from the above relations.

    B.   Variations on the General Form

        1.   Many categories or degrees on X, Y, and Z rather than just the categories of present or absent.

        2.   Many X's or input variables, Y's or output variables, and Z's or intervening variables, rather than just a single X, Y, or Z.

3.   Nonlinear relations whereby X bears a changing relation with Y rather than a constant relation, and likewise with the relations among the other variables.

4.   Constraints on the variables whereby X, Y, or Z cannot empirically or normatively vary infinitely upward or downward.

5.   Probabilities whereby X bears a relation with Y that only occurs a percentage of the time, and likewise with the other relations.

C.   Criteria of a Good Deductive Model

1.   Premises about reality should be empirically validated or at least be consistent with related empirical knowledge.

2.   Premises about normative goals should be reasonably related to the goals that potential policy makers are likely to have.

3.   The conclusions that are derived should follow from the premises by logical deduction without requiring outside information.

4.   The deductive model should serve a causal or prescriptive purpose or some other useful purpose.

5.   The model should indicate how its conclusions would change as a result of changes in its empirical and normative premises.

6.   Broadness in time, geography, and abstractness, but still applicable to concrete situations.

7.   Simple and understandable, but still capture the essence of an important complex phenomenon.

8.   The model should be revised in light of whatever empirical data is subsequently gathered relevant to either the premises or the conclusions.

II. CAUSAL MODELING

A.   Definition or General Form

1. Premises
    a.   X precedes Y

    b.   X covaries with Y

    c.   No Z can be controlled for that will substantially change the covariation.

2. Conclusion

    Therefore, X causes Y.

B. Main Uses

1. X as a given

    If X is increasing or decreasing, make adjustments for the effects of changes that would otherwise occur in Y.

2. Y as a given

    If it is desired to have Y change in a certain direction or remain constant, then X must be changed appropriately.

III. PRESCRIPTIVE MODELING

A. Definition or General Form

1. Premises

    a.   Y causes Y   (A perception or P)

    b.   Y is desirable   (A value or V)

2. Conclusion

    Therefore, adopt X   (A decision or D)

B. Main Uses

1. Determine D^*

    Given P and V, determine D^* (where D^* is the decision which should be reached in light of the premises).

2. Influence D

Try to change P and V to influence D (where D is the actual decision which is made, or the predicted decision which will be made).

3.   Determine V

Given D and P, determine V.

4.   Determine P

Given D and V, determine P.

5.   Changing D^* to Equal D

Revise the numerical quantities for V and P attributed by the researcher to the decision-makers he is dealing with (related to determining V and P, although V and P can be determined by empirical nondeductive methods such as surveys and participant observation.

6.   Changing D to Equal D^*

Try to get the decision makers to revise their notions of P and V (related to influencing D, although one can try to influence D directly without going through P and V by limiting the decision-makers discretion).

APPENDIX 6.2: A BIBLIOGRAPHY OF BOOKS ON DEDUCTIVE MODELING IN POLICY ANALYSIS

I. DEDUCTIVE MODELING IN GENERAL SOCIAL SCIENCE AND SOCIAL PROBLEMS

1. Hubert Blalock, Jr., *Theory Construction: From Verbal to Mathematical Formulations* (Prentice-Hall, 1969), 180 pp.

2. Fernando Cortes, Adam Przeworski, and John Sprague, *Systems Analysis for Social Scientists* (Wiley, 1974), 336 pp.

3. Gary Fromm et al., *Federally Supported Mathematical Models: Survey and Analysis* (NSF-FANN, 1974), 3 volumes.

4. Saul Gass and Roger Sisson, *A Guide to Models in Governmental Planning and Operations* (Environmental Protection Agency, 1974) 415 pp.

5. Martin Greenberger, *Models in the Policy Process* (Russell Sage, 1977).

6. David Heise, *Causal Analysis* (Wiley, 1975), 301 pp.

7. Charles Lave and James March, *An Introduction to Models in the Social Sciences* (Harper and Row, 1975), 421 pp.

8. Robert Singleton and William Tyndall, *Games and Programs: Mathematics for Modeling* (Freeman, 1974), 304 pp.

9. Ralph Stogdill et al., *The Process of Model Building in the Behavioral Sciences* (Ohio State U. Press, 1970), 179 pp.

II. DEDUCTIVE MODELING IN ECONOMICS, BUSINESS ADMINISTRATION, AND MONETARY PROBLEMS

1. William Baumol, *Economic Theory and Operations Analysis* (Prentice-Hall, 1965), 606 pp.

2. Michael Brennan, *Preface to Econometrics* (South-Western, 1973), 448 pp.

3. James Buchanan and Robert Tollison (eds.), *Theory of Public Choice: Political Applications of Economics* (Michigan, 1972), 335 pp.

4. Sheen Kassouf, *Normative Decision Making* (Prentice-Hall, 1970), 88 pp.

5. Richard McKenzie and Gordon Tullock, *The New World of Economics* (Irwin, 1975) 269 pp.

6. Ezra Mishan, *Cost-Benefit Analysis* (Praeger, 1976) 454 pp.

7. Samuel Richmond, *Operations Research for Management Decisions* (Ronald, 1968), 615 pp.

III. DEDUCTIVE MODELING IN POLITICAL SCIENCE AND POLITICAL PROBLEMS

1. Hayward Alker, *Mathematics and Politics* (Macmillan, 1965), 152 pp.

2. Hayward R. Alker, Karl Deutsch, and Antoine Stoetzel, *Mathematical Approaches to Politics* (Jossey-Bass, 1973), 473 pp.

3. James Buchanan and Gordon Tullock, *The Calculus of Consent: Logical Foundations of Constitutional Democracy* (Michigan, 1962), 361 pp.

4. Jack Byrd, Jr., *Operations Research Models for Public Administration* (Lexington-Heath, 1975), 276 pp.

5. Wayne Francis, *Formal Models of American Politics: An Introduction* (Harper and Row, 1972), 209 pp.

6. Stuart Nagel with Marian Neef, *Operations Research Methods: As Applied to Political Science and the Legal Process* (Sage Publications, 1976), 76 pp.

7. William Riker and Peter Ordershook, *An Introduction to Positive Political Theory* (Prentice-Hall, 1973), 386 pp.

8. Gordon Tullock and Richard Wagner (eds.), *Rational Models in Policy Studies* (Lexington Books, 1977) (Based on the symposium issue of the spring, 1977 *Policy Studies Journal.*)

IV. DEDUCTIVE MODELING AS APPLIED TO THE LEGAL PROCESS

1. Gary Becker and William Landes (eds.), *Essays in the Economics of Crime and Punishment* (Columbia, 1974), 268 pp.

2. Haif Bohigian, *The Foundations and Mathematical Models of Operations Research with Extensions to the Criminal Justice System* (Gazette, 1971), 282 pp.

3. Michael Finkelstein and Abraham Sofaer, *Quantitative Methods in Law* (Little, Brown, 1977).

4. Stuart Nagel (ed.), *Modeling the Criminal Justice System* (Sage Publications, 1977).

5. Stuart Nagel and Marian Neef, *Legal Process Modeling* (Sage Publications, 1977).

6. Richard Posner, *Economic Analysis of Law* (Little, Brown, 1972), 415 pp.

7. Simon Rottenberg (ed.), *The Economics of Crime and Punishment* (American Enterprise Institute for Public Policy Research, 1973), 232 pp.

8. Thomas Schelling and Richard Zeckhauser, *Law and Public Policy: Policy Analysis* (Harvard Kennedy School, 1974 mimeographed materials.)

9. Gordon Tullock, *The Logic of the Law* (Basic Books, 1971), 278 pp.

NOTES

1. On deductive modeling in general, see Charles Lave and James March, *An Introduction to Models in the Social Sciences* (Harper and Row, 1975); Robert Singleton and William Tyndall, *Games and Programs: Mathematics for Modeling*

(Freeman, 1974); and Ralph Stogdill et al., *The Process of Model Building in the Behavioral Sciences* (Ohio State U. Press, 1970).

2. On deductive modeling applied to criminal justice research, see Gordon Tullock, *The Logic of the Law* (Basic Books, 1971); Gary Becker and William Landes (eds.), *Essays in the Economics of Crime and Punishment* (Columbia, 1974); and Nagel (ed.), *Modeling the Criminal Justice System* (Sage, 1977).

3. On modeling aspects of jury decision-making, see Bernard Grofman, "Jury Decision-Making Models," in Nagel, op. cit. note 2; and Nagel and Neef, "Deductive Modeling to Determine an Optimum Jury Size and Fraction Required to Convict," 1975 *Washington University Law Quarterly* 933-978 (1976).

4. On causal modeling, see David Heise, *Causal Analysis* (Wiley, 1975); Hubert Blalock, Jr., *Causal Inferences in Non-experimental Research* (U. of North Carolina Press, 1964); and Nagel and Neef, "Causal Analysis and the Legal Process," in *The Legal Process: Modeling the System* (Sage Publications, 1977), pp. 41-68.

5. On decision theory and deterrence modeling, see *Readings in Correctional Economics* (Correctional Economics Center of the American Bar Association, 1975); James Q. Wilson, *Thinking about Crime* (Basic Books, 1975); and Nagel, Neef, and Schramm, "Decision Theory and the Pre-Trial Release Decision in Criminal Cases," 31 *University of Miami Law Review* 1433-1491 (1977).

6. On plea bargaining models, see Will McLauchlan, "Models of Plea Bargaining," in Nagel, op. cit. note 2 and Nagel and Neef, "Plea Bargaining, Decision Theory, and Equilibrium Models, 51 and 52 *Indiana Law Journal* 987-1024, 1-61 (1976).

7. On the civil rights example and optimum mix models, see Nagel and Neef, *The Application of Mixed Strategies: Civil Rights and Other Multi-Activity Policies* (Sage Publications, 1976); and Nagel and Neef, "Allocating Resources Geographically for Optimum Results," 3 *Political Methodology* 383-404 (1976).

8. The authors thank Steven Seitz of the University of Illinois for his help in developing some of the above ideas. On the application of logic to social science and deductive modeling, see Harry DeFrancesco, *Quantitative Analysis Methods for Substantive Analysts* (Melville, 1975); Herbert Costner and Robert Leik, "Deductions from Axiomatic Theory," 29 *American Sociological Review* 819-835 (1964); Kenneth Bailey, "Evolutionary Axiomatic Theories" in Edgar Borgatta and George Bohrnstedt (eds.) *Sociological Methodology* (Jossey-Bass, 1970); and Alan Anderson and Omar Moore, "The Formal Analysis of Normative Concepts," 22 *American Sociological Review* 9-17 (1957).

9. On prescriptive modeling, see Martin Greenberger, *Models in the Policy Process* (Russell Sage, 1976); Samuel Richmond, *Operations Research for Management Decisions* (Ronald, 1968); William Baumol, *Economic Theory and Operations Analysis* (Prentice-Hall, 1965); and Nagel and Neef, *Operations Research Methods: As Applied to Political Science and the Legal Process* (Sage Publications, 1976).

10. On the pretrial release example and optimum level models, see Nagel, Wice, and Neef, *Too Much or Too Little Policy: The Example of Pretrial Release as a Case in Point* (Sage Publications, 1977).

Chapter 7

APPLYING POLICY ANALYSIS AND SOCIAL SCIENCE RESEARCH TO DELAY REDUCTION

The purpose of this concluding chapter is to take a single policy problem, namely the problem of delay reduction in the legal process, and apply to it in a general way the methods previously discussed that are associated with social science research and policy analysis. These methods include (1) reaching a decision as to whether a hypothesis has been confirmed, (2) predicting from one variable to another, (3) determining causal relations, (4) measuring goals and related variables, (5) arriving at an optimum choice, level, or mix, and (6) deducing conclusions from empirical and/or normative premises.

Delay in processing court cases is a serious problem in both civil and criminal cases. Civil cases often take many years to process from the time the litigation is initially filed until the case goes to trial, if there is a trial. That kind of delay is harmful to the injured plaintiff, who must wait to be compensated for his or her injuries. It is also harmful to the judicial system in view of the likelihood that witnesses will forget, disappear, or die before the case can come to trial. Criminal cases generally do not take as long as civil cases, but the harm caused by delaying them may be even greater. If the defendant is confined to jail while awaiting trial, he may be jailed for a longer period of time than the sentence he could receive if convicted given the nature of the charges, but he may not even be convicted. If the defendant is not confined to jail while awaiting trial, long delay may increase substantially his opportunity to commit further crimes or to fail to appear when his trial is scheduled to occur.[1]

Management science, operations research, and policy analysis are concerned with developing methods whereby one can determine policies for maximizing given goals under varying conditions. A frequent goal of management science is to maximize the speed at which work is done while holding constant the quality of the product.[2] Applications of management science are increasingly being made outside the realm of business administration and industrial management, and in the realm of government, including the legal process.[3] Applications to the legal process have emphasized delay reduction, but the applications have generally only dealt with flow chart models and queueing theory rather than the fuller range of the management science methods that are potentially applicable. Those management science concepts and methods include queueing, sequencing, critical flow paths, optimum level analysis, allocation, choice under uncertainty, and Markov chain analysis. The analysis which follows will emphasize the value of these methods in not only reducing court delay, but also in obtaining a more insightful theoretical understanding of the relations among the relevant causal variables.

Queueing Theory

Queueing theory involves a set of mathematical models or formulas that are basically of two types. One type involves attempting to predict the amount of time that will be consumed (T) by various types of cases at various stages of the legal process. Those predictions are made from knowing the average number of cases that arrive (A) per day (or other unit of time) in the system (or at the stage being considered), and from knowing the average number of cases that are serviced (S) per day or other unit of time. The basic prediction formula is $T = 1/(S-A)$, which indicates that time consumed relates inversely to the servicing rate of cases and directly to the arrival rate. Those relations in that formula can be quite useful in predicting how much time can be reduced by increasing the service rate or by decreasing the arrival rate.

The other type of basic queueing formula involves attempting to predict the number (N) of cases backed up in the system or at a given stage. Those predictions are also made from knowing the arrival rate and the service rate. The basic prediction formula of that type is $N = (A/S)/(1-A/S)$. In other words, the size of the backlog varies directly with how bad the arrival/service ratio is and inversely with the complement of that ratio. A bad arrival/service ratio is one in which the arrival rate approaches or exceeds the service ratio.

Instead of talking about total time in the system or at a stage, we can talk about waiting time to be serviced (T_W) and actual servicing time (T_S). The formula for waiting time is $T_W = T(A/S)$. In other words, waiting time equals the total time discounted or multiplied by the arrival/service ratio. It also follows that $T_S = T - T_W$, since total time is waiting time plus servicing time. Likewise we can talk about the waiting backlog (N_W) which consists of the number of cases waiting to be serviced and the servicing backlog (N_S) which consists of the number of cases currently being serviced. The formula for the waiting backlog is $N_W = N(A/S)$, analogous to the formula for waiting time. It also follows that $N_S = N - N_W$, since total backlog is the waiting backlog plus the servicing backlog.

Other queueing formulas have been developed to enable one to predict the probability of having a certain number of cases arrive or be serviced given the average arrival and service rate. Still other formulas can be used to predict the time consumed and the size of backlogs when (1) the number of processors or judges is varied, (2) unusual arrival or service rates are present, and when (3) the system operates under special rules concerning priority servicing of certain types of cases, judge shopping by lawyers, and maximum quotas on cases of certain types.

Queueing formulas are useful for making reasonably accurate estimates of how the time and backlog would be reduced by changing the arrival rate, service rate, number of judges, and other queueing variables. The formulas are also helpful in emphasizing that the only way to reduce time and backlog is through those variables. For example, we can reduce the initial arrival rate by diverting cases to other processors such as administrative agencies, and we can reduce the arrival rate at subsequent stages by encouraging pretrial settlement. Likewise, we can reduce the service time and thus increase the service rate by having more judge-time, such as through delegation to quasi-judges, and by having fewer stages in the system, such as by eliminating grand juries for formal indictments. If an average two-day trial can be reduced to one day, and there are 500 cases waiting in line, then queueing theory brings out that the 500th case will be heard 250 working days sooner as a result of one day saved per case.

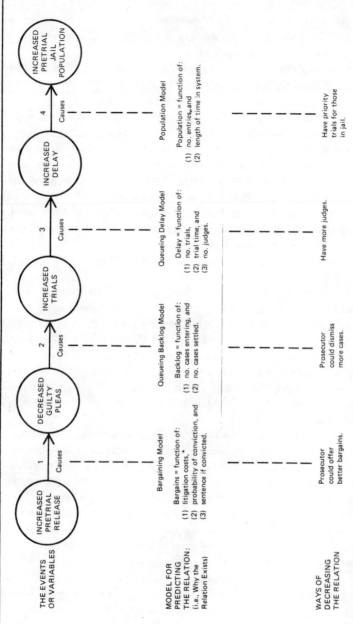

THE EVENTS OR VARIABLES

INCREASED PRETRIAL RELEASE

Causes 1

DECREASED GUILTY PLEAS

Causes 2

INCREASED TRIALS

Causes 3

INCREASED DELAY

Causes 4

INCREASED PRETRIAL JAIL POPULATION

MODEL FOR PREDICTING THE RELATION: (i.e., Why the Relation Exists)

Bargaining Model

Bargains = function of:
(1) litigation costs,*
(2) probability of conviction, and
(3) sentence if convicted.

Queueing Backlog Model

Backlog = function of:
(1) no. cases entering, and
(2) no. cases settled.

Queueing Delay Model

Delay = function of:
(1) no. trials,
(2) trial time, and
(3) no. judges.

Population Model

Population = function of:
(1) no. entries, and
(2) length of time in system.

WAYS OF DECREASING THE RELATION

Prosecutor could offer better bargains.

Prosecutor could dismiss more cases.

Have more judges.

Have priority trials for those in jail.

*including the cost of sitting in jail awaiting trial.

Figure 7.1: THE IMPACT OF PRETRIAL RELEASE ON THE PRETRIAL JAIL POPULATION (To Illustrate Queueing Theory)

To provide an illustration of where queueing analysis can be helpful in gaining insights that might otherwise be missed, one might look to the problem of the effect of increased pretrial release on the pretrial jail population, as is shown in Figure 7.1. One might logically think that increased pretrial release should result in a decreased pretrial jail population. The opposite effect might occur in view of the fact that increased pretrial release decreases the vulnerability of many defendants to the prosecutor's offer to reduce the sentence to time served or probation in return for a plea of guilty. If increased pretrial release thereby decreases guilty pleas, then our queueing backlog model tells us to expect increased trials, assuming all other things remain constant. Likewise our queueing delay model tells us to expect increased delay from the increased trials. If there is increased delay that means defendants sitting in jail awaiting trial probably will be there longer. That in turn means the pretrial jail population may increase even though fewer defendants are being sent to jail to await trial in view of the increased pretrial release.

A useful purpose that the queueing models and the other models involved in this analysis can serve is not only to provide a better understanding of the causal relations, but also to indicate ways of decreasing the occurrence of those relations. Thus increased pretrial release need not result in decreased guilty pleas if the prosecutor offers better bargains, such as probation to defendants out of jail who otherwise would receive jail sentences. Even if there are decreased guilty pleas, they need not result in increased trials if the prosecutor dismisses more cases to offset the decrease in cases settled. Likewise increased trials need not result in increased delay, if the system offsets the increased trials with more judges. Finally increased delay need not result in an increased pretrial jail population if priority trials are provided for those defendants who are in jail even though that might mean even greater delay for defendants out of jail.[4]

Optimum Sequencing

Optimum sequencing emphasizes that delay can be reduced simply by the order in which cases are heard, even if there is no reduction in arrivals, no acceleration in the servicing time per case, and no increase in judge time. For example, suppose we have only one judge and three cases, one of which takes 20 days to hear, one 10, and one 5. If the one judge hears those cases in the order in which they arrive, as is generally done, then the first case will take 20 days to process, the second case will take 30 days to process (10 days servicing time, and 20 days waiting for the first case), and the third case will take 35 days to process (5 days servicing time and 30 days waiting for the first two cases), as is shown in Figure 7.2. The average time per case is thus 85 days divided by 3 cases, or 28 days. If, however, the judge hears those cases by taking the shortest one first, then the first case will take 5 days, the second case 15 days, and the third case 40 days, for an average of only 60 days/3 cases, or 20 days per case. Thus by just reordering the way in which the cases are heard, we save an average of eight days per case, which represents a time reduction of 8/28, or about 30 percent.

One objection that might be raised immediately to a system of taking the shorter cases first is that the longer cases might then either never get processed or their processing plus waiting time would probably exceed some maximum statutory, constitutional, or socially desirable limit. If we specify that no case should be allowed to take as many as a certain number of days, such as 30 days, then there is no way to order those three cases so that none will take as long as 30 days. To satisfy that maximum constraint, we would have to change the problem by (1) specifying a shorter processing time for some or all the cases, or by (2) specifying that our one judge does not have to hear all three cases either because the arrivals have been reduced or, more likely, because a second judge has been added. If we have two judges, with the first judge hearing the 5-day case and the second judge hearing the

Order No. 1					Order No. 2					Order No. 3			
Case	T_W	+ T_S	= T		Case	T_W	+ T_S	= T		Case	T_W	+ T_S	= T
20	0	20	20		10	0	10	10		5	0	5	5
10	20	10	30		20	10	20	30		20	5	20	25
5	30	5	35		5	30	5	35		10	25	10	35
		SUM =	85				SUM =	75				SUM =	65
		AVG =	28				AVG =	25				AVG =	22

Order No. 4					Order No. 5					Order No. 6			
Case	T_W	+ T_S	= T		Case	T_W	+ T_S	= T		Case	T_W	+ T_S	= T
20	0	20	20		10	0	10	10		5	0	5	5
5	20	5	25		5	10	5	15		10	5	10	15
10	25	10	35		20	15	20	35		20	15	20	35
		SUM =	80				SUM =	60				SUM =	55
		AVG =	27				AVG =	20				AVG =	18

t_W = Waiting time, t_s = Servicing time, T = Total time.

Figure 7.2: WAYS OF ORDERING THREE CASES
(To Illustrate Optimum Sequencing)

20-day case and the 10-day case, then those three cases will take 5, 20, and 30 days respectively for waiting and processing time, or an average of 55/3, or 18 days. If, on the other hand, the first judge hears the 20-day case and the second judge hears the 5-day and 10-day case, then those three cases will take 20, 5, and 15 days respectively, or an average of 40/3, or only 13 days.

However, we could also get the average down to 13 days by giving the first judge the 10-day case and having the second judge hear the 5-day and the 20-day case. The question then becomes which of those two allocations and orders is best. If our only criterion is to minimize the average time per case, then they are tied for best. Logically though we could say that when two allocations and orders give the same minimum average time, pick the one in which the longest case also is minimized. This means our first 13-day example above would be best since its longest case takes only 20 days, whereas the longest case in the second 13-day example takes 25 days. The general rules with multiple courts to minimize average time per case and then minimize the longest case are (1) within each court the shorter cases should be taken first, and (2) the shortest case should be given to the court with the greater quantity of cases, where there is an uneven number of cases.

At this point one might logically ask how does one know in advance what cases are 5-day, 10-day, and 20-day cases. The best approach to answering that question is probably to do a statistical prediction analysis for different sets of cases such as criminal cases and personal injury cases with time consumed always being the variable predicted. For criminal cases, the predictor variables might be severity of the crime type, whether the defendant has asked for a jury or bench trial, and whether the defendant has private counsel or a public defender. For personal injury cases, the predictor variables might be the plaintiff's latest settlement demand, the defendant's latest settlement offer, and the type of personal injury involved. With the prediction coefficients from those kinds of analysis, one could then make reasonable predictions of the time that will be consumed by an incoming case knowing how it is positioned on the predictor variables. Many court systems are now using computers for calendaring purposes to avoid multiple court dates for the same lawyers or judges. Those computer programs could be supplemented to indicate the order in which a week's accumulation of new cases should be heard in light of the above sequencing principles.

Another type of optimum sequencing involves sequencing of stages within cases rather than sequencing of cases. It relates to such questions as whether the pleadings for two cases should be heard before the trial occurs on the first case. The general rule in optimum sequencing of stages is to do all the stages for case 1 before starting any of the stages for case 2 in order to minimize the average time per case. As above, one also should order the cases by taking the shorter ones first. The rule of processing the stages of a given case in uninterrupted succession applies regardless of the relative length of the time of the stages within each case or across cases so long as we are operating under the constraint that the pleadings must precede the trial in each case. The rule, however, assumes that the participants will be ready to begin the second stage immediately after the first stage. Otherwise it makes sense to start a new next case so the court will not be idle during the preparation time for the first case.

A related problem concerns whether the liability verdict stage should be decided separately from the damages stage in personal injury cases by two juries or trials. Doing so saves time because (1) personal injury cases in which the defendant is not found liable do not have to go to the damages stage, (2) personal injury cases in which the defendant is found liable can often be settled out of court after the liability stage without the damages stage since liability is usually more subjective and more difficult to settle than damages, and (3) by allowing the first jury to hear only the liability decision, they more frequently decide in favor of the defendant since they cannot offset the plaintiff's contributory negligence by reducing the damages. This, however, is not truly a sequencing problem since under either the combined trial or the split trial, liability precedes damages. This is more an allocation problem with regard to whether one or two decision-makers (i.e., one or two trials) should decide damages and liability. It does, however, nicely illustrate the fact that any management science method for reducing delay should be analyzed carefully to determine what effect it might have on changing the outcomes of cases, which we presumably do not want our delay reduction methods to do.[5]

Critical Path Method and Flow Chart Models

Critical path method (CPM), or Program Evaluation and Review Technique (PERT), emphasizes that if total time is going to be reduced in cases, one should not concentrate on reducing all the stages, but only those stages that are especially influential on the total time. Influential in this context means two things. First, the stage is essential to some subsequent stage which cannot be started until the earlier stage is completed. Second, the stage takes longer than other stages that are also essential to the subsequent stage. For example, preparation by the public defender and preparation by the prosecutor are normally both essential for going to trial, as is indicated in Figure 7.3. If, however, the public defender on the average takes three weeks to prepare for trial and the prosecutor takes only two weeks, then the critical path from pleading to trial is through the lower arrow of preparation by the public defender. This is so because reducing the prosecutor's preparation time would not make trials occur any sooner. Reducing the public defender's preparation time by, for example, providing him with additional resources would, however, enable trials to occur sooner. If the public defender's preparation time is reduced to less than two weeks, then preparation by the prosecutor becomes a critical path.

This kind of analysis could be expanded to include the total criminal justice process from arrest to parole or the civil justice process from complaint to collecting on the judgment. Many of the stages in either kind of legal process, however, do not involve two or more procedures coming together as prerequisites to a subsequent stage. Rather, the legal process tends to be more like the kind of assembly line in which each stage follows the preceding stage in boxcar fashion. Other jointly converging stages, however, include the bringing together of information by the defense and prosecutor on the matter of pretrial release, and the bringing together of information by the defense, prosecutor, and probation department on postconviction sentencing. Normally, the probation department's presentence report follows the conviction of the defendant, but substantial time might be saved by having the probation department prepare presentence reports on all defendants before they are convicted, rather than just for the about 70 percent who are convicted. The extra cost of preparing unnecessary reports for the 30 percent of defendants who are not convicted may be more than

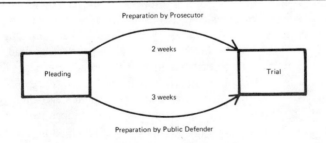

Figure 7.3: PREPARATION BETWEEN PLEADING AND TRIAL
(To Illustrate Critical Path Analysis)

offset by the time wasted waiting for reports whose preparation does not begin until conviction. More specifically, the extra cost of reporting on all defendants would be .30 times the number of defendants times the average cost per report, whereas the extra cost of not reporting on all the defendants equals (1) the extra cost of storing defendants in the county jail when they could be free if their release on probation is recommended, and (2) the extra cost to the county if the defendant could be shipped sooner to the state prison when imprisonment is recommended.

In Figure 7.3 we indicated that preparation by the prosecutor would be two weeks by impliedly averaging the prosecutor's preparation time over a set of cases and then doing likewise for the public defender. Often that kind of data is not available. A commonly used substitute is to ask the prosecutor for a subjective estimate, or better yet, three subjective estimates. One estimate would be the most likely or most common time (comparable to the mode in statistical analysis), the second estimate would be an optimistic time (which occurs about once in 100 cases), and the third estimate would be a pessimistic time (which also occurs about once in 100 cases). From these three estimates an average or mean time is computed by the formula: T_E (for expected time) equals the optimistic time plus four times the most likely time plus the pessimistic time, with the sum divided by six. That formula is based on (1) the idea that people cannot directly estimate averages, but they can more easily estimate optimistic, most likely, and pessimistic figures as above defined, (2) assumptions concerning how averages tend to relate to those figures, and (3) the usefulness of those input figures in PERT-CPM outputs.

By inputting into a PERT or CPM computer program information concerning the ordering of the stages and the optimistic, modal, and pessimistic estimates for each stage, one can obtain a variety of useful outputs. These outputs include (1) estimates of the date by which each stage is likely to be completed, (2) estimates of how much time will have accumulated as of each stage, (3) the stages that constitute the critical path from start to finish, (4) the amount of slack or dead time at the end of each stage that has to wait for an adjacent stage to be completed in order to bring the results from the two together at the next stage, and (5) the probability that a subsequent stage will have to wait for a previous stage that is not on the critical path. These informational outputs can be helpful in better planning of big cases and also routine cases. Such planning should not emphasize equally all stages that are on the critical path, but rather those stages on the critical path from start to finish (1) that consume the most time and (2) that are most subject to time reduction as indicated by the amount of spread between the optimistic, most likely, and pessimistic estimates. The more spread or diversity there is regarding how much time is consumed at a given stage, the more that stage may be subject to time reduction if one can determine what correlates with that variance or spread across cases, over time, or across courts.

Closely related to critical path analysis is the preparation of flow chart models. They consist of a series of rectangles or other geometric shapes which represent the beginnings or endings of stages in the legal process, and a series of arrows connecting the rectangles. On the arrows are generally written the quantity of time needed to go from the beginning to the end of each stage. The arrows also show how the stages flow into each other or how the stages represent either-or possibilities, including the possibility or probability of dropping out rather than going ahead. Flow chart models are useful as a visual aid for seeing the general case processing more clearly, which can be quite suggestive of ideas for how time can be reduced. They can also be computerized to show the output effects of changes in the times, case quantities, stages, or other inputs. More complicated variations of flow chart models include showing in one or more flow charts average time consumption for each passage, measures of spread or distribution, optimistic or desired time consumption as determined by asking experts, the proportion of cases that move from one event to another where there is provision for branching or dropping out, and the dollar cost of each event or time passage to the legal system or the parties. In addition to rectangles and arrows, one can also develop a great variety of geometric forms to show events or nodes that begin the process, end the process, or that are both beginning and ending points within the process, and to show time passages that always occur or that occur with given probabilities, and to provide queueing, critical path, and other information. That mass of information can then be used as input into a computerized simulation program which then provides a variety of outputs showing how all the numbers change if there is a change in such things as the number of cases entering the system or the proportion of cases which take one turn rather than another at a branching point.[6]

Optimum Level and Mix Analysis

Queueing theory tells us cases can be processed faster if we decrease arrivals, increase the servicing rate, and increase the number of processors. This is not meant to imply that we should strive to reduce arrivals to zero, or increase the servicing rate or number of processors to the point where time consumption becomes virtually zero. On the contrary, the speed-up costs may be greater than the delay costs such that we are better off keeping the delay. Optimum level analysis in the context of optimum time consumption is designed to tell us what is the optimum level of delay in the sense of minimizing the sum of the delay costs (Y_1) and the speed-up costs (Y_2).

Figure 7.4 in pictorial form shows what is involved in optimum level analysis for a hypothetical metropolitan court system. It consists of three curves. The delay cost curve shows that as time consumed increases, a set of costs referred to as delay costs also increase and at an increasing rate. To be more exact the relation between delay costs and time consumed is indicated by the equation $Y_1 = \$5(T)^2$. One thing the equation tells us is that if there are zero days consumed, there will be no delay costs. The \$5 tells us that if only one day is consumed, there will be \$5 in delay costs. Of that \$5 figure, \$7 represents wasted cost

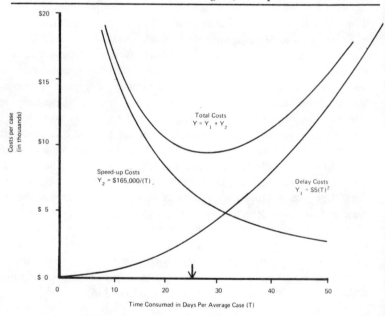

Figure 7.4: DETERMINING OPTIMUM TIME CONSUMPTION IN LIGHT OF SPEED-UP AND DELAY COSTS (To Illustrate Optimum Level and Mix Analysis)

per day per jailed defendant (discounted by the fact that only 50 percent of the defendants are jailed) and $3 represents wasted cost per day per released nonjailed defendant (discounted by the fact that only 50 percent of the defendants are released). That $7 figure can be broken into $2 wasted jail maintenance costs and $5 unnecessarily lost national income. The $2 figure reflects the fact that it costs $6 per day to maintain a defendant in jail, and one third of them have their cases dismissed or acquitted when they come to trial. The $5 figure reflects the fact that defendants could be earning about $15 a day if they were out of jail, and one-third of them will be out of jail when their trials occur. That $3 figure per released defendant is determined by calculating (1) the crime-committing cost or the rearresting cost for the average released defendant, (2) multiplied by the low probability of the occurrence of crime-committing or rearresting, (3) multiplied by the middling probability of being convicted and jailed if the case were to come to disposition, and (4) divided by the number of days released. The hypothetical 2 in the exponent of the equation tells us that as time consumed goes up 1 percent, delay costs go up 2 percent.

The second curve in Figure 4 is the speed-up cost curve, which shows that time consumed can be reduced toward zero by spending money to speed up the legal process. More specifically, the money that is referred to here is money for hiring additional judges at $40,000 per year or $110 per day, figuring 365 days to a year. The exact relation between speed-up costs and time consumed is indicated by the equation $Y_2 = \$165,000/(T)$. The $165,000 represents $110 per day multiplied by a 1500 figure, which was arrived at by statistically analyzing a set of data showing the average time consumed per case and the number of working judges at various years in the court system.

The third curve representing the total costs is simply the sum of the first two curves. Where that total cost curve bottoms out is the point where we are minimizing the sum of the delay costs and the speed-up costs. One can visually see that point in Figure 7.4 is at approximately 25 days. One could also prove that algebraically, given our equations. This means that 25 days or about one month is the optimum level of time consumption in order to minimize the sum of the relevant costs as we have calculated them. We could also say that the optimum level of judges to have is 60 judges, since we previously noted that the relation between number of judges (J) and days consumed (T) is about $J = 1500/T$, or 60 judges equals 1500 divided by 25 days.

We could make this optimum level analysis more realistic by taking into consideration that speed-up costs (Y_2) may only be accurately indicated as a combination of the cost of judges, prosecutors, public defenders, other personnel, courtrooms, and other costs, rather than just judges. A related perspective involves determining a separate cost equation for prosecutors and public defenders analogous to the way we determined the cost equation for judges. Such a cost equation for prosecutors might be $T = 98,400/\$P$, where T is time consumed in days and $\$P$ is dollars allocated to the prosecutor's office. That equation would follow if prosecutors get paid $30,000 a year or $82 a day over 365 days, and previous annual data show a relation between time consumed and the number of prosecutors of the form $T = 1200/P$. Likewise such a cost equation for defenders might be $T = 55,000/\$D$, where $\$D$ is dollars allocated to the public defender's office. That equation would follow if defenders get paid an average of $20,000 a year or $55 a day, and previous annual data show a relation between T and D of the form $T = 1000/D$.

With equations such as these for judges, prosecutors, and defenders, we can calculate the marginal rate of return in terms of time reduction for an extra dollar spent for each of these three types of court personnel. With those three figures we can then determine the optimum mix of our total court budget between those three types of personnel in order to minimize the average time consumed per case. We may, however, have to supplement those figures with some notion as to what minimum amount is required for each type of personnel. Instead of finding the mix that will minimize time consumption, we might also decide what is the maximum time consumption we are willing to tolerate, and then determine what minimum total expenditures (in light of those figures) will enable us to reach that maximum time consumption.[7]

Optimum Choice Analysis

Both optimum level and optimum mix analysis involve working with a variable to be optimized that has a continuum of categories as dollars does. Optimum choice analysis on the other hand involves a variable that has discrete categories like yes, no, or do it, don't do it. That type of analysis might be especially valuable in analyzing how to get judicial personnel like judges, prosecutors, and defense counsel to do the things that are most likely to lead to settlements, a reduction in servicing time, or other activities that will reduce the average time consumed per case.

Optimum choice analysis operates on the assumption that when individuals choose one activity over another, they are impliedly indicating that the expected benefits minus costs of the chosen activity are greater than the expected benefits minus costs of the rejected activity. The expected benefits equal the benefits to be received from an action discounted or multiplied by the probability of the occurrence of whatever events those benefits are contingent upon. Likewise, the expected costs equal the costs to be incurred by an action discounted by the probability of whatever events those costs are contingent upon. The general decision theory involved in optimum choice analysis is shown in Figure 7.5.

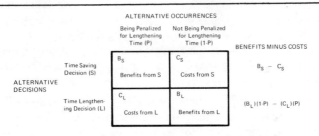

Abbreviations: P = probability of being penalized. B = benefits. C = costs. S = time saving decision. L = time lengthening decision.

To Increase the Likelihood That Time Saving Decisions Will be Chosen:

I. Increase the benefits from making time-saving decisions (i.e., increase B_S).

For example, reward assistant states attorneys with salary increases and promotions for reducing the average time consumption per case.

II. Decrease the costs of making time saving decisions (i.e., decrease C_S).

For example, establish a computerized system that informs assistant states attorneys concerning actual and predicted tims at various stages for all cases to minimize the trouble involved to the attorney in keeping track of cases. Also, provide more investigative and preparation resources.

III. Increase the costs incurred from making time-lengthening decisions (i.e., increase C_L).

For example, provide under the speedy trial rules for absolute discharge of the defendant whose case extends beyond the time limit rather than just release on recognizance.

IV. Decrease the benefits from making time-lengthening decisions (i.e., decrease B_L).

For example, increase release on recognizance so that lengthening the pretrial time will not make the jailed defendant more vulnerable to pleading guilty.

V. Raise the probability of the decision-maker being penalized for lengthening time (i.e., increase P).

For example, allow fewer exceptions to the speedy trial rules such as suspending their application "for good cause" or "exceptional circumstances."

Figure 7.5: INCREASING THE LIKELIHOOD THAT PROSECUTORS WILL REACH TIME-SAVING DECISIONS (To Illustrate Optimum Choice Analysis)

Figure 7.5 specifically applies optimum choice analysis to the problem of how to get prosecutors and assistant states attorneys to make decisions to accelerate the slow and difficult cases so they do not exceed a maximum time threshold. Doing that could involve (1) increasing the benefits and decreasing the costs from making time-saving decisions, (2) decreasing the benefits and increasing the costs from making time-lengthening decisions, and (3) increasing or decreasing the probabilities of relevant contingent events. To encourage favorable time consumption decisions, assistant states attorneys can be given monetary rewards (to increase the benefits) and be given work-saving resources (to decrease the costs). Likewise, to discourage unfavorable time consumption decisions, states attorneys can in effect be punished by providing for an absolute discharge not subject to reprosecution of excessively delayed defendants, and they can be deprived of the plea bargaining benefits of lengthy pretrial incarceration by providing more release on recognizance. These devices may incur substantial monetary and nonmonetary speed-up costs to the system which may outweigh the delay costs, as discussed under optimum level analysis. Optimum choice analysis, however, does stimulate one's thinking with regard to how decision-makers can be influenced to make time-saving decisions if one is at least for the moment primarily concerned with time-saving.

A similar optimum choice analysis could be applied to the decisions made in the public defender's office or the offices of private defense attorneys. The suggestions there for encouraging time-saving decisions may, however, conflict with the decisions applicable to the states' attorney. For example, one might recommend more pretrial release to decrease the delay benefit the prosecutor receives from the increased willingness to plead guilty by defendants held in jail. On the other hand, one might recommend less pretrial release in order to make the defendant and indirectly his attorney suffer more from delaying the case. In such conflicting situations, one has to decide which side is more responsible for the delay, or decide on the basis of criteria other than saving time. There are also benefit-cost suggestions stimulated by this analysis applicable to the defense side that do not conflict with the previous suggestions applicable to the prosecution. For example, providing monetary rewards to assistant public defenders and more resources does not conflict with the prosecutor suggestions unless one assumes there is a fixed quantity of resources available to the criminal justice system, and whatever the prosecutor gets must be taken away from the public defender or other parts of the system.

A similar optimum choice analysis could also be applied to judicial decisions that affect delay. For example, as of now, judges incur virtually no personal costs from granting repeated continuances or making other delaying decisions. If, however, records were publicized showing for each judge in a given court system how long on the average he takes to process cases of various types, that visibility might cause the especially slow judges to change their ways so as to come closer to the averages of the other judges. Such a publicizing system (even just among the judges rather than the general public) would have the effect of increasing the costs of making time-lengthening decisions. That kind of record-keeping can also be done for making comparisons across assistant states attorneys and assistant public defenders in a given court system, or across court systems if one calculates separate averages for cases of different types of severity and different expected time consumptions.[8]

Markov Chain Analysis

The essence of Markov chain analysis involves the prediction of subsequent events by knowing the probability of one event leading to another. As an oversimplified example, if we know that 60 percent of the convicted defendants in a given court system go to prison and 40 percent receive probation, those percentages or probabilities in effect tell us something about what would happen if the number of convictions increased from 200 to 300 per year. More specifically, they tell us that before the increase, the prison caseload was 120 cases per year (.60 times 200) and the probation caseload was 80 cases, and after the increase, the prison caseload will probably be 180 cases per year (.60 times 300) and the probation caseload 120 cases. That simple example could be made substantially more interesting if it were part of a chain of branching events, such that a change in one of the early events has a kind of domino effect moving out across the branches, where the ultimate effects are not so readily predictable in the absence of a Markov chain analysis.

Figure 7.6 provides an example of Markov chain analysis used to predict the effect on the public defender's caseload of a change in the probability of being held in jail pending trial. More specifically, if 100 cases enter the system and previously 10 percent were released on their own recognizance, 30 percent were released on bond, and 60 percent were held in jail pending trial, then how much of an increase or a decrease would there be in the public defender's caseload if those probabilities were to change to .40, .20, and .40 respectively as the result of a bail reform movement? To answer that question we need to

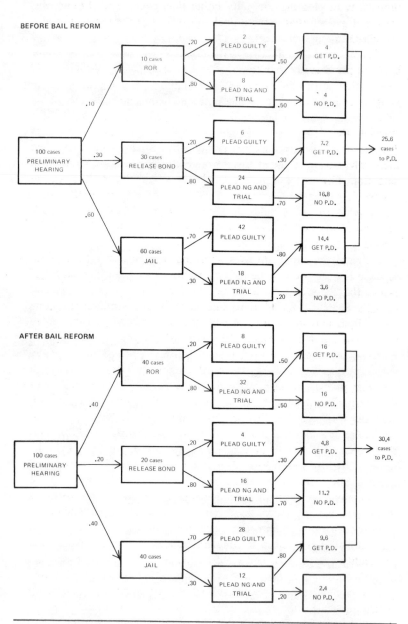

Figure 7.6: PREDICTING THE EFFECTS ON PUBLIC DEFENDER CASELOADS
OF CHANGES IN PRETRIAL RELEASE (To Illustrate Markov Chain
Analysis)

know for each of those categories of pretrial release what is their probability of pleading not guilty rather than guilty, and of those who plead not guilty, what is the probability of having the public defender appointed to represent them.

That data tend to indicate that those in jail pending trial are more likely to plead guilty than those released. The data also indicate that of those defendants who plead not guilty, the ones most likely to be indigent and thus eligible for the public defender are the defendants who have been kept in jail pending trial unable to make bond. Of those released, the defendants who put up bond money are possibly less likely to be indigent enough to have the public defender appointed than those who are released on their own recognizance. The hypothetical data impliedly assumes that about one-half of the ROR cases are middle-class defendants who are considered good risks for ROR but are not eligible for the public defender, and the other half are poor defendants who are also considered good risks for ROR but who are eligible for the public defender.

The analysis simply involves allocating the entering 100 cases in accordance with the first tier of probabilities to the second column of events; then allocating those allocations in accordance with the second tier of probabilities to the third column of events; and then allocating those allocations in accordance with the third tier of probabilities to the fourth column of events. The last step in the analysis involves summing the number of cases probabilistically allocated to the public defender in various rows of the fourth column of events to determine the total public defender caseload. The same thing is done both with the "before" probabilities and the "after" probabilities. Doing so indicates that the predicted "before" caseload for 100 cases is 25½ cases to the public defender and the predicted "after" caseload for 100 cases is 30½ cases. This means an increase of 19 percent in the public defender's caseload since (30.4-25.6)/25.6 is 19 percent. This means that if the public defender's office is going to continue to operate at the same caseload per assistant public defender, 19 percent more assistants should possibly be hired without waiting for the backlog to build up.

In the legal process literature, there have now appeared a number of examples of Markov chain reasoning as applied to trying to predict the probability that a given convicted defendant will reengage in criminal behavior within a certain number of time periods after being released from prison. The paper by David White, for example, finds that a released juvenile who was not referred back to the court during the first three months after being released has a .978 probability of not being referred back in the fourth month, a .019 probability of committing a minor crime in the fourth month, and a .003 probability of committing a major crime. Other probabilities can be calculated for subsequent months (either empirically from direct data or deductively from probability formulas) for other combinations of nonreferrals, minor crimes, and major crimes in the preceding months. That kind of analysis can be useful in predicting behavior, comparing different types of convicts or treatments, and developing recommendations for special supervision of certain types of convicts.[9]

Some Conclusions

The time-oriented models presented are all useful for saving time in the legal process. Queueing theory is especially useful for deducing the implications of arrival rates and servicing rates with regard to the amount of delay and backlog that is likely to occur. It also points up the importance in reducing delay and backlog of (1) decreasing the arrival rate and the number of stages, and of (2) increasing the service rate and the number of processors. Sequential optimizing is useful for arriving at an optimum ordering of cases and case stages as part of a scientific calendaring of judicial and other legal procedures. Critical path analysis and flow chart models emphasize what stages in the legal process are particularly important for concentrating one's time reduction efforts, and the effects of input and parameter changes on those stages. Optimum level analysis as a time-oriented model emphasizes minimizing the sum of the delay costs and the speed-up costs. Optimum mix analysis is useful in allocating scarce resources among different programs or groups of personnel in order to get (1) the most time reduction for a given budget or (2) the least expenditures under a maximum time constraint. Optimum choice analysis can be helpful in developing incentives for getting judges, prosecutors, and defense counsel to do the things that are most likely to lead to delay reduction. Markov chain analysis emphasizes how a given change can produce a domino-like chain reaction through a series of branching or successive probabilities and relations, especially where the change or the reaction relates to time consumed or arrivals in the system.

Partly by coincidence, the six time-oriented models presented also usefully for teaching purposes correspond to the six methodological problems emphasized in the previous six chapters. Thus, queueing theory represents an example of a deductive model (Chapter 6) whereby one deduces formulas for determining time consumed and backlog from the average rate at which cases arrive and are serviced assuming certain types of distributions around those averages. Optimum sequencing is a good example of optimizing analysis (Chapter 5) in that like many optimizing models it can aid in maximizing benefits or minimizing costs by just systematically analyzing the effects that alternative inputs have on desired outputs. Critical path methods emphasize measurement of a goal variable (Chapter 4), namely time consumed at various stages in the processing of cases. Optimum choice analysis is particularly concerned with understanding and manipulating the causal factors (Chapter 3) responsible for why decision makers sometimes make time lengthening decisions and sometimes time saving decisions. Optimum level analysis depends heavily on prediction methods (Chapter 2) for determining the relation between time consumed and total cost. Markov chain analysis involves probabilistic considerations (Chapter 1) and also combines the other methodological processes. Many other policy problems besides delay reduction could also be used to illustrate how a combination of the methods discussed can help generate insights for understanding and lessening policy problems.

NOTES

This chapter was coauthored with Nancy Munshaw of the Department of Urban and Regional Planning at the University of Illinois.

1. On the serious nature of the delay problem in the legal process, see Howard James, *Crisis in the Courts* (David McKay, 1969); Harry Jones (ed.), *The Courts, The Public, and the Law Explosion* (Prentice-Hall, 1965); Walter E. Meyer Research Institute, *Dollars, Delay and the Automobile Victim: Studies in Reparation for Highway Injuries and Related Court Problems* (Bobbs-Merrill, 1968); Glenn Winters (ed.), *Selected Readings: Court Congestion and Delay* (American Judicature Society, 1971); and Hans Zeisel, Harry Kalven, Jr., and Bernard Buchholz, *Delay in the Court* (Little, Brown, 1959).

2. General management science works include Samuel Richmond, *Operations Research for Management Decisions* (Ronald Press, 1968); Robert Thierauf and Richard Grosse, *Decision Making through Operations Research* (Wiley, 1970); Hamdy Taha, *Operations Research: An Introduction* (Macmillan, 1971); Harvey Wagner, *Principles of Operations Research with Applications to Managerial Decisions* (Prentice-Hall, 1969); and David Anderson, Dennis Sweeney, and Thomas Williams, *An Introduction to Management Science: Quantitative Approaches to Decision Making* (West, 1976). These works all include material on methods relevant to delay reduction.

3. Management science and operations research as applied to governmental and legal problems include Saul Gass and Roger Sisson, *A Guide to Models in Governmental Planning and Operations* (Environmental Protection Agency,

1974); Edward Beltrami, *Models for Public Systems Analysis* (Academic Press, 1977); Michael White, Michael Radnor, and David Tansik, *Management and Policy Science in American Government* (Lexington-Heath, 1975); Jack Byrd, Jr., *Operations Research Models for Public Administration* (Lexington-Heath, 1975); and Nagel and Neef, *The Legal Process: Modeling the System* (Sage Publications, 1977).

4. On queueing theory, see Jack Byrd, Jr., note 3, at pp. 198-208; Donald Gross and Carl Harris, *Fundamentals of Queueing Theory* (Wiley, 1974); Alec Lee, *Applied Queueing Theory* (Macmillan, 1966); S. Richmond, note 2, at 405-438; and Thomas Saaty, *Elements of Queueing Theory: With Applications* (McGraw-Hill, 1961). For additional examples of queueing theory applied to the legal process, see Haig Bohigian, *The Foundations and Mathematical Models of Operations Research with Extensions to the Criminal Justice System* (Gazette, 1971), pp. 191-209; Jan Chaiken and P. Dormont, *Patrol Car Allocation Model* (Rand, 1975); Jan Chaiken, Thomas Carbill, Leo Holliday, David Jaquette, Michael Lawless, and Edward Quade, *Criminal Justice Models: An Overview* (Rand, 1975); and John Reed, *The Application of Operations Research to Court Delay* (Praeger, 1973). Also see Hans Zeisel, Harry Kalven, and Bernard Buchholz, *Delay in the Court* (Little, Brown, 1959), since that book is organized in accordance with queueing concepts by being divided into parts on "Reducing the Trial Time" (i.e., increasing servicing rates), "Increasing Settlements" (i.e., decreasing arrival rates), and "More Judge Time" (i.e., increasing the channels or processors).

5. On dynamic and sequential programming, see Jack Byrd, note 3, at 139-156; Richard Conway, William Maxwell, and Louis Miller, *Theory of Scheduling* (Addison-Wesley, 1967); A. Kaufman, *Graphs, Dynamic Programing, and Finite Games* (Academic Press, 1967); Kenneth Baker, *Introduction to Sequencing and Scheduling* (Wiley, 1974); S. Richmond, note 2, at 461-480; George Nemhauser, *Introduction to Dynamic Programming* (Wiley, 1966); and Brian Gluss, *An Elementary Introduction to Dynamic Programming* (Allyn and Bacon, 1972). For additional examples of dynamic and sequential programming applied to the legal process, see Haig Bohigian, note 4, at 171-190; John Jennings, *Evaluation of the Manhattan Criminal Courts Master Calendar Project* (Rand, 1971); Raymond Nimmer, *The System Impact of Criminal Justice Reforms: Judicial Delay as a Case Study* (American Bar Foundation, 1974), pp. 62-96; Programming Methods, Inc., *Justice: Judicial System to Increase Court Effectiveness* (PMI, 1971); H. Zeisel, note 1, at 201-205; and Jack Hausner, Thomas Lane, and Gary Oleson, "Automated Scheduling in the Courts," in Sidney Bounstein and Murray Kamrass (eds.), *Operations Research in Law Enforcement, Justice, and Societal Security* (Lexington-Heath, 1976), p. 217.

6. On critical path method and flow chart modeling, see Russell Archibald and Richard Villoria, *Network-Based Management Systems (PERT/CPM)* (Wiley, 1967); Jack Byrd, note 3 at, pp. 115-138; H. Evarts, *Introduction to PERT* (1964); B.J. Hansen, *Practical PERT* (America House, 1964); Samuel Richmond, note 2, at pp. 481-500; and Gary Whitehouse, *Systems Analysis and Systems Design* (Prentice-Hall, 1973). Additional examples of flow chart modeling applied to the legal process include Jan Chaiken, Thomas Carbill, Leo Holliday, David Jaquette, Michael Lawless, and Edward Quade, note 5; Alfred Blumstein, "A Model to Aid in Planning for the Total Criminal Justice System," in Leonard

Oberlander (ed.), *Quantitative Tools for Criminal Justice Planning* (LEAA, 1975); Joseph Navarro and Jean Taylor, "Data Analyses and Simulation of a Court System for the Processing of Criminal Cases," in The President's Commission on Law Enforcement and Administration of Justice, *Task Force Report: Science and Technology* (Government Printing Office, 1967); R. Gordon Cassidy, "A Systems Approach to Planning and Evaluation in Criminal Justice Systems," 9 *Socio-Economic Planning Sciences* (1975), pp. 301-312; William Biles, "A Simulation Study of Delay Mechanisms in Criminal Courts," (Operations Research Society of America meeting, 1972); and Gary Hogg, Richard DeVor and Michael Handwerker, "Analysis of Criminal Justice Systems via Stochastic Network Simulation," (Workshop on OR in the Criminal Justice System at San Diego, California, 1973).

7. On optimum level analysis, see Michael Brennan, *Preface to Econometrics: An Introduction to Quantitative Methods in Economics* (Southwestern, 1973), pp. 111-192; Jack Byrd, note 3, at 183-198; Samuel Richmond, note 2, at pp. 87-126; and James Shockley, *The Brief Calculus: With Applications in the Social Sciences* (Holt, Rinehart, and Winston, 1971). For additional examples of optimum level analysis applied to reducing delay and other aspects of the legal process, see Nagel and Neef, *Legal Policy Analysis: Finding an Optimum Level or Mix* (Lexington-Heath, 1977); Nagel, Neef, and Wice, *Too Much or Too Little Policy: The Example of Pretrial Release* (Sage Publications, 1977); Hans Zeisel, note 1 at pp. 169-220; Llad Phillips and Harold Votey, "An Economic Basis for the Definition and Control of Crime," in Nagel (ed.), *Modeling the Criminal Justice System* (Sage, 1977), p. 89; Fredric Merrill and Linus Schrage, "Efficient Use of Jurors: A Field Study and Simulation Model of a Court System," 2 *Washington University Law Quarterly* (1969), pp. 151-183; and G. Thomas Munsterman and William Pabst, "Operating an Efficient Jury System," (International Meeting of the Institute of Management Sciences, 1975).

On optimum mix analysis, see Jack Byrd, note 3, at 85-114; Philip Kotler, *Marketing Decision Making: A Model Building Approach* (Holt, Rinehart, and Winston, 1971), Robert Llewellyn, *Linear Programing* (Holt, Rinehart, and Winston, 1963); Claude McMillan, *Mathematical Programming* (Wiley, 1970); and S. Richmond, note 2, at 314-404. For additional examples of optimum mix analysis applied to the legal process, see Werner Hirsch, *The Economics of State and Local Government* (McGraw-Hill, 1970), pp. 217-254; Nagel, *Minimizing Costs and Maximizing Benefits in Providing Legal Services to the Poor* (Sage Publications, 1973); and Donald Shoup and Stephen Mehay, *Program Budgeting for Urban Police Services* (Praeger, 1971).

8. On optimum choice analysis, see Robert Behn and James Vaupel, *Analytical Thinking for Busy Decision Makers* (Basic Books, 1979); Ruth Mack, *Planning on Uncertainty: Decision Making in Business and Government Administration* (Wiley, 1971); Howard Raiffa, *Decision Analysis: Introductory Lectures on Choices under Uncertainty* (Addison-Wesley, 1968); and S. Richmond, note 2, at pp. 301-60. For additional examples of choice theory applied to the legal process, see Nagel and Neef, *Decision Theory and the Legal Process* (Lexington-Heath, 1978); Nagel, Neef, and Schramm, "Decision Theory and the Pretrial Release Decision in Criminal Cases," *University of Miami Law Review* (1977), pp. 1433-1491; and Robert Stover and Don Brown, "Reducing Rule Violations by Police, Judges, and Corrections Officials," in Nagel (ed.), *Modeling the Criminal Justice System* (Sage Publications, 1977), pp. 297-312.

9. On Markov chain analysis, see Dean Isaacson and Richard Madsen, *Markov Chains Theory and Applications* (Wiley, 1975); John Kemeny and J. Laurie Snell, *Finite Markov Chains* (Prentice-Hall, 1960); S. Richmond, note 2, at 439-460; and Sidney Ulmer, "Stochastic Process Models in Political Analysis," in James Herndon and Joseph Bernd (eds.), *Math Applications in Political Science* (Virginia Polytechnic Institute, 1965). For additional examples of Markov chain analysis applied to the legal process, see Ronald Rardin and Paul Gray, "Analysis of Crime Control Strategies," 1 *Journal of Criminal Justice* 339-46 (1973); Ronald Slivka and Frank Cannavale, Jr., "An Analytical Model of the Passage of Defendants through a Court System," *Journal of Research in Crime and Delinquency* 132-140 (1973); S. Deutsch, J. Jarvis, and R. Parker, "A Network Flow Model for Predicting Criminal Displacement and Deterrence," 1977; David Greenberg, "Recidivism as Radioactive Decay," (1975); Thomas Schelling and Richard Zeckhauser, "Law and Public Policy: Policy Analysis," course materials, 1975; David White, Soo Hong Uh, and Kim Andriano, "Juvenile Court Records and Markov Chains: Their Use as Aids in Identification and Treatment of Delinquent Youth," 1 *Law and Human Behavior* 217-237 (1977); and J. Belkin, J. Blumstein, and W. Glass, "Recidivism as Feedback Process: An Analytical Model and Empirical Validation, 1 *Journal of Criminal Justice* 7-26 (1973).

EPILOGUE

This book has discussed a number of basic problems in social science research and policy analysis. It has done so mainly in accordance with the idea that social science and policy analysis should be more than ivory tower matters, but rather they should attempt to develop causal and evaluative relations that are useful for obtaining a better understanding and control over inputs and outputs in social problems. That kind of concern is becoming increasingly important in all fields of scientific knowledge, but especially in the social sciences. It especially manifests itself in an increasing involvement in research that is relevant to important governmental policies and decisions. That increasing involvement has appeared in recent years in the development of new articles, books, journals, book series, convention papers, organizations, courses, curricula, grants, job openings, and other indicators of academic activity.

The increased concern began especially in the late 1960s as part of the general public's concern for civil rights, the war on poverty, peace, women's liberation, environmental protection, and other social problems. The implementation of that concern was facilitated by the development and spread of computer software, statistical and mathematical methods, and interdisciplinary relations. The relative attractiveness of the government as an employer and sponsor also increased, as the role of universities in employment and research funding decreased.

Policy analysis or policy studies can be broadly defined as the study of the nature, causes, and effects of alternative public policies. Sometimes policy analysis is more specifically defined to refer to the methods used in analyzing public policies. The main methods, however, are no different from those associated with social science and the scientific method in general, except that they are applied to variables and subject matters involving relations among policies, policy causes, and policy effects. In that sense, policy analysis is not something new methodologically. There are, however, at least two relatively new and exciting developments that are becoming increasingly associated with policy analysis.

One new development involves a concern for deducing the effects of alternative public policies before the policies are adopted, as contrasted to the more usual approach of quantitatively or non-quantitatively evaluating policies after they have been adopted. Deductive modeling involves deducing conclusions about the effects of policies from empirically tested premises, although the conclusions have not necessarily been empirically tested. A second new development involves a concern for determining an optimum policy or combination of policies for achieving a given goal or set of goals. This evaluative approach can be contrasted with the more common situation where policies are taken as givens and the researcher attempts to determine the extent to which they are achieving their desired effects.

Those two dimensions of deducing effects of policy changes and optimizing alternative public policies have been discussed in Chapters 6 and 5, which in turn are based on the more fundamental problems of inference, prediction, causation, and measurement discussed in the previous four chapters. Although those two dimensions have an element of newness to them, they both relate back to a traditional social philosophy concern for logical and normative analysis quite prevalent in the writings of such classical social philosophers as Aristotle, Saint Thomas Aquinas, and other pre-twentieth century thinkers. They also relate back to a more recent behavioral science concern for quantifying relationships which has been quite prevalent in the post-World War II social science literature. Policy analysis research thus represents a kind of synthesis of classical social philosophy and modern behavioral science as applied to important policy problems.

Policy analysis also represents an interdisciplinary synthesis of methodological and conceptual contributions from such disciplines as economics, business administration, industrial engineering, and social psychology. Political science and public administration also contribute a perspective that emphasizes the need to consider problems of policy adoption, implementation, and political philosophy. The examples we have presented generally come from the substance of legal policy problems, but one can easily reason by analogy to policy problems from a broad variety of substantive fields. Both deductive modeling and optimization have wide potential applicability. What is especially needed now are even more researchers who are interested in developing that applicability for its theoretical and practical usefulness.

OVERVIEW APPENDIX 1:
SUMMARY OF THE MAIN FORMULAS
IN STATISTICAL ANALYSIS

The following appendix is designed to provide a summary and review of the main formulas used in statistical analysis. This book does not presuppose a knowledge of these formulas since many of them are explained at various points in the text relative to the subjects being discussed. This appendix, however, does pull together many basic ideas so as to further clarify their relationships. The following formulas emphasize the kind of statistical analysis that is relevant to social science and policy analysis. Expressing nonlinear relations is particularly relevant to benefit-cost analysis where benefit curves and cost curves are usually nonlinear because of such principles as the principle of diminishing incremental utility with successive input units. For a better understanding of these formulas, see such standard statistics textbooks as H. Blalock, *Social Statistics* (McGraw-Hill, 1972), and J. Guilford, and B. Fruchter, *Fundamental Statistics in Psychology and Education* (McGraw-Hill, 1973).

I. BASIC SYMBOLS

X   = A score of a person, place, or thing on a variable, generally a variable used to predict from.

Y   = A score of a person, place, or thing on a variable, generally a variable used to predict to.

Σ = Sum the scores that follow.

N = The number of persons, places, or things being analyzed.

$1, 2, \ldots n$ = Subscripts to show the first, second, and last case.

m = Subscript to show the mean or average score.

p = Subscript to show the predicted score, i.e., the predicted score of a case on a Y variable given the score of the case on an X variable.

Δ = Change in

II. MEASURES OF CENTRAL TENDENCY

A. The Mean: $(X_1 + \ldots + X_n)/N = \Sigma X/N = X_m$

B. The Median: Arrange the X's in rank order and find the middle one.

C. The Mode: The most common X.

III. MEASURES OF SPREAD

A. The Range: The highest X minus the lowest X.

B. The Mean Deviation: $\Sigma| X-X_m| / N$, where vertical bars mean ignore the sign of the difference.

C. The Variance and Standard Deviation: $\Sigma(X-X_m)^2 / N$, and the square root of that expression for the standard deviation or S.

IV. MEASURE OF GOODNESS OF FIT OR CORRELATION CO-EFFICIENT

A. In words: The complement of unexplained variance divided by total variance.

B. In symbols: 1.00 minus $\Sigma(Y-Y_p)^2 / \Sigma(Y-Y_m)^2 = r^2$

V. THE PROBABILITY OF A RELATION BEING DUE TO CHANCE

A. In a four-cell table: Chi-Square $= r^2 N$

B. In general: Chi-Square = $\Sigma\,[(O\text{-}E)^2\,/\,E]$, where 0 is an observed score, and E is an expected-by-chance score. $E = $ (row total) (column total) /N

VI. EXPRESSING A LINEAR RELATION BETWEEN TWO VARIABLES

A. Linear relation: $Y_p = a + bX$

B. Y-intercept or a: The predicted value of Y when X equals 0.

C. Slope or b: The predicted change in Y when there is a one unit change in X. Symbolically, $b = \Delta Y / \Delta X = (Y_2\text{-}Y_1)/(X_2\text{-}X_1)$.

VII. EXPRESSING A NONLINEAR RELATION BETWEEN TWO VARIABLES

A. Curves which slope in only one direction with constant elasticity:

   1. The relation: $Y_p = a(X)^b$

   2. Scale coefficient or a: The predicted value of Y when X equals one.

   3. Elasticity coefficient or b: The predicted percentage change in Y when there is a change of one percent in X. Symbolically, $b = \Delta\%X/\Delta\%Y = (Y_2\text{-}Y_1)/Y_1$ divided by $(X_2\text{-}X_1)/X_1$.

   4. Slope for such a curve at any point = $ba(X)^{b\text{-}1}$

B. Curves which change directions:

   1. The relation: $Y_p = a + b_1X + b_2X^2$

   2. Slope for such a curve at any point = $b_1 + 2b_2X$

   3. The value of X which produces a minimum or maximum Y for such a curve = $-b_1/2b_2$

C. Curves which slope in only one direction, but change elasticity:

   1. The relation: $Y_p = a + b_1X + b_2X^2 + b_3X^3$

2. Slope for such a curve at any point $= b_1 + 2b_2X + 3b_3X^2$

D. Other Curves:

1. There are an infinite number of curves, but the above three are likely to fit most social science data.

2. The above three can also be expressed as linear relations by logging the X and Y variables in curve 1, squaring the X variable in curve 2, and cubing the X variable in curve 3.

3. Slopes for the above three are also easy to express by knowing that (1) if Y equals a constant, the slope is 0; (2) if Y equals a + bX, the slope is b; and (3) if Y equals aX^b, the slope is baX^{b-1}.

VIII. CRITERIA FOR FITTING LINES OR CURVES TO DATA

A. Least squares: Minimize $\Sigma(Y-Y_p)^2$, i.e., minimize the sum of the deviations squared between the actual and predicted scores.

B. Mean residual: Minimize $\Sigma| Y-Y_p |$, i.e., minimize the sum of the absolute deviations or residuals between the actual and predicted scores.

NOTE: Correlation coefficients and slopes can be expressed as relations between a Y variable and an X variable with or without holding one or more Z variables constant.

OVERVIEW APPENDIX 2: METHODS FOR HANDLING MISSING DATA

One of the most common and controversial problems in data processing is how to handle missing information. The purpose of this appendix is to describe a variety of ways of doing so. In the outline below, roman numerals always refer to methods or groups of methods, capital letters refer to specific methods, the arabic numeral 1 defines a specific method, and arabic numeral 2 indicates advantages and disadvantages of a specific method. All the methods described below can be handled by SPSS, SOUPAC, or other programs.

I. IGNORE THE PROBLEM

1. Input a data matrix of entities by variables into an SPSS, SOUPAC, or other program without taking into consideration that blanks, nines, or some other code means missing information.

2. Advantage = simplicity. Disadvantage = results are likely to be meaningless because entities with blanks are likely to be treated as if they are scored zeroes or whatever number is used for missing information.

II. FURTHER REDUCE THE DATA

These methods have the advantage of considering the presence of missing information and of handling it in a relatively simple way. They have the disadvantage of decreasing the number of useable variables or entities.

    A.   Variable Deletion

        1. Eliminate variables that have missing data.

        2. This can be disastrous to the research project if those variables are essential.

    B.   Casewise Deletion

        1. Eliminate entities that have any missing data

        2. This purifies the sample but it may unduly decrease the sample size.

    C.   Equation-Wise Deletion

        1. Eliminate entities that have missing data, but only on the variables being used in each separate regression equation so the sample size will vary by regression equation.

        2. This may, however, make comparisons across the equations meaningless.

    D.   Pairwise Deletion

        1. Eliminate entities that have missing data, but only on the variables being used in a given bivariate correlation.

        2. This may also make comparisons across correlations meaningless.

III. SUBSTITUTE SOMETHING FOR THE MISSING DATA

These methods have the advantage of preserving data and using information available. They have the disadvantage of requiring some extra work, and sometimes may involve arbitrary substitutions.

    A.   Substitute a Measure of Central Tendency

        Substitute the mean score or modal score on variable X_i for those entities that are blank on X_i. The mean or mode on X_i is determined from those entities that have information on X_i.

    B.   Substitute a Predicted Score

        For those entities that have information on X_i and on other variables, obtain a regression equation predicting X_i from those other variables. Use that regression equation to get predicted scores for those entities that lack information on X_i. This is probably the best method from the point of view of preserving information and making an accurate substitution, but it does involve the most work.

C.   Substitute in Light of One's Knowledge of the Subject Matter

For example, where a person fails to provide their sex on the student course evaluation questionnaire, one could perhaps assume the respondent is a female on the theory that females are more sensitive about revealing their sex than males are. This is in effect predicting from the known prior distribution of the variable among respondents and nonrespondents. Another example might involve guessing as to a respondent's economic class from the respondent's answers to other questions which is a form of subjective regression analysis. Any substitution method must be clearly explained and justified in any research report in which it is used.

D.   Make Missing Data a Category and/or a Variable in Itself

For example, on a sex variable, one could have males, females, and blanks. That would cause no problem in a subsequent cross-tabulation analysis. It would, however, create a variable in which the categories have no inherent order. To remedy that, one could place blanks between males and females on the assumption some are males and some are females. More specifically, one could code males as 0's, females as 1's, and blanks as .5. If one knows that 60 percent of the responding sample consists of females, one could code blanks as .6, but that is the same as substituting the mean score for blanks. One could also add a separate variable called, "Did the respondent provide information on sex?" which is coded 0 for no, and 1 for yes. By including that variable in the regression analysis, it partials out the effect of making missing data a category on the basic variable while at the same time not losing any respondents.

IV. USE A MISSING DATA CORRELATION MATRIX AS INPUT

1. Input the data matrix of entities by variables into the SPSS missing data correlation program asking for pairwise deletion. The correlation matrix of variables by variables can then be used as input into the multivariate regression, stepwise regression, or factor analysis programs as if each correlation coefficient was based on the same sample size. This method in effect operates on the assumption that although the sample sizes differ for each correlation coefficient, all the correlation coefficients tend to be representative of the true correlation coefficients.

2. Advantage = simple, and uses all the data available. Disadvantage = may only be meaningful for the first few variables in a stepwise regression because of inconsistencies that make longer regression equations not capable of being outputted.

NAME INDEX

Abt, Clark, 170
Alker, Hayward, 194
Anderson, Alan, 196
Anderson, David, 217
Andrews, E.M., 102
Andriano, Kim, 219
Aranson, Peter, 176
Archibald, Russell, 174
Armstrong, R.D., 67

Bailey, Kenneth, 196
Baker, Kenneth, 174, 218
Bauer, Raymond, 128, 130
Baumol, William, 127, 167, 176, 194, 196
Becker, Gary, 195, 196
Behn, Robert, 170, 219
Belkin, J., 219
Beltrami, Edward, 173, 217
Bennett, Carl, 169
Benson, Oliver, 95, 99
Bernd, Joseph, 219
Biles, William, 218
Black, Guy, 128, 169, 175
Blackstone, William, 20, 22, 23, 24, 25, 31
Blalock, Hubert, 17, 27, 31, 62, 65, 95, 97, 99, 100, 193, 196, 223
Blumstein, Alfred, 127, 168, 218
Blumstein, J., 219
Blydenburgh, John C., 67
Bohigian, Haig, 174, 176, 195, 217, 218
Bohrnstedt, George, 102, 196

Book, John, 168
Borgatta, Edgar, 102, 196
Bounstein, Sidney, 218
Brennan, Michael, 172, 194, 218
Brown, Don, 219
Brown, Peter, 176
Brown, Rex, 171
Buchanan, James, 168, 172, 194
Buchholz, Bernard, 217
Bush, R.R., 65
Byrd, Jack, Jr., 130, 174, 176, 194, 217, 218, 219

Campbell, Donald, 97, 101
Cannavale, Frank, Jr., 219
Carbill, Thomas, 217, 218
Caro, Francis, 169
Cassidy, R. Gordon, 218
Caulcott, E., 97
Chaiken, Jan, 174, 217, 218
Champagne, Anthony, 97
Clark, Elizabeth, 171
Clarke, Stevens, 37, 62
Clayton, Ron, 167
Cochrane, James, 127
Conway, Richard, 217
Cortes, Fernando, 174, 193
Costner, Herbert, 62, 68, 196
Crenson, Matthew, 127, 169
Crissey, Brian, 127, 169

Dean, Gerald, 171
Dean, Gillian, 83, 100
DeFrancesco, Harry, 196

de Neufville, Richard, 168
Deutsch, Karl, 194
Deutsch, S., 219
DeVor, Richard, 218
Dolbeare, Kenneth, 129, 175
Dormont, F., 217
Drake, Alvin, 168
Dutta, M., 66, 67

Easton, Allan, 127, 171
Edwards, Ward, 68, 127, 129
Eimermann, Thomas, 128, 176
Erlanger, Howard, 100
Evarts, H., 218

Feigenbaum, 65
Feldman, Julian, 65
Finkelstein, Michael, 195
Finney, D.J., 67
Fischoff, Baruch, 171
Fisher, Gene, 172
Francis, Wayne, 194
Frankfurter, Felix, 99
Freeman, Jean, 62
Frome, E.L., 67
Fromm, Gary, 168, 193
Fruchter, Benjamin, 35, 62, 97, 223

Gage, N.L., 97
Gardiner, Peter C., 127
Gass, Saul, 127, 168, 193, 217
Gergen, Kenneth, 128, 130
Gibson, James L., 98, 99
Glass, Brian, 218
Glass, Gene, 101
Glass, W., 219
Golding, Martin, 176
Goldman, Thomas, 173
Gray, Paul, 219
Green, Leon, 95
Greenberg, David, 100, 219
Greenberger, Martin, 127, 169, 193, 196
Gregg, Phillip, 176
Grofman, Bernard, 128, 196
Gross, Donald, 174, 217
Grosse, Richard, 168, 217
Grossman, Joel, 98, 99
Guenther, Anthony, 31

Guilford, J.P., 35, 62, 97, 223
Guttentag, Marcia, 128, 170, 176

Halter, Albert, 171
Hamilton, Diane, 168
Hamilton, William, 168
Handwerker, Michael, 218
Hansen, B.J., 218
Harberger, Arnold, 169
Harris, Carl, 174, 217
Hausman, Warren, 67
Hausner, Jack, 218
Haveman, Robert, 169, 173
Hays, William, 31, 33
Heise, David, 102, 130, 193, 196
Helly, Walter, 127, 169
Henkel, Ramon, 31
Henry, S., 172
Herndon, James, 219
Hildebrand, David, 62, 63
Himmelblau, David, 67
Hinrichs, Harley, 170
Hirsch, Werner, 127, 219
Hite, James, 172
Hogg, Gary, 218
Holliday, Leo, 217, 218
Howard, R., 171

Isaacson, Dean, 219

Jaquette, David, 217, 218
Jarvis, J., 219
Jeffrey, R.C., 171
Jennings, John, 218
James, Dorothy, 175
Jones, Harry, 217

Kahn, Andrew, 171
Kahneman, Daniel, 68
Kalven, Harry, Jr., 217
Kamrass, Murray, 127, 168
Kaplan, Martin, 127
Kassouf, Sheen, 167, 194
Kaufman, A., 218
Keeney, Ralph, 127, 168, 171, 175
Kemeny, John, 219
Kessler, Ronald, 100
Kiresuk, Thomas, 130

Kloek, Teun, 168
Koch, Gary, 62
Kotler, Philip, 173, 219
Kritzer, 98

Labovitz, Sanford, 31
Ladd, John, 176
Laidlaw, C., 173
Laing, James, 63
Lamm, David, 32, 130
Landes, William, 195, 196
Lane, Thomas, 218
Lave, Charles, 193, 195
Lawless, Michael, 217, 218
Layard, Richard, 169
Lee, Alec, 217
Lee, Sang, 173
Lee, Wayne, 171
Leik, Robert, 196
Lichtenstein, Sara, 171
Lineberry, Robert, 100
Liske, C., 100
Llewellyn, Robert, 173, 219
Logan, Charles, 100
Lumsdaine, Arthur, 169
Lyden, 173

MacIver, Robert, 95
Mack, Ruth, 171, 219
MacRae, Duncan, Jr., 168, 176
Madsen, Richard, 219
Mahan, Linda, 31
Makridakis, Spyros, 174
March, James, 193, 195
Margolis, Julius, 169, 173
Marks, David, 168
Matheson, J., 171
Maxwell, William, 217
McKean, Roland, 127, 170, 175
McKenzie, Richard, 194
McLauchlan, Will, 196
McMillen, Claude, Jr., 173, 219
Meehan, Eugene, 176
Mehay, Stephen, 219
Mellay, Stephen, 173
Merrill, Fredric, 218
Miller, A., 100
Miller, D.W., 172, 173

Miller, Louis, 217
Mishan, E.J., 127, 128, 169, 194
Moore, Omar, 196
Morris, Philip, 175
Morrison, Denton, 31
Morse, Philip, 168
Mosteller, Frederick, 65
Mueller, John, 62, 68
Munshaw, Nancy, 14, 128, 217
Munsterman, G. Thomas, 219

Nagin, Daniel, 100
Nass, Gilbert, 31
Navarro, Joseph, 218
Nemhauser, George, 218
Nimmer, Raymond, 218
Niskanen, William, 169
North, D., 171

Oberlander, Leonard, 218
Oleson, Gary, 218
Ordeshook, Peter, 195

Pabst, William, 219
Paley, Hiram, 62
Parker, R., 219
Pelz, D., 102
Peterson, Cameron, 171
Phillips, Llad, 172, 218
Portnoy, Stephen, 62
Posner, Richard, 195
Przeworski, Adam, 174, 193

Quade, E.S., 128, 168, 169, 175, 217, 218

Radnor, Michael, 217
Raiffa, Howard, 127, 171, 219
Rardin, Ronald, 219
Rawls, John, 44
Reed, John, 174, 217
Reinbolt, Kathleen, 128
Richmond, Samuel, 63, 66, 130, 168, 194, 196, 217, 218, 219
Riker, William, 195
Rosenthal, Howard, 63
Ross, Laurence, 101

Rossi, Peter, 170
Rottenberg, Simon, 195

Saar, Shalom, 170
Saaty, Thomas, 217
Sales, Bruce, 32, 130
Schaefer, Elmer, 128, 130
Schelling, Thomas, 195, 219
Schrage, Linus, 218
Schramm, Sarah Slavin, 128, 175, 196, 219
Schuessler, Karl, 62, 68
Schwartz, Steven, 127
Seitz, Steven, 196
Selvin, Hanan, 31
Sherman, Robert, 130
Shockley, James, 172, 218
Shoup, Donald, 173, 219
Siegel, Sidney, 17, 31
Simon, Herbert, 45, 65, 97
Simon, Rita, 14, 31, 97, 130
Singleton, Robert, 193, 195
Sisson, Roger, 127, 168, 193, 217
Sjoberg, Gideon, 176
Skipper, James, 31
Slivka, Ronald, 219
Slovic, Paul, 171
Snell, J. Laurie, 219
Sofaer, Abraham, 195
Spaeth, Harold, 99
Spetzler, C., 171
Spielman, Stephen, 31
Sprague, John, 174, 193
Stanley, J., 97
Starr, M.K., 172
Stigler, George, 172
Stoetzel, Antoine, 194
Stogdill, Ralph, 193, 196
Stokey, Edith, 168
Stover, Robert, 219
Struening, Elmer, 128, 170
Suchman, Edward, 170
Sweeney, Dennis, 217

Taha, Hamdy, 217
Tansik, David, 217
Taylor, Graeme, 170
Taylor, Jean, 218

Thaler, Richard, 67
Theil, Henri, 168
Thierauf, Robert, 168, 217
Tittle, C., 98
Tollison, Robert, 194
Tribe, Laurence, 176
Tullock, Gordon, 168, 172, 194, 195, 196
Tversky, Amos, 68
Tyndall, William, 193, 195

Uh, Soo Hong, 219
Ulmer, Sidney, 219

van Horn, Andrew, 171
Vaupel, James, 170, 219
Villoria, Richard, 174, 218
Viek, Charles, 127
Votey, Harold, 172, 218

Wagner, Harvey, 67, 217
Wagner, Richard, 195
Weiss, Armand, 127, 168
Weiss, Carol, 170
Weitzman, Lenore, 98
Wendt, Dirk, 127
Wheelwright, Steven, 174
White, David, 215, 219
White, Michael, 217
Whitehouse, Gary, 218
Wholey, Joseph, 170
Wice, Paul, 172, 196, 218
Wilde, James, 168
Williams, Thomas, 217
Williams, Walter, 170
Wilson, Hoyt, 67
Wilson, James Q., 196
Winkler, Robert, 31, 33
Winsborough, Halliman, 100
Winters, Glenn, 217
Wonnacott, Ronald, 62, 64, 67
Wonnacott, Thomas, 62, 64, 67

Zeckhauser, Richard, 128, 130, 169, 195, 219
Zeisel, Hans, 95, 99, 168, 217, 218
Zeleny, Milan, 127

SUBJECT INDEX

Accommodations, public, 144
Accuracy of prediction methods, 35-68
    Predicting randomly, 37-41, 62
    Central tendency measures, 41-45
    Correlation, 48-52
    Equations, 52-56
    Event-matching, 45-48
Acquittal errors, 18-19, 23-25, 110
Activism of judges, 99
Alternative policies, 134-136
    Continuum of, 140-145
Analysis of variance, 96
Anti-crime allocation, 109-111
Appearance at trial, predicting, 37-41
Approaches to methodological problems, 9-14
Arraignment judges, 187
Arrests, delay, 148
Assaults, felonious, 80-81
Assigned counsel, 134-136
Attitudes of judges, 11, 74, 88
Attorney-client relations, 76-81
Average deviation approach to prediction, 35-68

Backgrounds of judges, 98
Bail bonds, 134-136
Bayesian prediction, 63, 66
Benefit-cost approach to statistical significance, 17-33
Beyond a reasonable doubt, 19
Blacks, differential treatment, 80-81
Blacks, voter registration, 183

Bond-setting, 134-136, 138-140
Business administration, 222

Campaign expenditures, 107
Cases, civil, delay, 148, 197-219
Catholics, and divorce, 85
Causation, 9-14
    Coeffects and intervening variables, 70-76
    Deductive, 181-185
    Determining and rejecting, 69-102
    Joint causation, 76-81
    Modeling, 190-191
    Reciprocal causation, 82-88
Certainty of being caught, 98
Chance probability, 9-14
Chi square, 31
Choice, optimum, 210-212
Choosing counsel, 89
Civil cases, delay in, 197-219
Civil liberties, 111
Civil rights activities, 144
    Organizations, 108
Civil settlements, 139
Clarifying goals, 9-14
Client-attorney relations, 76-81
Cocausation, 76-81
Coeffects causation, 70-76
Combined causal impact, 76-81
Combining and relating goals, 9-14, 105-131
    Conflicting goals, 106-113
    Relating goals, 113-120

Common units of measurement, 109-111
Compositing of variables, 123-126
Confirmation of hypotheses, 9-14, 24
Conflicting goals, 9-14, 105-131
Contingent probabilities, 136-138, 138-140
Continuums of alternatives, 116-118, 140-145
Controlling for variables, 35-68, 69-102, 118-120
Controversies in methodological problems, 9-14
Conviction criterion problem, 18-19, 23-25, 110
Corrections, 107-109
Correlation, prediction, 48-52, 65, 67
Cost-benefit approach to statistical significance, 17-33
Costs, holding, 19
Costs of errors, evaluating, 17-33
Counsel, choosing, 89, 134-136
Court precedents, 14
Courts, 107-109
Crime, allocation, 109-111
Crime rates, 182
Crime reduction, 111
Criminal justice, 144
Critical path method, 13, 204-207, 218
Cross-lagged panel analysis, 82-88, 101

Damages in personal injury cases, 35-68
Data, missing, 227-229
Data processing symbols, 223-226
Decision-making alternatives, 133-159
Decision theory, 196
    Method for statistical significance, 22-27, 30-31
Decisional propensities of judges, 99
Decriminalization of marijuana, 101
Deduction, 9-14
    Deductive modeling, 177-196
Defendants held in jail, 187
    Number to hold, 134-136
Defender, public, 134-136
Delay, arrests, 148
    Civil cases, 197-219

Critical path method, 204-207
Markov chain analysis, 212-215
Optimum choice, 210-212
Optimum level and mix, 207-210
Optimum sequencing, 201-204
Queueing theory, 198-201
Determination of probation, 80-81
Determining and rejecting causation, 69-102
Deterrence modeling, 196
Deviation, average, in predicting, 35-68
Differential treatment of blacks, 80-81
Discrete policy choices, 114-116, 136-138
Discrimination, racial, minimizing, 21-22, 25-27, 31, 88
Disposition of cases, delay in, 148
Distribution of data, use in prediction, 41-48
Divorce law, 82-88, 120
Due process, optimum level, 140-143
Dynamic programming, 217, 218

Economics, 222
Education, as intervening variable, 98
Effects of feedback, 82-88
Elementary statistical symbols, 223-226
Empirical data, in deductive premises, 180
Employment, 144
Engineering, industrial, 222
Environmental protection, 141
Environmental variables, 118-120
Errors of not convicting the guilty, 9-14, 18-19, 23-25, 32, 33, 110
Evaluating the costs of errors, 17-33
Exclusionary rule, 111
Expenditures, campaign, 107
Explanatory causal analysis, as goal, 89

F-test, 31
Factor analysis, 124-125
Failing to appear at trial, predicting, 37-41
Fair procedure, optimum level, 140-143
Feedback effects, in causation, 82-88

Felonious assaults, 80-81
Female-dominated juries, 98
Flow chart models, 204-207, 218

General modeling, 178-181
General optimizing, 134-136, 139, 144-145
Gestalt approach, 111-112
Goals, clarifying, 9-14
    Combining, 106-113
Goodness of fit, 224
Grand larceny, 80-81
Guilty, error of not convicting, 9-14, 18-19, 23-25, 32, 33

Handling missing data, 227-229
Hierarchy of methodological problems, 9-14
Holding errors, 18-19, 23-25
Housing, 144
Hypotheses, confirmation of, 9-14, 24

Impact effects, 76-81, 82-88
Imprisonment, 182-183
Industrial engineering, 222
Inference, 9-14
Innocent, error of convicting, 9-14, 18-19, 23-25, 32, 33, 110
Integrating diverse forms of causation, 88-89
Integration benefits, 142
Interactive causation, 76-81
Interracial equality, 183
Interrupted time series, 82-88, 101
Intervening variable causation, 70-76, 183
Inventory level for statistical significance, 19-22, 30, 31-32

Jail, defendants held, 187
    Maintenance costs, 109
    Number to hold, 134-136
Joint causation, 76-81
Judges
    Activism, 99
    Arraignment, 187
    Attitudes, 11, 74, 88
    Backgrounds, 98

Decisional propensities, 99
Judicare, 114-116
Juries, size of, 9-14
Jurors, decision-making, 130
    Optimum number, 134-136
    Size problem, 128, 180-181
    Threshold probability for convicting, 9-14, 18-19, 23-25, 32-33

Larceny, 80-81
Law reform activities, 107-109, 149
Lawyers and unpopular clients, 76-81
Least squares criterion in prediction, 35-36, 52, 55, 64
Legal counsel for poor, 114-116
Legal services agencies, 75, 107-109, 134, 149
Level and mix, optimum, 207-210
Level of statistical significance, desirable, 17-33
Lexicographic ordering, 128
Liberties, civil, 111
Linear regression, 116-118
Linear relations, 225
Litigants, 76-81
Log-linear regression, 116-118
Logical deduction, 177-196

Maintenance costs, jails, 109
Management science, 217
Marijuana decriminalization, 101
Markov chain analysis, 13, 212-215
Mass media, 107
Matching, events, 45-48
Maximizing net benefits, general rule, 134-136
Mean, use in prediction, 41-48
Mean residual approach to prediction, 35-68
Measurement, common units, 109-111
Measures of central tendency, 41-45, 224
Media, 107
Median category, for predicting, 63
Methodological problems, hierarchy of, 9-14
Methods for handling missing data,

227-229
Methods for predicting, 35-68
    Central tendency, 41-45
    Correlation, 48-52
    Equations, 52-56
    Event-matching, 45-48
Methods of reducing variables, 123-126
Minimizing squared deviations, in pre-
    diction, 35-36
Missing data, 227-229
Mode, use in prediction, 41-48, 63
Models, causal, 181-185, 190-191
Monotonic relations, 157-158
Multiple goals, 9-14, 106-113

National crime occurrence, 144
Negative test, in causation, 74
Noncausal relations, 70-72
Nonlinear relations, 225
Nonmonotonic relations, 158-159
Non-optimum prediction, 68
Normal curve, 31
Normative conclusions, 180
Normative weights, 111-112
Numbers of variables, reducing,
    123-126

Operations research, 217
Optimum level of due process, 140-143
Optimizing, 9-14
Optimum choice, level, or mix,
    133-159, 210-212
    Alternative policies in general,
        134-136
    Contingent probabilities, 138-140
    Discrete alternatives, 136-138
    Optimum levels, 140-143
    Optimum mixes, 143-145
    Sequencing, 201-204
    Simultaneous choices, 145-147
    Value decisions, 147-149
Optimum level analysis, in hierarchy,
    9-14, 207-210, 218-219
    Decision theory approach, 22-27
    Inventory modeling approach,
        19-22
    Statistical significance, 17-33
Optimum mix analysis, 9-14, 207-210

Optimum sequencing, 201-204
Optimum time, 197-219
Organizations, civil rights, 108
Organizations, precinct, 107-109
Outage costs, 19
Overlapping goals, 129-130

Partitioning, 118-120
Party affiliation, 97
Personal injury cases, damages, 35-68
PERT analysis, 147, 204-207
Plea bargaining, 108, 129, 139
Police, 107-109, 111-112
Poor, legal counsel for, 114-116,
    136-138
Portfolio analysis, 146
Positive test, in causation, 74
Power of tests, 31
Precedents, court, 14
Precinct organizations, 107-109
Prediction, 9-14, 35-68
    Bayesian, 63, 66
Prediction methods and criteria, 35-68
    Central tendency measures, 41-45
    Correlation, 48-52
    Equations, 52-56
    Event-matching, 45-48, 68
    Predicting randomly, 37-41, 62
Predictor variables, 37
Prescriptive modeling, 185-188,
    191-192
Pretrial jail populations, 148
Pretrial release, 35-68, 128, 141
Prior information, use in prediction,
    45-48, 48-52
Probabilities, contingent, 136-138,
    138-140
Probability of relationships due to
    chance, 9-14, 224-225
Probation, determination, 80-81
Probit regression analysis, 67
Processing court cases, delay in,
    197-219
Processing data, symbols, 223-226
Providing counsel, 134-136
Psychology, social, 222
Public accommodations, 144
Public defender system, 134-136

Punishment, severity of, 98

Quasi-legislation, 14
Queueing theory, 13, 147, 198-201, 207, 215, 217

Racial discrimination, 88
Racial disparity, minimizing, 21-22, 25-27, 31
Random prediction, 37-41, 62
Rates of crime, 182
Rates of divorce, 82-88
Rational prediction, 45-48
Reasoning from analogy, 185
Reasonable doubt level, 19
Reasoning, syllogistic, 177-196
Reciprocal causation, 82-88, 120
Recoding of variables, 126
Redistricting, 110, 114, 128-129
Reducing delay in legal process, 9-14
Reducing numbers of variables, 123-126, 227-228
Reduction of crime, 111
Region, as intervening variable, 98, 183
Registration, voter, 183
Regression equations, in predicting, 35-36, 52, 116-118
Rejection of hypotheses, 9-14, 24, 69-102
Relating goals to policy alternatives, 9-14, 105-131
Relations between attorneys and clients, 76-81
Research methods, hierarchy of, 9-14
Residual analysis, 119-120
Risks of accepting wrong hypotheses, 9-14, 24
Routine case handling activities, 107-109, 149

Sampling error, 9-14
Scalogramming, 125
Schools, 144
Search and seizure, 111, 129
Segregation, 142
Sentence determination, 80-81
Sequencing, optimum, 13, 201-204
Sequential handling of goals, 106-109, 216
Sequential programming, 217, 218
Setting of bonds, 138-140
Settlements, civil, 139
Severity of punishment, 98
Sex of juries, 98
Simultaneous choices, levels, or mixes, 145-147
Simultaneous handling of goals, 109-113
Size of juries, 9-14, 128, 134-136, 180-181
Slopes, 97
Social psychology, 222
Sociology of law, 83
Solutions, optimum, 9-14
Spread, measures of, 224
Squared deviations, minimizing, 35-36, 55
Statistical significance, benefit-cost approach to, 17-33
Statistical prediction, 9-14
Statistical symbols, 223-226
Statutes, 14
Stepwise regression, 125-126
Subgoals, 105-131
Subjective clustering of variables, 126
Supreme Court, 108
Syllogistic reasoning, 177-196

T-test, 31
Threshold probability of guilt, determining, 18-19, 22-25
Time, optimum, 197-219
Time-oriented models, 147
And delay reduction, 197-219
Time series, interrupted, 82-88, 101
Trials, failure to appear, 37-41
True or false hypotheses, 9-14, 24, 33
Two-stage prediction, 82-88
Type 1 or type 2 errors, 9-14, 22
Of holding or releasing defendants, 145-147

Units of measurement, 109-113
Unpopular clients, 76-81
Unrestricted regression analysis, in predicting, 52-56, 57, 67

Unsquared deviations, in predicting, 55
Urbanism, as intervening variable, 88, 98, 183

Validity of hypotheses, 180
Value decisions, 147-149, 186
Variables, compositing of, 123-126

Controlling for, 35-68, 69-102, 118-120
Variance accounted for, 35-68, 69-102
Voluntary counsel, 134-136
Voter registration, blacks, 183
Voting activities, 144

Weighting scores, 111-112

ABOUT THE AUTHORS

STUART S. NAGEL is a professor of political science at the University of Illinois and a member of the Illinois bar. He is the author with Marian Neef of *Decision Theory and the Legal Process* (1978), *Legal Policy Analysis: Finding an Optimum Level or Mix* (1977), *The Legal Process: Modeling the System* (1977). He is the author or editor of *Policy Studies and Review Annual* (1977), *Modeling the Criminal Justice System* (1977), *Policy Studies and the Social Sciences* (1975), *Policy Studies in America and Elsewhere* (1975), *Improving the Legal Process: Effects of Alternatives* (1975), *Environmental Politics* (1974), *The Rights of the Accused: In Law and Action* (1972), and *The Legal Process from a Behavioral Perspective* (1969). He has been an attorney to the Office of Economic Opportunity, Lawyer's Constitutional Defense Committee in Mississippi, National Labor Relations Board, and the U.S. Senate Judiciary Committee. Dr. Nagel has been a fellow of the Ford Foundation, Russell Sage, NSF, ACLS, SSRC, East-West Center, Illinois Law Enforcement Commission, and the Center for Advanced Study in the Behavioral Sciences. He has also been a grant recipient through the Policy Studies Organization from the Departments of Justice, Labor, HUD, Energy, Agriculture, Transportation, and HEW, and from the Rockefeller and Guggenheim Foundations.

MARIAN G. NEEF teaches and does research in political science at the University of Illinois. In addition to the above-mentioned books, she is the author with Stuart Nagel of such monographs as *Too Much or Too Little Policy: The Example of Pretrial Release* (1977); *Operations Research Methods: As Applied to Political Science and the Legal Process* (1976); and *The Application of Mixed Strategies: Civil Rights and Other Multiple-Activity Problems* (1976). She has also coauthored numerous articles in such journals as *Policy Analysis, American Bar Association Journal, Judicature, Political Methodology, Public Administration Review, Journal of Criminal Justice, Human Behavior, Journal of Legal Education, PS,* and various law reviews.